# BIBLE STUDY
# NOTES

Volume 5

# BIBLE STUDY NOTES

## MEMORIAL EDITION

By Anita S. Dole

Edited By Wm. R. Woofenden

AMERICAN NEW CHURCH
SUNDAY SCHOOL ASSOCIATION
1979

*Library of Congress Catalog Card Number: 76-24081*
*Complete set    ISBN  0-917426-00-2*
*Volume 5        ISBN  0-917426-05-3*

Sales Agent:

Swedenborg Library
79 Newbury Street
Boston, Massachusetts 02116

*"Well done, good and faithful servant."*
—*Matthew 25:23*

Printed in U.S.A.

# TABLE OF CONTENTS

# INTRODUCTORY NOTES FOR TEACHERS

As we may see by the accompanying chart, this program was planned as a four-year Bible course, but it was originally arranged so that the whole Word was covered by periods each year, in order that the child might early realize that the Bible is one book—not only a continuous story but a completed one—and also that children might not so often enter the Sunday School for the first time in the middle of the Bible story with no idea of what has gone before. While this plan might in any one year seem to leave many important stories untouched, the retelling of the background of the successive periods from year to year in the context of different stories built up gradually in the child's mind both a surer knowledge and a better understanding of the whole letter of the Word. The plan insured that the beginning of the Bible story was not forgotten before the end was reached, and that the Old and New Testaments were seen in their proper relation and proportion. Although the lessons are now arranged in Bible sequence, it is still possible, by using the chart, to use the original four-year plan.

The notes for the various age groups are written with two purposes in view. It is *not* intended that the teacher should read them to the class. Neither is it intended that copies should be given out to the pupils in advance. Only the Bible reading should be done in advance. For the teacher, the notes are meant to suggest the points to be covered in the lesson, a possible order of presentation, and the general level of meaning which pupils in the particular age group may be expected to comprehend. For the pupil, if he has his own set of the books, they are meant to be taken home, read as a review during the week, and preserved for future reference.

It is very important that the teacher plan his use of the class time carefully. Five minutes or less at the beginning of the period are enough for review questions. Then give five minutes to a carefully thought-out covering of the background of the lesson for the day before going into the lesson proper. In the Old Testament build the background as far as possible about persons and places in order to fix these in their proper sequence in the pupils' minds. In the New Testament the background should be the factual story of the Lord's life on earth.

The writings of the church tell us that "generals" must be grasped before "particulars" can be understood in their proper context; so we may feel sure that our first object in the Sunday School should be to impress the general outline of the whole Bible story on the minds of our pupils. The covering of the whole story each year has this objective in view.

The two survey lessons (nos. 22 and 24 on the accompanying chart) are general lessons but are based on a different passage each year in order to give the pupils a wider variety in the study of the Prophets than has been possible in previous courses. They are also optional lessons, written in such a way that Sunday Schools with a school year of less than forty sessions may omit them without losing continuity. Each series also contains fifteen lessons from the New Testament. A different Gospel is studied each year. Two of the fifteen lessons are written as optional lessons; three are the special lessons for Christmas, Palm Sunday, and Easter; and three are from the book of Revelation.

# FOUR-YEAR LESSON COURSE FOR NEW CHURCH SUNDAY SCHOOLS

## Assignments in the Old Testament

| Lesson | Subject | Series I | Series II | Series III | Series IV |
|---|---|---|---|---|---|
| 1. | The Creation | General View | First Four Days | Days Five and Six | The Seventh Day |
| 2. | The Most Ancient Church | The Garden of Eden | Helpmeet for Adam | The Serpent | Cain and Abel |
| 3. | The Ancient Church | Noah Builds an Ark | End of the Flood | The Rainbow | Tower of Babel |
| 4. | Abraham | The Call of Abram | Abram and Lot | Birth of Ishmael | Abraham & the Angels |
| 5. | Isaac | Birth of Isaac | Sacrifice of Isaac | Isaac and Rebekah | Isaac & Abimelech |
| 6. | Jacob | Jacob & Esau | Jacob's Dream | Wives & Sons | Jacob's Return |
| 7. | Joseph | Joseph & Brothers | Joseph in Prison | Ruler of Egypt | Sons and Death |
| 8. | Moses | Birth of Moses | The Burning Bush | The Ten Plagues | The Passover |
| 9. | Escape from Egypt | Crossing Red Sea | Marah & Elim | Quails and Manna | Rephidim & Amalek |
| 10. | Mount Sinai | Ten Commandments | Ark of Covenant | The Tabernacle | The Golden Calf |
| 11. | Wilderness Wanderings | Nadab & Abihu | The Twelve Spies | Korah, Dathan, Abiram | Aaron's Rod |
| 12. | Entering the Holy Land | Balaam | Call of Joshua | Crossing the Jordan | Gilgal |
| 13. | Conquest of Holy Land | Jericho | Ai | The Gibeonites | Conquest & Division |
| 14. | The Judges | Deborah & Barak | Gideon | Jephthah | Samson |
| 15. | Samuel | Birth of Samuel | Lord Calls Samuel | Capture of the Ark | Asking for a King |
| 16. | Saul | Choosing of Saul | Saul's Impatience | Saul & Jonathan | Sparing Agag |
| 17. | David | Anointing of David | David & Goliath | Ark to Jerusalem | David & Bathsheba |
| 18. | Solomon | Wisdom of Solomon | Glory of Solomon | Building the Temple | Decline & Death |
| 19. | Kingdom of Israel | Elijah & Ahab | Elijah at Horeb | Elijah's Mantle | Elisha & Naaman |
| 20. | Kingdom of Judah | Reign of Asa | Hezekiah & Isaiah | Josiah | Zedekiah & Jeremiah |
| 21. | Book of Psalms | Psalm 1 | Psalm 19 | Psalm 91 | Psalm 119 |

| Lesson | Series I | Series II | Series III | Series IV |
|---|---|---|---|---|
| *22. Major Prophets—Survey | Isaiah 6 | Jeremiah 1 | Ezekiel 47:1-12 | Daniel 5 |
| 23. Major Prophets | Fiery Furnace | Ezekiel's Vision | Daniel & the Image | Daniel & the Lions |
| *24. Minor Prophets—Survey | Micah 6 | Joel 3:9-21 | Amos 8 | Zechariah 4 |
| 25. Minor Prophets | Haggai 1; 2 | Jonah & the Fish | Malachi 3; 4 | Jonah & the Gourd |

## Assignments in the New Testament

| Lesson | Series I | Series II | Series III | Series IV |
|---|---|---|---|---|
| 26. | Matthew 1:18-25; 2:13-23 | Mark 1 | Luke 1 | John 1 |
| 27. | Matthew 3 | Mark 2 | Luke 7:1-30 | John 2:1-11 |
| 28. | Matthew 4:1-11 | *Mark 3 | Luke 9:1-36 | *John 3:1-21 |
| 29. | *Matthew 4:12-25 | *Mark 4 | Luke 10:25-42 | John 4:1-42 |
| 30. | Matthew 5; 6; 7 | Mark 5 | *Luke 11 | John 5:1-16 |
| 31. | Matthew 8 | Mark 6 | Luke 14 | John 9 |
| 32. | *Matthew 13 | Mark 10 | Luke 15 | *John 10 |
| 33. | Matthew 17:1-13 | Mark 14 | *Luke 16 | John 11:1-46 |
| 34. | Matthew 26; 27 | Mark 15 | Luke 24:13-53 | John 15 |
| 35. | Revelation 1 | Revelation 4 | Revelation 6 | Revelation 12 |
| 36. | Revelation 2; 3 | Revelation 5 | Revelation 8; 9 | Revelation 13; 19:11-21 |
| 37. | Revelation 21; 22 | Revelation 20:11-15; 21:1-7 | Revelation 21:9-16 | Revelation 22:8-21 |

### Special Lessons

| | Series I | Series II | Series III | Series IV |
|---|---|---|---|---|
| Christmas | Matthew 2:1-15 | Luke 2:1-20 | Matthew 2:1-15 | Luke 2:1-20 |
| Palm Sunday | Matthew 21:1-27 | Mark 11 | Luke 19 | John 12:12-50 |
| Easter | Matthew 28 | Mark 16 | Luke 24:1-12 | John 20; 21 |

*Optional Lessons

# BIBLE STUDY NOTES

## MARK-LUKE

# THE LORD'S BAPTISM
## Mark 1

The general introduction for all classes should be concerned with the fact that there are four Gospels and the value to us of having four accounts of the Lord's life given us by Him through different individuals.

═══════

## Doctrinal Points

*The Lord came on earth among the Jews because they had the Word and lived in the Holy Land of the Old Testament story.*

*John the Baptist fulfilled the prophecy in Malachi, tying together the Old and the New Testaments.*

*People had to see and put away their sins before they could accept the Lord.*

*It was those who truly wanted to be good who accepted the Lord.*

═══════

## Notes for Parents

In this course [in the original four-year cycle], when we come to the New Testament we study the life of the Lord from a different Gospel each year. Now we have come to the Gospel of Mark. The four Gospels were all written under inspiration from the Lord: that is, the Lord dictated to the writers the words they were to use just as He spoke to the old prophets. But He always used words and facts which were in the mind of the writer. So the four Gospels give us four different viewpoints and altogether present a complete picture.

Mark does not give us the Christmas story but begins immediately with the first public appearance of the Lord when He came from Nazareth to the Jordan to be baptized by John. We are told in all the Gospels that John was the messenger promised in the Old Testament by Malachi and also by Isaiah, the messenger who was to go before the Lord "to prepare His way." The way of the Lord has to be prepared with all of us. You know how your children, at those times when they are bent on having their own way, will not listen to any loving, gentle arguments from you, but go on until they have to be punished for their naughtiness. We grown people are pretty much the same way, aren't we? When we are determined to get something for ourselves, we won't listen to advice even from our best friend. And before we will listen to the Lord's teaching about being unselfish and loving the neighbor, we have to be brought somehow to realize the bad things that are in us and to want to get rid of them. This was the kind of preparation the people received from John the Baptist, which opened their minds and hearts to recognize and welcome the Lord.

Baptism with water is a symbol of the desire to have our souls made clean by truth from the Lord. The Lord Himself by being baptized made it the Christian sign, and He afterward commanded His apostles to baptize in His name. Baptism shows that we want to be His followers and to bring up our children to follow Him, too. It opens a place for Him in our hearts and minds.

### Primary

The story of the Lord's baptism should be made the basis of telling the children in a simple way why they were baptized and connecting this with their coming to Sunday school to learn about the Lord and how He wants us to live. As part of the introduction the prophecies in Malachi should be read, and the children should be told why it was necessary for someone to prepare the way of the Lord.

What event marks the beginning of the New Testament?
Where was the Lord born?
Where did He grow up?
Who was sent before the Lord to prepare His way?
How did he prepare it?
Where did John live?
What was his clothing?
What was his food?
Where did he baptize?
How did he say the Lord would baptize?

When you were a baby, your parents brought you to church to be baptized. The minister took you in his arms, put a little water on your head, gave you the name your parents had chosen for you, and received you into the Christian Church. Your parents promised to do all they could to bring you up to be a true follower of our Lord Jesus Christ, and the angels who were near knew that now you belonged among Christians in this world and in their world too. Baptism is the Christian sign.

Our story today tells us how our Lord, when He was in the world, taught us this by being baptized Himself.

The Lord was about thirty years old when He came to John to be baptized. Most of the people knew nothing about Him.

Only a very few had even heard of the wonderful signs which were given at His birth.

But they knew from the prophecies in the Old Testament that someday the Lord would come.

They knew from Isaiah 9:6 that He would be called the Son of God but that He would really be God Himself.

Baptism with water was a sign that the life of the person was to be clean.

What appeared when He was baptized?

What did the voice from heaven say?

So John and all the people who saw and heard knew that this was the promised savior.

Where did the Lord go as soon as He was baptized?

What happened to Him there?

## Junior

The history of the return from captivity will be interesting to this class, as will also the facts we know concerning Mark. The necessity of the preparation of the people by John the Baptist should be discussed in its application to our own lives. The correspondence of baptism can be given.

When Babylon conquered the kingdom of Judah, some of the poorest of the people were left in the land, and it was promised through the prophets that the faithful among the captives would one day be allowed to return. The books of Ezra and Nehemiah— which, although they do not have an inner sense, are historical records of this return—follow the two books of Chronicles. Read the first chapter of Ezra. Ezra 2:64 tells us that 42,360 people, besides over seven thousand servants and maids, returned to Judah when Cyrus gave them permission. Later another group returned, although many were too well satisfied with Babylon to uproot themselves and go back. Jerusalem and the temple were rebuilt, and the descendants of the returned captives were in the Holy Land when the Lord was born in Bethlehem some four hundred years later.

Now we are studying the life of the Lord as we find it in the Gospel of Mark. Mark was not one of the twelve apostles. He is first mentioned in Acts 12:12, where we learn that his mother was one of the early Christians in Jerusalem. Mark's Hebrew name was John, but it was customary in those days, when the Holy Land was under the rule of Rome, to have a Roman name also. His Roman name was Marcus, which in English becomes Mark. He had undoubtedly known the Lord and witnessed some of the events which he records, and he was also one of those who traveled about with Peter on his missionary journeys. We remember that Peter was one of the first and closest followers of the Lord. So the events of the Lord's ministry were all well known to Mark and were in his memory in much detail so that the Lord could use him for the writing of this Gospel. But Mark's concern is with the three years of the Lord's public life, and he does not mention His birth or early life.

What is the last book in the Old Testament?

Read Malachi 3:1 and 4:5-6 and then Mark 1:2-3. The promised messenger was John the Baptist. We learn from Luke 1:36 that John's mother was a cousin of Mary the mother of Jesus. She and her husband knew that Mary's child would be the Messiah and that their own son was to be His messenger. If you will read Luke 1:16-17 you will see just how John was to fulfill the prophecy in Malachi 4:5-6. Later the Lord Himself confirmed this (Matthew 11:14 and 17:10-13). *Elias* [KJV] is the Greek form of the name *Elijah*. The Lord had to come into the world because He could no longer reach by means of the Word of the Old Testament even those who wanted to learn of God and obey Him. He Himself tells us why in Matthew 15:1-9. You remember how unwilling Jonah was to take the Lord's message to Nineveh. The Jews were the only ones in the world who had the Word, and they were not only keeping it from the Gentiles, but their scribes and the Pharisees had also added so many rules and sayings of their own that the people, few of whom could even read, did not know what was really right and wrong in the sight of God.

Before we can do right we must see what we are doing that is wrong and stop doing it. John the Baptist was a prophet, the first prophet the people had had for four hundred years. The people were helped to see this by the fact that John lived and looked like the old prophets of whom they had heard. Read II Kings 1:8.

Where did John live?
What did he wear?
What was his food?

The people flocked to hear him and believed that what he told them came from God. He first pointed out the sins into which they had fallen and told them to repent. Then he baptized them in the water of the Jordan. We all know that water is the symbol of truth. Baptism with water is the sign that we want to make our lives clean by learning the Lord's truth and obeying it. You know perhaps that when you were baptized, your parents promised to try to bring you up to obey the truth as our Lord Jesus Christ showed it to us. He Himself made baptism the Christian sign.

In verse 7 of our chapter, what did John say?
With what did he say the Lord would baptize?
What was seen after Jesus was baptized?
What did the voice from heaven say?

This showed John and all the people present that Jesus was the promised Messiah or Christ—*Messiah* is the Hebrew word and *Christ* the Greek word meaning "the anointed one." Read Isaiah 9:6. They knew from this prophecy that the Messiah would be called the Son of God while He was in the world but that He would really be "the everlasting Father" come down into a form which men could see.

Where did the Lord go after His baptism?
What happened to Him there?

The rest of our chapter tells of the beginning of the Lord's ministry. He went about teaching, preaching, and healing. People began to follow Him in crowds. Some came just to see the wonderful things He did, but others came because they wanted to learn and obey. The Lord knew that He could not stay in the world very long. So part of His work was to give special instruction to a few chosen followers who would be able and willing to carry the Gospel—the "good news"—of His life to all the world after He should have left their visible presence. We learn in this chapter how He found and called the first four of these chosen disciples.

What were their names?

We shall learn about the others in a later lesson.

The Lord began almost immediately to perform miracles. A miracle means simply a "wonderful" thing, but we use the word to describe acts which only the Lord could do. Three miracles are described in this chapter and many others referred to. We also learn that he taught in the synagogue in Capernaum.

## Intermediate

The reason for the return from captivity should be stressed in introducing the lesson, as well as the way in which the scribes and Pharisees had confused the people by their added regulations. The correspondence of baptism, of the Jordan, and of the dove are important, and the class should also be told why the Lord was called the Son of God.

Four hundred years elapse between the close of the Old Testament and the beginning of the New. In all that time no prophet was sent. You remember that, although the people of Israel never came back after they were carried away to Assyria, it was promised by the prophets that the people of Judah would be allowed to return. The story of their return is told in the historical books of

Ezra and Nehemiah, which our teachings tell us do not have an inner meaning. Swedenborg tells us the reason these people were allowed to return. It was because the Lord, when He came into the world, was to "fulfill" the Law and the Prophets, to live out before the eyes of men the divine truth which was within the Word. So He had to come among the people who had the Word and in the country where the names of the places had been used in the Word to correspond to things in that inner truth. The returned captives rebuilt Jerusalem and the temple and re-established the forms of their religion. They did not go back to the open idolatry which they knew had been the cause of the fall of their nation, but instead they built up such a body of additional laws and regulations for the carrying out of their worship that by the time the Lord came into the world, He could tell them truly, "Ye have made the commandment of God of none effect by your tradition." (Matthew 15:6) The simple good people, who could not read the Word for themselves, did not really know what it taught. Read Matthew 23:23.

Now read Malachi 3:1 and 4:5-6. You see that the very last prophet to speak to the people before the Advent, and indeed the very last words of that prophet, told them that when the Messiah was about to appear, someone—who would be like Elijah—would come as a messenger of the Lord to prepare the people to receive Him. This messenger was John the Baptist. Read II Kings 1:8. John the Baptist dressed as Elijah did. Like Elijah he lived in the wilderness. He had all the marks of a great prophet, and this made people listen to him and believe what he said. Even Herod believed him to be a prophet.

Like Elijah and all the prophets, John pointed out the sins of the people and told them to repent. You know that when you are in a selfish and willful state, you do not want to be told the truth about yourself. You will not listen, and then you are punished because you were told what was right and refused to do it. If people had not been led by John to see and put away their sins before the Lord began to preach, they would not have accepted what He said and acknowledged Him to be the Messiah. We always have to put away wrongdoing before we can do right. John the Baptist stands for this first necessary step in the Christian life. That was why he baptized in the Jordan, because baptism pictures making the life clean according to the truth, and the Jordan pictures the truths which introduce us into the good life—truths like the commandments. We know that if we break the commandments we are not good, no matter what other seemingly good things we may do.

John told the people that the Lord, when He came, would baptize them with the Holy Spirit. The Holy Spirit is the Lord's own spirit of unselfish love, which comes into our hearts from Him after we put away selfishness and wrongdoing.

In the account of the Lord's baptism in Matthew 3:13-17 we learn that John recognized the Lord when He came to be baptized and wanted the Lord to baptize him instead. Read Matthew 3:15. You see that the Lord taught that baptism was the orderly beginning of the kind of life He came to show us, the Christian life. If we take the Lord as our example, we begin by being baptized.

The dove which, descended on the Lord was a representation of the Holy Spirit. When we believe in the Lord and want to obey Him, His spirit comes down into our good desire and shows us the truth of the things we have learned from the Word about Him. Swedenborg says the dove which descended on the Lord at His baptism pictures "the Holy of faith." This means that the truths of the Word are holy because they come from the Lord. In heaven when the angels are talking about the holy truths which their minds are receiving from the Lord, doves appear about them. Whenever we read the word "dove" in the Word, the angels who are with us immediately think about some holy truth that comes from the Lord.

We need also to understand why the voice from heaven said, "Thou art my beloved Son," and why the first verse of our chapter says, "the gospel of Jesus Christ, the Son of God." Read carefully Isaiah 9:6. You see that in this prophecy it is said that a "son" would be given to the world and yet one of His names would be "the everlasting Father." When the Lord came into the world in fulfillment of this prophecy, He was often called the "Son of God" and yet He said of Himself (John 14:9), "He that hath seen me hath seen the Father." The people thought of Him at first as a man like themselves; so He allowed them to think of Him as the Son of God until they had learned enough of the wonderful things He did and said to be ready to believe that He was really their heavenly Father Himself.

His wonderful works began immediately after His baptism. He went into the wilderness for forty days to conquer the temptations which were in the natural body and mind in which He was living. Then He began His ministry. The three parts of this ministry were preaching, teaching, and healing. Preaching has to do with the heart, teaching with the mind, and healing with the body. Our chapter contains the story of three different miracles of healing. It also tells of His preaching in the synagogue in Capernaum and later in the synagogues throughout Galilee. And it tells of the calling of the first four disciples who were to become apostles. We shall have more to say about all these things in later lessons.

*Basic Correspondences*

baptism = cleansing the life
according to the truth

the Jordan = introductory truths

the dove = the Holy of faith

## Senior

Show this class the reason why some of the captives of Judah had to return from Babylon to the Holy Land and also the reason why their history after the return is not part of the Word. The first two quotations at the end of the lesson furnish the basis for this discussion. The necessity for John's work, according to the statement in Malachi 4:6, should be discussed, together with the application to our own lives and the care of divine providence in protecting us from accepting truth which we are unwilling to use in life. Stress the meaning of baptism and its importance as a sacrament.

When the people of Judah were carried away captive to Babylon, some of the poorer people were left in the land, and it was also prophesied that the faithful among the captives would eventually be allowed to return. The books of Ezra and Nehemiah (which do not have an inner sense) tell the story of this return. After seventy years of captivity "the Lord stirred up the spirit of Cyrus king of Persia," who was at this time ruling over Babylon, to proclaim that all the captives who wished to return and rebuild Jerusalem and the temple might do so. He also commanded that those who did not choose to return should help their brethren with money and other gifts, and he himself restored to them the gold and silver vessels of the temple which had been taken to Babylon by Nebuchadnezzar. About fifty thousand people returned at this time and another thousand or more returned later with Ezra under Artaxerxes. The temple was rebuilt and all the forms of worship were re-established. The prophets Haggai, Zechariah, and Malachi belong to this period. Their mission was to promote the rebuilding of the temple, to rebuke the people for the evils into which they had fallen, and to foretell the coming of the Messiah. But we should note that after Malachi no prophet arose for four hundred years. Although those who returned did not fall back into open idolatry and continued to read the Law and the Prophets and to observe the rites which preserved the connection between heaven and earth, their history no longer represented anything spiritual. So it does not appear as part of the Word. We are told in the writings of Swedenborg that it was necessary for them to return because the Lord had to come into the world among those who had the Word and in the land whose mountains and rivers and forests had been used representatively in the Word. But the writing of the Word itself was not continued until He came.

We are studying the story of the Lord's life from the Gospel of Mark. The four Gospels give us this story from four points of view, complementing each other. We notice immediately that Mark does not give us any account of the Lord's birth and childhood. He takes up the story at the time when the Lord—at about the age of thirty—came forth from Nazareth to begin His active ministry. We remember from the Christmas lessons that very few people actually knew of Him at the time of His birth. So the beginning of the Gospel of Mark helps us to understand how most of the people must first have heard of Him.

We must remember that all the people were brought up on the story of the wonderful history of their nation, of the miracles Jehovah had wrought for them in the old days and the great prophets who had been sent to them. Now suddenly in their own day they again had a prophet. John the Baptist lived in the wilderness. He wore the hairy mantle and leathern girdle of the old prophets. And he spoke with the same powerful, chiding voice which they heard from the scrolls in their synagogues. They flocked to hear him. He showed them their sins, and they saw and confessed them and were baptized by Him in Jordan. They were familiar with ritual washings. But John also, like the earlier prophets, spoke of the long-awaited Messiah. Indeed he said that the time was at hand, that he himself was the messenger of the Advent spoken of by their last prophet, Malachi (Malachi 3:1; 4:5-6). Then one day, as John was baptizing, a stranger from Nazareth appeared, and when He was baptized, the heavens opened, a dove descended upon Him, and a voice told them that this was the Son of God.

The Lord came to "fulfill" the Law and the Prophets. We know that this meant that He lived out before men the inner truth of the Word. But He also in many instances fulfilled the literal prophecies. The people were accustomed to think of the Messiah as the "Son of God," but they knew that this "Son" would be no other than Jehovah Himself wearing the form of a man of flesh and blood. Read Isaiah 9:6. All who were truly prepared by recognizing their own sins and need of help received Him. In Malachi 4:6 we learn that if John had not been sent to prepare His way, the Lord's coming would have smitten the earth with a curse. Does this seem strange? We can understand it by a very simple example. The man or woman today who professes to believe in the Lord while in his heart he does not desire or intend to obey Him is the person who not only does the Christian Church on earth most harm but also is himself a hypocrite and is most surely headed for the hells. Read what the Lord said of the scribes and Pharisees in Matthew 23:23-33. Read also John 3:19. The great body of the people rejected and crucified the Lord not because He did not fulfill the Law and the Prophets and prove Himself to be the Messiah, but because they did not want to live the truth He showed them. The good in heart, who are represented by those who listened to John, repented, and were baptized—washed clean by the truth—were the ones to whom the Lord's coming was a blessing. It is the same today.

Mark gives only two verses to the Lord's forty days in the wilderness tempted of the devil, which Matthew and Luke describe in more detail. He passes immediately to the calling of the first disciples, the beginning of the Lord's preaching in the synagogues, and His miraculous healings. Mark himself was not one of the apostles although, since his mother was prominent among the early Christians (Acts 12:12), he undoubtedly knew the Lord and witnessed some of the things he describes. He was later a close companion of Peter. So he had in his mind the facts which enabled the Lord to use him as one of the writers of the Word.

---

### Adult

Interesting discussion topics are the reason for the return from captivity, the nature of the four-hundred-year period following, the value of having four Gospels, the facts we know about Mark as an individual, and the reason why John had to come before the Lord.

Each of the Gospels makes the connection with the Old Testament in a different way. Matthew and Luke give the genealogies and cite the fulfillment of certain prophecies by the coming of the Lord. John shows the inner connection with all that went before from the beginning of creation. Mark makes the most immediate direct connection with the end of the Old Testament, quoting in his second verse the prophecy of Malachi, the last of the Old Testament prophets.

We now begin the study of the Gospel of Mark. The four Gospels complement each other. Although for the most part they present the same facts, each one adds details not mentioned in the others, and each offers a slightly different viewpoint. This has always been recognized. The first "harmony" of the Gospels was produced by Tatian as early as 170 A.D. The first thing that strikes us about the Gospel of Mark is his omission of any account of the Lord's birth and childhood. We know that the Lord in dictating the Word made use of the things which were in the minds of the individuals through whom He wrote. Mark's mind was apparently preoccupied with the marvelous works of the Lord in His public ministry. Mark was not one of the apostles. He is not mentioned by name in any of the Gospels. That he had personal acquaintance with the Lord we may assume from the first mention of him in Acts 12:12, where it is evident that his mother's home was a rendezvous for Christians in Jerusalem. We learn here that Mark's Hebrew name was John. *Mark* is the English form of the Latin *Marcus*. During the time of Roman rule, many boys were given double names in this way. In Acts 13:5 we hear of John Mark again as assisting Paul and Barnabas on their missionary journeys. In Acts 13:13 he leaves them and returns to Jerusalem, and we find that his return prejudiced Paul against him and caused a separation between Paul and Barnabas (Acts 15:36-41). Colossians 4:10 gives us the information that Mark was a nephew of Barnabas, and by that time he had also been re-accepted by Paul as a companion. Paul again speaks of him favorably in II Timothy 4:11. In I Peter 5:13 we learn that he was with Peter in Babylon, and tradition says that it was from Peter that he received most of his knowledge of the Lord's life. At least it is apparent that he was in a position to learn from Peter, one of the three disciples who had been with the Lord most constantly from the beginning of His public ministry.

The general impression we get from the opening chapter of Mark is that of the impact of the first public appearance of the Lord upon the common people. The immediate reference to the prophecy of Malachi bridges the four-hundred-year gap in the coming of the Word of the Lord. Malachi prophesied a messenger of the Advent. John the Baptist is that messenger. Malachi (Malachi 4:5-6) had also prophesied that Elijah would be the one sent. The fact that John looked and dressed like Elijah and that he lived in the wilderness, thus fulfilling the prophecy of Isaiah 40:3, must have disposed the people to accept him and welcome his instruction. Even Herod recognized him as a holy man and feared him (Mark 6:20).

John's preaching in the wilderness may well be compared to the wilderness period in Jewish history. The relation of his mission to the Lord's ministry is the same as that of the wilderness journey to the conquest of the Holy Land. We recall that the Israelites had to remain in the wilderness until all those had died who were unwilling to face the sacrifices and dangers involved in the conquest, and that this pictured that our regeneration cannot begin until we are willing to recognize and with the Lord's help fight the evils within ourselves. Malachi 4:6 tells us that unless John had prepared the way, the Lord's coming would have smitten the earth with a curse. Sin is to acknowledge the truth and be unwilling to try to obey it. Again and again in the writings we read that the Lord enlightens only those who are seeking the truth for the sake of life. The Lord teaches this same lesson when He says to Nicodemus (John 3:19): "This is the condemnation, that light is come into the world, and men loved darkness rather than light, because their deeds were evil." It is taught also in many passages in which the Lord is said to have blinded men's eyes lest they see.

We do not read of baptism as such before John, but the people of that day were familiar enough with washings and purifications to accept it as necessary, and the Lord made it a Christian sacrament by His example first and later by command (Matthew 28:19). It is the symbol of our desire to cleanse our lives according to the truths which the Lord gives us in the Word. We recall that the Jordan, the boundary of the Holy Land, pictures introductory truths.

Mark does not record the story of John's hesitation to baptize the Lord and the Lord's answer. He gives us the simple, powerful picture of the sudden appearance of the stranger from Nazareth coming to be baptized with the rest and then, as He came up from the water, the opening of the heavens, the descent of the dove, and the voice proclaiming this to be the "beloved Son," the long-awaited Messiah. It is not surprising that in the first verse of this Gospel as well as in verse 11 the Lord is referred to as the Son of God. The people had been taught to think of the Messiah, as they would see Him in the flesh, as the Son of God, but they knew also that He would be Jehovah Himself. We may be certain of this by studying the familiar prophecy in Isaiah 9:6.

## From the Writings of Swedenborg

*Arcana Coelestia*, n. 10559[3]: "The church had been in the land of Canaan from the most ancient times, and . . . the Word could not have been written elsewhere, thus except with the nation which possessed that land; and where the Word is, there is the church. That the Word could not have been written anywhere else was because all the places that were in the whole of that land, and that were round about it, such as the mountains, the valleys, the rivers, the forests, and all the rest, had become representative of celestial and spiritual things; and it was necessary that the sense of the letter of the Word, in both the historical and the prophetical parts, should consist of such things, because the interior things of the Word, which are celestial and spiritual, must close in such things, and as it were stand on them like a house upon its foundation."

*Apocalypse Explained*, n. 1029[17]: "Since the Lord was to be born in that nation and make Himself manifest where the church then was and where His Word was, so that nation after a captivity of seventy years was brought back from Babylon, and the temple was rebuilt. And yet no other church remained with them except a church like that called Babylon, as can be seen from many things which the Lord himself said about that nation, and from the way they received Him; and for this reason Jerusalem was again destroyed, and the temple burnt with fire."

*True Christian Religion*, n. 144: Of the descent of the dove: "This took place because baptism signifies regeneration and purification; and a dove has the same signification. Who cannot see that the dove was not the Holy Spirit; and that the Holy Spirit was not the dove? Doves often appear in heaven; and whenever they appear the angels know that they are correspondences of the affections and consequent thoughts concerning regeneration and purification of some who are near by."

## Suggested Questions on the Lesson

J. What is the whole story of the Old Testament about?  *history of Israel*

P. What event marks the beginning of the New Testament?  *birth of Jesus Christ*

J. Why were the Jews allowed to return from Babylon?  *to re-establish Judaism in Canaan*

J. What three prophets prophesied after the return?  *Haggai, Zechariah, Malachi*

P. Who was the last of these?  *Malachi*

J. How many years passed after the time of Malachi before the Lord was born?  *about four hundred*

S. Why are the events of these years not described in the Word?  *no prophet arose*

P. How many Gospels are there?  *four*

J. Why did the Lord give us so many accounts of His life?  *fill out one another*

J. What can you tell about Mark?  *John Marcus, mother Christian, traveled with Peter*

P. At what point in the Lord's life does Mark's Gospel begin?  *baptism of the Lord*

J. What prophecy did John the Baptist fulfill?  *Malachi's*

P. Where did he live?  *wilderness*

P. What did he wear?  *camel's hair, leather belt*

P. What was his food?  *locusts and wild honey*

J. What was his message?  *Repent!*

I. What does baptism represent?  *cleansing lives with the Lord's truth*

P. Who came from Nazareth to be baptized?  *Jesus*

P. What happened when the Lord was baptized?  *Spirit descended like dove*

J. What did the voice from heaven say?  *"Thou art my beloved Son"*

J. Who were the first four men the Lord called to be His disciples?  *Simon Peter, Andrew, James, John*

I. What is the rest of our chapter about?  *beginning of Lord's ministry of teaching, preaching, and healing*

# NEW WINE
## Mark 2

Review briefly the last lesson, calling attention especially to the latter part of chapter 1, as the connection with today's lesson can be made most easily by speaking of the miracles, and pointing out again that the Lord's ministry had three parts: preaching, teaching, and healing, and that the physical healings were always done as signs of His power to heal the souls of men.

---

### Doctrinal Points
*The Lord performed miracles in order to teach spiritual lessons.*
*The Lord "broke" the laws only in the Jewish interpretation of them.*
*Faith had to be present if a man was to be healed by a miracle.*
*It is right to do good on the sabbath day.*

---

### Notes for Parents
There were three parts of the Lord's ministry: preaching, teaching, and healing. He preached in the synagogues. He taught in many surroundings, on mountaintops and by the seashore to great crowds of people, and in houses and quiet places apart to His close disciples. And everywhere He went He healed people of all kinds of diseases. The people probably thought that the miracles of healing were the most important part of His work. We all tend to think that our bodies are the most important part of us. But the Lord's miracles were just evidences of His power to do more important things for us, to help us get rid of selfish passions and wrong thoughts which make our souls sick. So the palsied man in our chapter for today is a picture of every one of us in the times when we mean to do right but just don't seem able to do it. The Lord shows us in the story of this miracle that first we must see our faults and want

17

to be forgiven, and then we must make a real effort to walk in the
right way.

The scribes and Pharisees were called hypocrites by the Lord
because they pretended to keep all the laws more strictly than
other people and yet were proud and scornful and hard and selfish.
The new wine He came to bring was a new spirit of unselfish love
and service to all mankind, and this could not be contained in the
little petty regulations with which the scribes and Pharisees had
burdened the people. The Lord never broke the commandments,
but He brushed aside all the man-made rules which interfered with
His ministry. He emphasized keeping the spirit of the Law. So He
said that the sabbath was made for man. The sabbath is our opportunity to put aside a lot of the things that keep us so busy and
tired during the week, and to think about the really important
things which will last forever. Our bodies do need rest, but our
souls need rest in the Lord; they need spiritual food, knowledge
of the Lord and of what He wants us to be, and time to do some
of the kind and helpful things for others which are crowded out
during the week. Sunday should be the happiest day of the week
because it brings us closer to the Lord, from whom all real happiness comes.

### Primary

Although this lesson is oriented toward the latter part of the chapter, it is suggested that the better passage for the teacher to read aloud is the story of the
healing of the palsied man, which will be easier for the children to understand.
However, they can understand verses 21 and 22 in the literal sense and will be
interested in what "bottles" [KJV] were in those days. Be sure they understand who the scribes and Pharisees and the publicans (tax collectors) were.

Where did the Lord grow up?
Who was sent to prepare the people to receive Him?
How did John prepare them?

You remember how the Lord came to John the Baptist to be
baptized. That was the first time most of the people had seen Him,
but He soon became known to many as He went about through

Galilee doing good. He preached in the synagogues, and He healed many sick people who were brought to Him.

In our lesson today the Lord had come back to Capernaum.
The first part of the chapter tells about how He healed a man who had the palsy and was paralyzed so that he had to be carried about on a bed.
The people all flocked about the Lord.

You can imagine how eager people were to see the Lord and how they listened to what He taught them. But you know there are always people who want to be important themselves and don't like to see people paying attention to someone else. In the Lord's time the scribes and Pharisees were like that. The scribes were the men who knew how to read and write and spent most of their time copying the books of the Law and the Prophets, and so thought they knew more than anyone else. And the Pharisees were a group who prided themselves on keeping every little bit of the Law. They set themselves up as the most religious people in the country and thought everyone ought to obey them. So the scribes and Pharisees were always finding fault with the Lord and asking why He didn't do just as they did. Our chapter tells about some of their foolish complaints.

What fault did they find first?
What was the Lord's answer to this complaint?
The publicans were hated because they earned their living by collecting taxes for the Romans from their own people.
The Lord came to help all who really wanted help.
What was the next complaint against Him?
What did He answer?

He could not be hindered in His work by the silly rules of the Pharisees. He compared these rules to old cloth into which you could not put a new piece, and to old wine skins too weak to hold new wine. The "bottles" [KJV] of that day were not glass bottles such as we have, but the skins of animals drawn off whole and then tied tightly at the legs so that they would hold liquid.

New ideas necessarily change our ways of living.
The Lord came to give a new understanding of what real goodness is.
The old ways did not fit this new understanding.

## Junior

This is a good opportunity to discuss the New Testament division of the Holy Land, comparing it with the earlier division between Israel and Judah and with the even earlier division among the twelve tribes. We shall not be using a map much in our study of Mark, but the children need to have the geography clearly in mind. Have the class look up the Bible references. Explain who the scribes, Pharisees, and publicans were, and the nature of the "bottles" [KJV]. Emphasize the purpose of the sabbath.

Where was the Lord brought up?
Who was sent to prepare his way?
How did He prepare it?
In what river did John baptize?

During the three years of His ministry the Lord made His head-quarters at Capernaum on the Sea of Galilee. At this time the Holy Land was divided into three districts, Judea, Samaria, and Galilee. The greatest concentration of people was in Judea, although there were many Jews in the northern part of the land also. Samaria was largely occupied by the descendants of the "strangers" brought in from the east when Assyria conquered Israel. Galilee was called "Galilee of the Gentiles" because there were so many Greeks and other foreigners there. Bethlehem and Jerusalem were in Judea, Nazareth and Capernaum in Galilee. Most of the Lord's ministry was in Galilee, but He went down to Jerusalem for the great feasts, going and coming through Samaria, and also frequently crossing the Jordan or the Sea of Galilee into the territory on the other side, which was called Perea by the Romans.

Which of the twelve tribes had originally settled in this cross-Jordan country?
Who were the first four disciples of the Lord?
Where did He find them?

After the Lord's baptism He went about Galilee preaching in the synagogues and healing all kinds of diseases. In our lesson for today He has come back to Capernaum. Because of His miracles of healing His fame had grown and people in Capernaum flocked to see Him and brought their sick to be healed.

What miracle is described in our chapter?

Palsy is a form of paralysis and this man was so palsied that he was not able to walk.

How was he brought within reach of the Lord?
What did the Lord do for him first?
What did the scribes think?
How did the Lord silence them?

The scribes were men who copied the Scriptures—printing had not yet been invented—and also various commentaries written by the rabbis. They prided themselves on their knowledge of the Law and were looked up to as authorities. And the Pharisees were the sect who placed great weight on observing every little detail not only of the Law but of the sayings of the rabbis. The Lord called both the scribes and the Pharisees hypocrites. Read what He says about them in Matthew 23:13-33, especially verses 23 to 28. The scribes and Pharisees were jealous of anyone who seemed to be drawing the attention and respect of the people. They saw in the Lord a threat to their own authority, and throughout His ministry they tried in every possible way to find fault and to lead Him into saying something which they could use against Him.

In this chapter whom did the Lord call to be His disciple?
What was this man's business?

The publicans were Jews who earned their living by collecting the taxes imposed on the Jews by Rome. The Jews of course resented the Roman rule and also the taxation, and so they despised any of their own people who went into this occupation. Look up Matthew 9:9 to see who this Levi was whom the Lord called to be His disciple. As we learned in our lesson on the first chapter of Mark, it was not uncommon for a man to have two names and to be called sometimes by one and sometimes by the other.

What fault did the scribes and Pharisees now find with the Lord?
How did the Lord answer?

The only people whom the Lord cannot help are those who are so satisfied with themselves that they think they do not need His help. We should constantly be on our guard against becoming self-satisfied because this, above everything else, closes the door of our souls against the Lord.

What was the next criticism of the Lord?

The Lord's answer may seem hard to understand unless we think of what fasting is and why people fast. Literally fasting means going without food or at least without certain foods we especially like. People fast when they are physically sick or when they are feeling very sorrowful. The fasts of Bible days were prescribed to bring the people into a state of repentance and humility. So the disciples of John did fast. But the Lord's presence always made His disciples happy and as long as He was with them they could not grieve or fast. Read John 15:11.

Now let us see what the Lord meant by verses 21 and 22. We can very easily understand about the cloth because we all know how thin and weak the edges of a hole in old cloth are. To understand about the "bottles" we need to know that they were not the kind of bottles we use, but wineskins, made of the skins of animals, usually goats, drawn off very carefully and tied tightly at the legs so that they would hold liquid. These skins of course gradually wore thin and might easily break under the fermenting pressure of new wine. But we should know that both these verses are parables with a deeper meaning within the letter. Read again Matthew 23:23. The old garment and the old wineskin were like the tithes which the scribes and Pharisees made so important that they forgot "the weightier matters of the law, judgment, mercy, and faith" which were the real "wine" inside. The Lord came to bring to men a new understanding of what goodness is, goodness of heart, kindness, unselfishness, service of the Lord and the neighbor. These were the new "cloth" to be woven, the new "wine" which could not be contained in the old formal observances of rites and ceremonies.

What was the final complaint in this chapter against the Lord?

In this case the Lord silenced His accusers by reminding them that David himself, who was their great hero, had broken the sabbath in the sense in which they were using it. We need to read this part of the lesson carefully. The Lord, when He said that the sabbath was made for man, was not doing away with the sabbath. He was pointing out why it was ordained. It is set apart so that we may have time to learn of the Lord and do things for others which we have no time for during the week. The Lord often healed on the sabbath day. He was criticized for it, but his way of using the sabbath was a "new bottle" to hold the "new wine" He brought.

────────

### Intermediate

There are several important lessons in correspondence here, especially the palsy, the wine, and the "bottles" or wineskins. The meaning of verses 21 and 22 can be discussed in connection with the lesson on the sabbath.

The first chapter of Mark tells us that after His baptism and His forty days' temptation in the wilderness the Lord went about Galilee preaching in the synagogues and healing all manner of diseases. The Lord did heal the sick, but we know that it was the souls of the people rather than their bodies in which He was primarily interested and that His physical healings were a picture of what He can do and wants to do for our souls. It is a good thing to have a healthy body if we use our bodies for good purposes. Our bodies are tools given us for use in this world and we should take care of them just as a good workman takes care of his tools, but the really important thing is what we make or build with our tools.

In the Scriptures diseases always picture spiritual weaknesses, each disease a different weakness. In our chapter for today we have the story of the man who was sick of the palsy. Palsy or paralysis pictures the inability to carry out our good intentions. We often know what is right and say that we want to do it, but we just can't seem to make ourselves do it. This is spiritual palsy. Notice that the Lord pointed out that the first need the man had was to get rid of his sins. Then He told him to take up his bed and walk. We need first to acknowledge that the failure to do right is our own fault—not the fault of our inheritance or of anything in the world around us—and then we must force ourselves to do what we know we ought to do. If you have forgotten the Lord's charge to Joshua, re-read Joshua 1:7.

Then in our lesson we have the calling of another disciple. The first four, you remember, were fishermen, but this one was a tax collector, or publican, an occupation despised by the Jews because they hated the Roman rule and taxation. You may wonder why we do not hear more of this Levi, as we do of Peter and some of the others. But Levi had another name by which we know him well. Read Matthew 9:9.

The scribes and Pharisees were afraid of this new preacher whom the people were flocking to hear. They had always been considered the authorities as to the Law and they were very jealous of their authority. So they constantly looked for some breaking of the Law of which they might accuse the Lord. The Gospels frequently tell of the Lord's encounters with the scribes and Pharisees. The Lord called them hypocrites (Matthew 23:13-33), and He always was able to answer their criticisms in such a way as to silence them. Even when they put Him to death, He rose again from the dead. In our chapter they first accuse Him of eating with publicans and sinners and He merely points out—what they cannot deny—that the duty of a preacher, as of a physician, is to help those who need his help. The religious leaders despised all who were different from themselves. You remember how Jonah resisted the Lord's command to preach to the people of Nineveh. The Scriptures, both the Old and the New Testaments, are full of condemnations of the church for its attitude toward Gentiles. No one who sets himself up as better than other people is in a state to receive instruction or help from the Lord.

The next fault the scribes and Pharisees found was with the fact that the Lord's disciples did not fast. The Lord answered this time by pointing out that there is a time for everything and that His disciples were not in any need of fasting so long as He was with them. Fasting is a symbol of sorrow, especially sorrow during temptation. The Lord himself fasted during the forty days of His temptation in the wilderness. But the disciples were happy when they were with the Lord; so during His lifetime on earth there would have been no point in their fasting.

The Lord sums up this teaching in the verses about the new cloth and the new wine. Garments picture truths with which we clothe our affections. When we receive new truth, everything in our old ideas which is not in agreement with it has to go. For example, people used to think that the earth was flat. Maps were drawn with this in mind and you can imagine how everything had to be changed when they discovered that the earth is round. New wine is a picture of new spiritual truth, new truth about the Lord and our relation to Him. Up to this time, people had always thought of God as like themselves in the sense of wanting praise and glory for Himself, loving only those who served and flattered Him, and punishing those who disobeyed Him. In addition to the Law given them in the Word, the scribes and Pharisees had built up a man-made system of rules of all kinds which they made the people obey. These were the old "bottles" which the new "wine" would break.

We have another clear example of what the Lord meant in the last few verses of our chapter. The Pharisees had made the sabbath a very hard and trying day. Others have sometimes done this too. Perhaps you have read how the Puritans in the early days of America thought the sabbath should be observed. Such mistakes come from putting more importance on outward than on inward things. All through His ministry the Lord was condemned by the Pharisees for "breaking" the sabbath, because He went about freely on that day, healed the sick, and did whatever was necessary to help others. The fact was that the sabbath of the Pharisees was an old bottle that had to be broken.

The Lord, when He said "the sabbath was made for man," did not do away with the sabbath: He merely told us what it is for. In Luke 4:16 we read, "As his custom was, he went into the synagogue on the sabbath day." The sabbath is a day set apart for the special purpose of learning of the Lord, joining in public worship, resting from the rush of our worldly activities, and doing some of those kind and helpful things for which we do not have time during the week. It should be different from every other day of the week, but it should be our happiest day because it should bring us closer to the Lord and to each other. The commandments had to be given in the negative because it is so easy for us to carry our weekday habits and occupations over into Sunday and so to spoil it for its real use; but we should get over the old idea of Sunday as a day on which we are *not* to do this or that, and think of it as our opportunity *to do* the most important things of all.

### Basic Correspondences

|                           |   |                                              |
|--------------------------:|---|----------------------------------------------|
| palsy or paralysis        | = | inability to do right                        |
| fasting                   | = | sorrow because of temptations                |
| "bottles" or wineskins    | = | outward forms in which truth is to be contained |

---

Senior

It is important for the young people to understand why we do not keep all the laws of the Old Testament in the letter and the difference between the ancient Jewish and the early Christian churches. This can be brought out well by a discussion of the meaning of the new wine and the old "bottles" or wineskins. Be sure that they understand that all the laws in the Old Testament are still valid in their internal meaning, and that the ten commandments still hold in their letter also.

In our lesson on the first chapter of Mark we considered principally the mission of John the Baptist and the meaning of the Lord's baptism. But that chapter, after mentioning the Lord's forty days' temptation in the wilderness and the calling of the first four disciples, goes immediately to the account of some of the Lord's miracles. The Gospel of Mark is the shortest of the Gospels and omits some of the important events and teachings of the others, but it contains almost as many of the stories of the miracles as do Matthew and Luke. It was the reports of the Lord's miracles which made the people flock to see and hear Him wherever He went. But we are not left in any real doubt as to the purpose of the miracles. The emphasis is steadily on the casting our of evil and falsity from the heart and mind and restoring the person to usefulness.

Our chapter for today begins with the healing of the palsied man, in which the Lord's first concern is with the man's sins. Palsy or paralysis is a picture of inability to walk in right ways. Spiritually we are all subject to this disease. We mean to lead good lives but we often fail to live up to our good intentions. A bed is a symbol of "doctrine." Doctrine may be religious truth or it may be a system of thinking derived from our environment and past experience. When we excuse ourselves for our shortcomings by saying, "Everybody does it," or "I can't change my nature," or, "Under the circumstances anyone would have acted as I did," we are lying down on our bed and letting others carry us. When we come to the Lord for help, the first step is to acknowledge that the sin is ours and that we need forgiveness, and the next step is to get up on our own feet spiritually and pick up the bed on which we have been carried and take it in the direction in which we ought to go.

The scribes and Pharisees could not deny the miracles. The Lord's power to heal was obvious to everyone. But they refused to believe that it was God's power. Swedenborg tells us that this was the very reason why miracles could be performed then, whereas they could not be performed today. Such miracles today would force men to believe in the Lord even when they did not want to obey Him. The Lord never forces us to believe in Him against our wills. Even among the people of Bible days the miracles were accepted and believed only by those who already believed.

The greater part of our chapter is concerned with efforts of the scribes and Pharisees to discredit the Lord. Their first complaint was that He ate with publicans and sinners. This is introduced by the incident of His calling Levi—Matthew (see Matthew 9:9)—from his place as tax collector to be one of His disciples. Matthew was a publican, one of the Jews despised by the Pharisees because they collected taxes for the Roman rulers. Several times the Lord's enemies tried to trick Him into saying something which they could report as treasonable, but He foiled each attempt by putting His finger on the root of the complaint. In this case He pointed out that it is the duty of the truly strong and great to help the weak and unfortunate. There was no answer to this obvious truth.

The rest of the chapter finds its keynote in verses 21 and 22. The scribes and Pharisees, as we read in Matthew 23:13-33, were sticklers for the Law but had no interest in the virtues which the Law was intended to develop and express. The Lord came to fulfill the Law and the Prophets, to live out before men the inner quality of divine truth. We are familiar with the fact that every little regulation commanded in the books of Moses has a spiritual meaning which is its timeless meaning. The regulation itself is like the husk in which the nourishing kernel of wheat is preserved. The Lord came to bring the wheat to view and the husks had to be broken in the process. The charge that His disciples did not fast and the frequent charges that He and His disciples "broke" the sabbath showed that to the scribes and Pharisees the husks were the all of religion.

New wine is a new interpretation of divine truth, which requires new forms for its expression. In the sermon on the mount we read several times: "Ye have heard that it was said by them of old time. . . . But I say unto you . . ." (Matthew 5:21-48). The Lord thus contrasted old forms with the new spirit which He had come to give. And He said (Mark 10:5) of one of the regulations of the Law of Moses: "For the hardness of your heart he wrote you this precept." Yet the Lord did not come to "destroy the law, or the prophets." He came to point out that the Law was not in the letter but in the spirit and that the spirit of the Law was love to the Lord and the neighbor.

This is brought out clearly in His teaching with regard to the sabbath. He said that "the sabbath was made for man, and not man for the sabbath." He and His disciples transgressed the law of the sabbath as the Pharisees had interpreted it, but they never "broke the sabbath." They used the sabbath for worship, for instruction, and for works of healing and charity. This is the purpose for which the sabbath was ordained, a regularly recurring opportunity to rest from the worldly occupations which claim so much of our time and strength and to recognize and develop the higher spiritual faculties which alone make us truly human beings.

―――――

### Adult

A profitable discussion topic is the attitude of the scribes and Pharisees toward the Lord and its counterpart in our modern world. One of the prime tasks of the New Church is to counteract the prevailing superficial materialistic trend. The new wine of which the Lord spoke is spiritual truth, and this cannot be confined in materialistic forms of thought.

As we saw in our lesson on chapter 1, the impression made by Mark's Gospel is that of the sudden appearance of the Lord at the beginning of His ministry. So we are almost immediately confronted with the miracles and with the reaction of the scribes and Pharisees against the new prophet to whom all the common people were flocking. John the Baptist had prepared the way of the Lord literally as well as spiritually. Because John dwelt in the wilderness and wore the hairy mantle of the prophets, and especially because nothing he said or did interfered with the position or convenience of the scribes and Pharisees, they had been willing enough to recognize John's claim to be a prophet. In fact, we can imagine that the appearance of such an authentic prophet after four hundred years in which the prophetic voice had been silent might be regarded as a strengthening of the position of religious orthodoxy. But now a person appears of very unorthodox demeanor who nevertheless has the sanction of John. As we learn later (Mark 11:29-32), they were afraid to discredit John because he had been generally accepted as a prophet. So it was a long time before they dared to do more than harass the Lord.

Swedenborg tells us that the miracles could be wrought among the people of that day because they would not interfere with their freedom, as they would have with people of greater spiritual sensitiveness. We read in Luke 10:13, "Woe unto thee, Chorazin! woe unto thee, Bethsaida! for if the mighty works had been done in Tyre and Sidon, which have been done in you, they had a great while ago repented, sitting in sackcloth and ashes." But the scribes and Pharisees could witness the miracles and merely say, "He hath Beelzebub, and by the prince of devils casteth he out devils." (Mark 3:22) The Lord never performed miracles to create faith. Faith had to be present before the miracle was performed. We read in connection with Nazareth, "He did not do many mighty works there because of their unbelief." (Matthew 13:58) The Lord did have compassion on the sick and maimed and obsessed, and He healed as many as were in humble and receptive states, but we are told that the miracles were wrought principally for the sake of the Word, that they might serve as pictures of the works of healing which the Lord can perform in our souls.

This is clearly illustrated in the miracle performed in our chapter. When the palsied man on his bed was let down through the roof into the Lord's presence, we read, "When Jesus saw their faith, he said unto the sick of the palsy, Son, thy sins be forgiven thee." His first concern was with the state of the man's faith and His second with the removal of his sins. Then he healed the man of his sickness "that ye may know that the Son of man hath power on earth to forgive sins." There is a lesson in this miracle for us. The man had faith but could not walk. We often mean to do right but somehow are too weak to carry out our good intentions. We fall back on the mental "bed" we have made to support us in our weakness, excusing ourselves on the ground of our inherited limitations or of our worldly environment or of the provocation under which we labor. If we look to the Lord for help, He shows us that we must first fully trust Him, then recognize that the fault is our own and desire to be forgiven, and finally that we must "take up our bed and walk" in the strength that He can give us.

Our chapter is really a series of encounters with the scribes and Pharisees. They were present at the miracle and objected to the Lord's claim to the power to forgive sins. The physical miracle silenced them only temporarily. When the Lord called a despised publican to be one of His disciples, Levi or Matthew (Matthew 9:9), they immediately found occasion to criticize Him for consorting with publicans and sinners. The new prophet was not following their pattern and so became a threat. The Lord's answer reminds us of the story of Jonah's experience when he refused to take the Lord's message to Nineveh. The religious leaders were proud, hard, contemptuous of everyone outside their own class and especially of Gentiles. We recall the Lord's condemnation of them in Matthew 23:13-33. The Lord is "no respecter of persons" (i.e., He does not show partiality). Humility and need are the gateway to His mercy. The scribes and Pharisees could not answer Him. They knew He was right. But their opposition was merely turned into another channel.

The next attack was on the fact that the Lord's disciples did not fast, and here they took pains to remind Him that the disciples of John did fast. And the Lord pointed out to them that fasting has a meaning and a purpose and that apart from its meaning it is of no value. Fasting, Swedenborg says, is a representation of sorrow, especially of sorrow during temptation. The Lord Himself fasted during the forty days' temptation in the wilderness. But the consciousness of the Lord's presence brings only joy to His disciples. Fasting under such circumstances would be a mockery.

The same distinction between substance and shadow is made in answer to the final complaint in this chapter in regard to the observance of the sabbath. The Lord did not say that either fasting or the sabbath is to be abandoned. Each is to be observed in the time and way for which it was ordained. The individual human soul is the thing in whose interest all observances were commanded, and the way in which these observances are to be kept is the way which promotes the welfare of the soul. The church then was an empty shell, merely the representative of a church, with no spiritual life within it. The Lord came to restore the church, to fulfill the Law and the Prophets, to live out before men the divine truth contained within them. Observance of the old outward forms was not adequate to express the spiritual power which He brought down to men. We know that for the Christian Church the sacrament of baptism is substituted for all the ceremonial washings of the ancient Jewish Church, and the sacrament of the Lord's Supper for all the sacrifices and feasts. There are laws, such as the ten commandments, whose letter can never be abrogated because they are the basic general laws of divine order. But most of the Old Testament ceremonial and civil laws took their literal form, as the Lord noted concerning the law of divorce, "because of the hardness of their hearts."

The teaching of the whole chapter is summed up in verses 21 and 22. (See the quotation from AE 376[28] below.) We need to remember this teaching in our thought about the New Church in its relation to the first Christian Church. When the Lord came into the world He brought new "wine," new truth from the Divine. It required new forms of expression, new "bottles." When He came the second time, He again brought new "wine" and the old forms will not contain it. The new truths revealed in the opened Word vastly expand our concept of our duty to the Lord and the neighbor. They cannot be lived adequately within the boundaries and forms of other churches. While there are all over the world in all religions people who "will be" of the New Church in the other life, they are not yet of that Church. With them the old "bottles" are merely being broken by the new "wine." There must be the specific New Church in the world to keep the new "wine" from being spilled and lost. The organized New Church is a new "bottle" with which its members are entrusted.

## From the Writings of Swedenborg

*Arcana Coelestia*, n. 9182[10]: "That 'the sons of the wedding do not mourn so long as the bridegroom is with them' denotes that they are in a blessed and happy state, thus with the Lord, when they are in truths conjoined with their good; 'they shall fast when the bridegroom is taken away from them' denotes that they are in an unhappy state when good is no longer conjoined with truths."

*Apocalypse Explained*, n. 376[28]: [referring to new wine and old bottles] "This comparison, like all others in the Word, is from correspondences, 'wine' signifying truth, 'old wine' the truth of the old or Jewish Church, and 'wine-skins' things that contain, 'old wine-skins' the statutes and judgments of the

Jewish Church, and 'fresh wine-skins' the precepts and commandments of the Lord. That the statutes and judgments of the Jewish Church, which related especially to sacrifices and representative worship, are not in agreement with the truths of the Christian Church is meant by 'they do not put new wine into old wine-skins, else the wine-skins burst and the wine is spilled; but they put new wine into fresh wine-skins, and both are preserved together' (Matthew 9:17)."

## Suggested Questions on the Lesson

P. Who prepared the way of the Lord? *John the Baptist*

P. What happened when the Lord was baptized? *dove appeared*

J. Who were the first four disciples called? *Peter, Andrew, James, John*

J. What three forms did the Lord's ministry take? *preaching, teaching, healing*

J. Where did he preach? *in the synagogues, many other places*

J. Into what three parts was the Holy Land divided in the Lord's time? *Galilee, Samaria, Judea*

J. In what part was He born? *Judea*

J. In what part did He grow up? *Galilee*

J. Where did most of His ministry take place? *Galilee*

J. Where did He live during His ministry? *Capernaum (by the Sea of Galilee)*

P. What miracle is described in our chapter? *healing paralytic or palsied man*

P. How was the palsied man brought to the Lord? *on a bed or pallet*

J. What did the Lord do for him first? *forgave his sins*

J. What disciple was called in our chapter? *Levi (Matthew)*

J. What was his occupation? *tax collector*

J. Who were (1) the scribes, and (2) the Pharisees? *(1) those who copied Scripture, (2) legalists*

J. Why did the people despise the publicans? *collected taxes for Rome*

J. What was their first complaint against the Lord? *He ate with tax collectors*

J. What was their second complaint? *His disciples didn't fast*

P. What did the Lord say about the new cloth and new wine? *need to go together*

J. What was the third complaint? *He broke the sabbath (picking grain)*

I. What did the Lord say about the sabbath? *made for man*

S. How should the sabbath be used? *to worship, to learn about God, to do good*

# THE TWELVE APOSTLES
*Mark 3*

The connection with the last lesson is easily made through the teaching in regard to the sabbath. Draw from the classes first what the Lord said about the sabbath and what its true purpose is, and then use the miracle in the beginning of today's chapter as an illustration.

―――――

## Doctrinal Points

*The Lord sees to it that everyone receives enough truth to save him if he tries to live according to what he learns.*
*The Word produced the church, not the church the Word.*
*Faith belongs to the understanding or thought plane.*
*Charity belongs to the plane of the heart or will.*
*Selfish motives in the heart destroy charity, no matter how many outwardly good deeds a person may do.*

―――――

## Notes for Parents

In our chapter for today we have an opportunity to see how different kinds of people reacted to the Lord's presence and teaching. We are apt to think that if we had been in the Holy Land when the Lord was on earth, we should certainly have loved and followed Him. But would we? Everyone certainly did not. The scribes and Pharisees resented Him so bitterly that they said that it was the devil from whom He got His power, and they even plotted against Him with their own avowed enemies, the Herodians, who approved of the Roman rule. The Lord's own family thought He was "beside Himself"—crazy—and wanted to force Him to stop His work. The crowds were so much more interested in being healed of their diseases than they were in what the Lord taught that He had to have a ship at hand in which He could get away from them if necessary. Only a very few people really followed Him to learn

34

the truth He came to teach. In which group would we have been?

We can answer this if we ask ourselves honestly in which group we are today. Do we, like the scribes and Pharisees, try to silence the voice that tells us we ought to be kinder and more faithful than we are? Do we, like the Lord's human relatives, think the Lord's teachings are too impractical to believe in? Do we, like the crowd, follow the Lord only for what we can get out of it for ourselves? Or do we, like the true disciples, put the Lord first in our thinking and in our lives and try to learn more and more of what He would have us do?

It was from these true disciples that the Lord chose twelve to be His apostles, to go out into the world after He should leave them and carry the Gospel—the good news—to all people, thus founding the Christian Church.

---

### Primary

After your introductory story, read verses 7 to 20 of our chapter, and talk about the twelve apostles. Teach the children the names of Peter, James, and John. Read the names of the others two or three times so that the names will become familiar. Tell them why they were called *apostles* and what their work was to be. They should also know which ones wrote books of the Bible.

Do you remember how in our lesson for last Sunday we read the story of the man who was sick of the palsy? This was only one of many diseases which our Lord healed when He was living in the world. Such great crowds came to Him to be healed that He often had to go away from them. Our chapter for today begins with the story of how He healed a man who had a withered hand. Because He did this on the sabbath His enemies tried to make trouble for Him. The Lord was never afraid of His enemies. He could always either shame them into silence or else leave them.

Where did He go to escape them?
What did He ask His disciples to provide for Him?
Where did He go to teach His disciples?
How many of them did He ordain to go out and preach?
What powers did He give them?

See how many of their names you can remember.
Which ones have we heard of before?

You will hear very often about the twelve apostles. Their names
are given in this chapter. Let us read how the Lord chose them.
[Read Mark 3:7-19.] We know most about Peter and James and
John. See if you can remember these three names and remember
that this was a different John from John the Baptist. These three
were the Lord's closest followers and were often taken with Him
when the others were not.

Do you know what *disciple* means?
It means "a learner."
The twelve special disciples whom the Lord ordained came to be called the
apostles, because *apostle* means "one sent forth."
They were the ones who were to go out into the world after the Lord left
them and begin the Christian Church.
Three of them—Peter, James, and John—were closer to the Lord than the
others.
He often took them with Him when the others did not go.
Which two apostles were chosen to write Gospels?
John was also the one to whom the revelation was given which is described
in the last book of our Bible.

---

## Junior

Give this class as much information as is available about the less-well-known
apostles, having them look up and read all the references. They should understand the importance of these twelve men in the beginning of the Christian
Church.

What miracle of healing did we learn about in our last lesson?
Who were the scribes?
Who were the Pharisees?
Why did they hate the Lord?
Of what did they accuse Him?
What did the Lord say about new wine?
What did He mean?
What did He say about the sabbath?

You remember that wherever the Lord was He always went to
the synagogue on the sabbath day. Our chapter begins, as the last

one ended, on the sabbath, and the scribes and Pharisees are still standing by to see how they can find fault with the Lord.

What miracle does He perform in the synagogue?
What did He ask the scribes and Pharisees?

Then we are told that He withdrew to the seashore and that He asked His disciples to have a small ship at hand in case the crowd became too great. Read Mark 4:1. You remember that the first four disciples were fishermen; so they had boats at their disposal. The people crowded about the Lord in such great numbers that He often had to withdraw from them. In addition to the seashore another favorite place from which the Lord taught is mentioned in our chapter. Read verse 13. Perhaps you remember the sermon on the mount. Read Matthew 5:1. In the Bible many important things happen on mountain tops. This is because going up on a mountain is a picture of lifting our minds above the plane of worldly thinking and drawing closer to the Lord. If you have ever been on a mountain, you know how small everything down below looks and how far you can see. That is the way this world looks to the Lord and the angels, and it is good for us to get the "angel view" of things sometimes. One of the best-loved of the Psalms (Psalm 121:1) teaches this lesson. You remember that the commandments were given from the top of Mount Sinai.

Who were the first four disciples called by the Lord?
What other disciple did we learn about in our last lesson?

A *disciple* is a "learner." Now we read that the Lord ordained twelve of His disciples to receive special instruction from Him so that they could go out and preach. They have come to be called the twelve apostles, because the word *apostle* means "one sent forth." See if you can learn the names of all twelve. Three of them—Peter, James, and John—were the Lord's closest followers and were taken with Him sometimes when the others were left behind. Andrew was Peter's brother, one of the first four.

The next four are Philip and Bartholomew, Matthew and Thomas. Philip came from Bethsaida, a village near Capernaum at the northern end of the Sea of Galilee. You may read about his call in John 1:43, and if you will read on a little, you will find that Philip brought another disciple, named Nathanael, to the Lord. It is thought that Nathanael may be the personal name of Bartholomew, for Bartholomew means "the son of Tolmai," and this name is not mentioned except in the lists in which all twelve are named. So this disciple might easily have been Nathanael the son of Tolmai. Matthew we can remember from the story of his call, which we had in our last lesson, and also because he was the writer of the first Gospel. To fix Thomas in your mind read John 20:24-29. Sometimes people today call a man who is hard to convince a "doubting Thomas."

Then there is another James, who is referred to sometimes as "James the Less" to distinguish him from the brother of John. He later became a great leader of the early Christians, having charge of the first church in Jerusalem. The disciple called Thaddaeus in this list is elsewhere called both Lebbaeus and Judas "not Iscariot" and is said by Luke to be the brother of the second James. He wrote the Epistle of Jude. Simon the Canaanite is sometimes called Simon Zelotes, and so was apparently one of a very strict sect called the Zealots. And finally there was Judas Iscariot, who became the betrayer of the Lord.

What powers did the Lord give the apostles?

The last part of our chapter teaches us a lesson which we all need. Verse 21 tells us that the Lord's "friends," when they heard the attention He was attracting, "went out to lay hold on him: for they said, He is beside himself." And verse 22 tells us that the scribes and Pharisees said that His power came from the devil. The same thing happens today. When one of our friends starts out on an entirely new course which we do not understand, we are very apt to think he is "crazy." And when someone we dislike does something very good, we are sure that he must have some bad motive behind his act. We are all too ready to think what we like to think instead of finding out what is really true. And in verse 29 the Lord teaches us that this is very dangerous. It is from this verse that people have come to speak of the "unforgivable sin." To "blaspheme against the Holy Spirit" is to be unwilling to acknowledge truth which condemns our evils. It is unforgivable only because it closes our minds to the truth and so makes it impossible for the Lord to reach us.

The last five verses of our chapter sometimes puzzle people, but this is because they want to think of the Lord just as a good man. The Lord was God Himself come into the world and to Him all men and women were equally dear. He wanted to help everyone, but He could come close only to those who were good.

---

### Intermediate

Stress the correspondence of the twelve apostles as a whole and of Peter, James, and John in particular. The difference between a disciple and an apostle can be taken up as it relates to our own activity. We need to be both.

Our chapter for today is very closely connected with the last one. You remember that the Lord told the scribes and Pharisees that the sabbath was made for man and not man for the sabbath, and immediately He had an opportunity to illustrate what He meant. For in the synagogue itself on the sabbath, He finds a man who needs healing, and He asks the scribes and Pharisees, "Is it lawful to do good on the sabbath days, or to do evil? to save life, or to kill?" The same story of the man with the withered hand is told in Matthew 12:9-13, and there He also asks them if they themselves would not rescue one of their sheep which happened to fall into a pit on the sabbath day. The Pharisees could not answer Him, because again they knew He was right; but they went out and "took counsel with the Herodians" against Him. This shows how bitter and determined they were, for the Pharisees and the Herodians were enemies. The Herodians were a political group who supported Herod and favored the Roman rule, while the Pharisees, as we have seen, hated the Roman rule.

The withered hand has a similar correspondence to the palsy, for the hand is always the symbol of power—we carry out most of our intentions by means of our hands. The man with the withered hand pictures those who, for lack of proper spiritual nourishment, have lost the power to do good. The good people in the Lord's time were in this state, and the Lord's teaching and example restored this power just as He restored the man's hand.

The Lord was in the habit of teaching by the seaside and also on a mountain—you remember the sermon on the mount—because the sea pictures knowledges gathered in the memory, and a mountain pictures an elevated state of thought.

Read Mark 4:1. This shows why the Lord asked His disciples to have a small ship at hand. You can see that most of the people who "pressed" upon the Lord to touch Him wanted to be healed of particular diseases and afflictions. The Lord taught such people by the seaside because He can help each of us only through what truths we have in our memories. Whenever we see that there is something wrong in what we are feeling or thinking or doing (this is spiritual disease) the Lord in a secret way brings up in our minds something we have learned from the Word which helps us to understand our fault and overcome it with His help. But then He went up into a mountain and called to Him "whom He would." A great many people want to live good lives and get rid of their faults, but they do not all want to think deeply about the Lord and His truth. The ones whom the Lord calls up into the mountain are those who want to lift their thoughts above the plane of worldly things and learn all they can about heavenly living. These are the people who are concerned not only with being good themselves but with bringing the Lord's truth and healing power to others. It was those who went up into the mountain with the Lord who could be sent out as His apostles.

The word *apostle* means "one sent forth." *Disciple* means "a learner." There were twelve apostles because the number twelve signifies "all things in a complex" or all the things which go together to make a whole. The twelve apostles, like the twelve sons of Jacob, picture all the qualities of faith and love which make a whole person, a person capable of loving, knowing, and serving the

Lord. So each apostle represents some particular quality in us. We cannot consider them all, but we should know about the three who were closest to the Lord—Peter, James, and John. You remember that in every one of us, as in the Lord, there is a trinity, the trinity of will, thought, and act. We would never do anything if we did not have some desire which prompted us. We cannot carry out any desire without thinking about it and learning how to do it. And we are never satisfied until our desire and thought are carried out into action. In the church faith and charity are common terms. Faith belongs to the understanding or thought plane, and charity belongs properly to the plane of the heart or desire. Sometimes people think of charity as just outward good deeds, but these are merely the carrying out into act of charity in the heart. The Lord says that our outward good deeds are not really good at all when they are done, as they sometimes are, from selfish motives like the desire to seem good and to be praised. Peter, James, and John represent the trinity in us: faith, charity, and the good of charity.

The apostles were those who, after the Lord left them, went out into the world and founded the Christian Church. Judas was the only one who did not serve the Lord in this way. We shall learn more about him later.

### Basic Correspondences

|            |   |                          |
|-----------:|---|--------------------------|
| a mountain | = | a high plane of thought  |
|      Peter | = | faith                    |
|      James | = | charity                  |
|       John | = | the good of charity      |

### Senior

The lesson of the unforgivable sin should be discussed with this class and the importance of an attitude of openness to the truth even when it condemns us.

The question which the Lord asked the Pharisees in the synagogue, "Is it lawful to do good on the sabbath days, or to do evil? to save life, or to kill?" carried on the teaching about the sabbath in our last week's lesson. The Pharisees could not answer it, and the Lord then healed the man whose hand had been withered. We know that the hand corresponds to the power to act. Things wither when they are deprived of the necessary nourishment, especially water. The scribes and Pharisees had come between the people and the Word, cutting off the supply of truth which they needed. So they had lost the power to live good lives. The common people were like the man with the withered hand. Note the fact that the Pharisees went out and "took counsel with the Herodians" against the Lord. This shows that they recognized that they had no legitimate means of silencing Him, for the Herodians, the political party who favored Herod and the Roman rule, were normally regarded by the Pharisees as enemies.

There is an interesting contrast presented in this chapter by the Lord's teaching the multitude by the seaside and then going up into a mountain to give special instruction to particular disciples and to commission the twelve apostles. The sea represents knowledges gathered in the memory. The Lord sees to it that everyone has the opportunity to receive into his memory sufficient truth for his salvation, if he chooses to obey it. But not all care to know more than the bare essentials of a good life. Those who want the truth not for their own salvation alone but that they may serve the Lord and the neighbor as fully as possible are pictured by those who were called up into the mountain to the Lord.

The twelve apostles, like the twelve sons of Jacob, represent "all things of faith and love," all the qualities in us which enable us to know and serve the Lord. The three closest to the Lord—Peter, James, and John—represent faith, charity, and the good of charity, the three essential elements of a good life, goodness in the mind, heart, and outward act. The other nine are subsidiary qualities, all good and useful in their proper place—even Judas who, representing the ancient Hebrew nation, pictures the interest in the externals of worship. It is only when the externals are placed in a position of first importance and observed without a true internal that they become perverted. The apostles, with the exception of Judas, were to go out into the world, after the Lord left them, and found the

Christian Church. They were men of different talents and different characters, but the Lord saw in each one capabilities which fitted him for his task. We should note, however, that the power each one had was from the Lord, and that the Gospel they were to preach was from the Lord, not their own. The Lord's life and teachings were the foundations of the Christian Church. The apostles were not the authors of the Gospels. The facts were drawn from their minds and arranged and expressed under inspiration from the Lord. The Word produced the Church, not the Church the Word.

As the Lord's fame grew, His kinsmen from Nazareth, who thought of Him only as one of themselves, were disturbed and said, "He is beside himself" (that is, crazy). We tend to doubt the ability of anyone whom we have known in childhood and youth to become a really great person. And the scribes said, "By the prince of the devils casteth he out devils." When one we dislike does great things, we are all prone to try to read some bad purpose into his seeming good works. The teaching in this chapter is that we should cultivate the habit of judging good and truth impersonally, and ask of any statement not, "Who said it?" but, "Is it true?" and of any deed or project not, "Who began it?" but, "Is it a good and useful thing?" Blasphemy against the Holy Spirit, which has come to be referred to as "the unforgivable sin," is unwillingness to recognize as truth from the Lord anything which condemns our own evils. When we are in this attitude it is impossible for the Lord to reach and help us. So we go on confirming evil in ourselves, which is the road to hell. Humility is the only ground in which the seeds of truth can take root.

The Lord's seeming indifference to His family, described in the last few verses of the chapter, should be considered in connection with their purpose in coming as described in verse 21. The Lord knew the hearts and minds of all men then as He knows them today. We come into relationship with the Lord only as we keep the commandments because they are from Him. This is the thought which is expressed in the last verse of our lesson.

## Adult

You will find that many of the adults will actually know very little about the twelve apostles and will be interested in such details as you can give them. In general, discussion should center on the various ways in which the people of the Lord's time reacted to His presence, and their counterparts in the life of today.

The Lord's life and teaching in the world accomplished the consummation of the ancient Jewish dispensation and the beginning of the first Christian dispensation. The scribes and Pharisees were the official spokesmen of the decadent church, and throughout the Gospels their attitude toward the Lord is one of stubborn and willfully blind rejection. It is interesting that in verse 5 of our chapter for today the word translated "hardness" is actually "blindness." Blindness of heart is the rejection of the truth by the selfish will. It is the "unforgivable sin" of verse 29. Again and again the charges of the scribes and Pharisees were countered by the Lord with such unanswerable truth that they could not argue. But in each case their opposition to Him was increased. In our chapter they "went forth, and straightway took counsel with the Herodians against Him, how they might destroy him." The Herodians were a political party which supported Herod and favored dependence upon Rome. They were enemies of the Pharisees. So a joining of forces with the Herodians was an acknowledgment by the Pharisees that they had no legitimate means of silencing the Lord.

The state of the common people at the end of this dispensation is pictured by the man in the synagogue whose hand was withered. The hand is the symbol of power. Whatever the physical cause of the man's affliction may have been, the use of the word *withered* involves in the spiritual sense the result of a lack of truth. It is lack of water which causes things to wither, and water corresponds to truth. The people had been deprived by the scribes and Pharisees of the truths of the Word. They had lost the power to do good because they did not know what was good. In Matthew 23:13 we read, "But woe unto you, scribes and Pharisees, hypocrites! for ye shut up the kingdom of heaven against men: for ye neither go in yourselves, neither suffer ye them that are entering to go in." The man in the synagogue is a picture of those who were devout and really desired to be able to live good lives.

Another class of people—the most numerous perhaps—is represented by the multitude who "pressed" (literally "rushed") upon the Lord at the seaside, desiring only to be healed of their diseases. Even in the natural sense, these people were thinking of themselves, not of each other or even of the Lord. They recognized their wretchedness and sought relief wherever it was promised. The Lord healed and taught these people by the seashore, a picture of how He is able in the Church universal of any age to lead men to better states by recalling to their minds whatever of truth they have stored in their memories. Verse 11 expresses a truth which is illustrated in several places in the Gospels—the truth that the hells and evil spirits cannot stand in the presence of the Lord. This should teach us that when we are struggling with a temptation, our ability to resist the evil will come only as we admit the Lord into our thoughts.

Then the Lord went up into a mountain and called unto Him whom He would. Those who are called to go up into the mountain with the Lord are those who want more than to be saved from suffering and disaster themselves. They really want to learn of the Lord and serve Him. The Lord found among this group His apostles, men in whom He saw the capacity to learn and also to transmit what they learned to others. Even here we should note that it was He who gave them all the power they had. After the Lord left them, the apostles did go out into the world and establish the Christian Church. But the Gospel they preached was the life of the Lord, and the miracles they performed were done in His name and by His means. One of the most subtle fallacies of our times is the assumption that the beginnings of the Christian Church and the Gospel records of the life of Christ were simply products of the minds and deeds of the apostles. Many conclusions of some modern theologians can be traced to this false premise, and we need to be able to recognize its influence and to discount such conclusions accordingly.

The twelve apostles were all different. Like the twelve sons of Jacob they represent "all things of faith and love in the complex" (AC 9643[4]). The particular correspondence of Peter, James, and John is given us a number of times in the writings: "faith, charity, and the good of charity" (AC preface to 2135) or "truth in the understanding," "truth in the will," and "truth in act" (AE 444[11]). AE 821[3] gives the correspondence of Andrew as "the obedience of faith." The difference between Andrew and John is probably analogous to the difference between the good of truth and the good of love. AE 740[8] says that Judas represents the ancient Jewish nation.

None of the other apostles is discussed specifically in the writings, but an interesting study could be made of them from the little we learn of each from the letter of the Word taken in connection with the correspondence of the sons of Jacob. Philip, whose home was at Bethsaida, is mentioned several times in the Gospel of John, first as bringing Nathanael to the Lord (John 1:43-46), then in connection with the feeding of the five thousand (John 6:7), then as a means of access to the Lord for "certain Greeks" (John 12:20-22), and especially in the incident in John 14:8-11, when it is Philip's request, "Show us the Father," which brings forth the Lord's clearest statement of His identity. Bartholomew, which means "son of Tolmai," may possibly have been that same Nathanael of John 1:47-51, since the name Bartholomew appears only in the lists of the twelve, and Nathanael, whose home was in Cana of Galilee, is included with several of the apostles in John 21:2 when the Lord appeared to them after His resurrection beside the sea of Tiberias. Thomas has come into our common speech as "doubting Thomas" because of his slowness to believe in the Lord's resurrection (John 20:24-29), but we should read also John 11:16 and 14:5. The second James, James the son of Alphaeus, is often referred to by commentators as "James the Less," but he became after the Lord's resurrection a great leader of the early Christians, the head of the Church in Jerusalem. Thaddaeus is the surname of Lebbaeus (Matthew 10:3) and is identical with "Judas the brother of James" in the list in Luke 6:16. He is the Judas "not Iscariot" of John 14:22 and the writer of the Epistle of Jude. Simon the Canaanite is also called Simon "Zelotes." This means that he was a member of the Zealots, a fanatical sect who worked especially for the overthrow of the Roman rule and the re-establishment of a theocracy.

An interesting thought is presented to us of the New Church by the statement in TCR 4: "It is a noteworthy fact that some months ago the Lord called together His twelve disciples, now angels, and sent them forth throughout the spiritual world, with the command to preach the gospel there anew, since the church that was scarcely a remnant of it survives." From this we may presume that all twelve became angels. In the letter of the Word (John 6:70) the Lord Himself speaks of Judas Iscariot as a devil. But Judas the man who, when he found that the Lord actually was taken prisoner by his means, tried to return the purchase money in order to release Him and, finding that impossible, went out and hanged himself (Matthew 27:3-10), evidently had in him the basis of salvation like all the others.

## From the Writings of Swedenborg

*Apocalypse Explained*, n. 820[2]: "Peter was the first of the apostles because truth from good is the first thing of the church; for, from the world a man does not know anything about heaven and hell, nor of a life after death, nor even about God. His natural light teaches nothing except what has entered through the eyes, thus nothing except what relates to the world and to self; and from these is his life; and so long as he is in these only he is in hell; and therefore, that he may be withdrawn from these and be led to heaven he must needs learn truths, which teach not only that there is a God, that there is a heaven and a hell, and that there is a life after death, but also teach the way to heaven. From this it is clear that truth is the first thing through which man has the church. But it must be truth from good, for truth without good is mere knowledge that a thing is so; and mere knowledge does nothing except to make a man capable of becoming a church; but this is not effected until he lives according to knowledges. Then truth is conjoined to good, and man is introduced into the church. Moreover, truths teach how a man ought to live; and when man is affected by truths for the sake of truths, which is done when he loves to live according to them, he is led by the Lord, and conjunction with heaven is granted him, and he becomes spiritual, and after death an angel of heaven. Nevertheless it is to be known that it is not truths that produce these effects, but good by means of truths; and good is from the Lord. Because truth from good, which is from the Lord, is the first thing of the church, Peter was the first to be called, and was the first of the apostles . . .''

## Suggested Questions on the Lesson

J. What did the Lord do first for the man who was sick of the palsy? *forgave sins*

J. What did the man have to do himself? *rise, pick up bed, walk*

J. What disciple was called in our last lesson? *Matthew (Levi)*

J. What faults did the scribes and Pharisees find with the Lord? *ate with sinners, disciples didn't fast, broke sabbath*

P. What did the Lord say about new wine? *needs new containers*

J. What did He mean? *old ideas and new truth don't go together*

J. What did He say about the sabbath? *made for man*

P. In our lesson today what miracle of healing was performed? *withered hand*

J. Why did the scribes and Pharisees object to it? *sabbath, challenged their authority*

J. With whom did they plot against the Lord? *Herodians*

P. Where did the Lord go to talk to the multitudes? *seashore*

P. Where did He go teach His disciples? *mountain*

P. How many did He choose to be apostles? *twelve*

J. What powers did He give them? *preach, cast out demons*

J. Name as many of the apostles as you can.

J. What did the Lord's family think about what He was doing? *thought He was crazy*

J. Where did the scribes say His power came from? *the devil (Beelzebub)*

S. What is the "unforgivable sin"? *rejecting truth that condemns our evils*

S. Why? *makes it impossible for the Lord to help us*

I. What did the Lord say when He was told that His mother and His brethren were looking for Him? *Whoever does the will of God is my mother and brother . . .*

I. Why did He seem to disown them? *because He knew why they came*

# PARABLES
*Mark 4*

The connection can be made very simply by explaining what a parable is and the fact that the whole Word—everything we have been studying—is actually a parable. Then point out that the meaning of this first parable in our chapter was explained by the Lord Himself, and go on from there. Even the little children can understand this much.

———

## Doctrinal Points

*All the Word is parable.*

*The Lord can enlighten all those who want the truth for the sake of living better lives.*

*Our eternal home is determined by the state of our hearts when we die—whether love to the Lord and the neighbor or the love of self rules there.*

———

## Notes for Parents

People often ask, "Why does the Lord speak to us in parables? Why does He not tell us plainly what He wants us to do?" But suppose He did: would we always do it? Yet it is when we refuse to do what we know the Lord is telling us to do that we commit sin. The Lord is our savior. He came into the world not to condemn, but to save. So He teaches us little by little in hidden ways, giving us an understanding of the truth only as fast as He sees we may accept and obey it.

Read in our chapter for today the parable of the sower and then read the Lord's own explanation of it. The Word of God is like the seed sown broadcast. Everyone may read it. But only in the good ground does it sink in, take root, and bring forth fruit. The good ground is the mind of any person who truly wants to be good. The parables are simple stories, easy to understand and easy to remember. They stay in the mind as stories until we need the lesson they are given to teach us, and then suddenly we think, "Oh, this is just like such-and-such a parable," and then we really understand and are helped.

And, do you know, we do the same with everything we read in the Word of God. At first we take it just as a story of something that happened long ago, but sooner or later it comes home to us with meaning. For all of the Word is a parable which the Lord is speaking to us, just as we tell or read to our children little stories which they can understand and enjoy and which, we hope, will sooner or later help them to decide rightly in the face of some temptation. In the sight of the Lord we are all little children and He leads us gently in the same way, giving us the truth we need but leaving us free to make our own decisions.

Read the whole chapter, remembering that the seed is the Word of God, and that the truth that is within it is the light of the lamp which we should let shine into all the dark corners of our minds and hearts.

---

### Primary

Tell the children the parable of the sower, reading a verse here and there, including some of the Lord's interpretation to show how the story has a hidden meaning. Then read verse 21 and explain simply what it means. Finally, read verses 26 to 34 and see what ideas the children draw from the two parables. You may be surprised at their understanding. Encourage them to think about what kind of ground they are and what kind they ought to be.

Our lesson today is about some of the Lord's parables. A parable is a story which has a meaning hidden within it. Did your mother ever say to you at night, "I know someone who is very sleepy"? What did she mean? She meant you, didn't she, although she seemed to be talking about someone else. That is a kind of parable. If she had said, "You are sleepy," perhaps you would have tried to make her believe you were not, because you didn't want to go to bed. But she made you look at yourself as if you were someone else, and you knew she was right. That is the way the Lord talks to us in the Word. He tells us stories about other people, but they are really about us. One verse in our chapter, as you will hear, says, "Without a parable spake he not unto them."

You know that none of us likes to have his faults pointed out to him.
But we are all quite willing to see other people's faults.
The Lord knows us through and through.
So He can use even our weaknesses as a means of teaching us.
In the Word He tells us stories about other people, and we easily see the point of these stories when we are thinking of the other people.
Then He shows us that the stories are really about us.
The parable of the sower, with which our chapter begins, is very well known.

Afterward the Lord told His apostles the inner meaning of this parable, saying that the seed is the truth the Lord gives us in His Word and that the different kinds of ground are different kinds of people. The good ground means the people who learn the truths of the Word and try hard to live according to them.

When you are listening to the Word, which kind of ground do you want to be?
Do you know the song which begins, "Jesus bids us shine"?
That song will help you to understand verse 21.
The other two parables in our lesson are both about seeds.
The things you are learning in Sunday school are some of these seeds of the kingdom of heaven.
Once they fall into your mind, the Lord can take care of them there so that when you need them, you will remember them—that is, if you want to be good.
But if you don't come to Sunday school, you miss many of these seeds.
What did the Lord say about the mustard seed?
Sometimes what we are told doesn't seem very important to us at the time.
But what does the mustard seed become?
What lesson does this teach us?

## Junior

After explaining what a parable is, have the class look up Nathan's parable (II Samuel 12:1-19) and read it. Discuss it as showing why the Lord speaks to us in parables. Then have the children take up each parable in our chapter, thinking how it applies to themselves. The Juniors are old enough to begin to practice reading the Word in this way, and it is one way to stimulate their interest in reading it daily.

What is a parable?
In our chapter, where is the Lord teaching?
Who are listening to Him?
What parable did He tell them?
To whom did He explain the parable?

In verses 11 and 12, the Lord tells us why He spoke to the multitude in parables. To help us understand what He means, let us read II Samuel 12:1-9. King David had committed a great sin. If Nathan the prophet had come to him and immediately charged him with it, David would have been angry and would have tried to justify himself. But Nathan told him about another man who had done wrong. The story seemed to have nothing to do with David; so he condemned the wrong-doer immediately. Then Nathan said, "Thou art the man," and David could not help seeing that he himself was guilty.

The whole Word of God is a parable. It seems to be talking about the doings of people who lived long ago. We can read their history and judge them, saying, "This was a good deed, and this a bad one. How could people turn to the worship of idols when the Lord had done so much for them? These people brought their own punishment upon themselves." Then there comes the voice of the Lord saying to us, "Thou art the man." We begin to look honestly at our own feelings and thoughts and conduct, and we see that we have done the same things just in a little different form. The Lord teaches us in this way because He knows how prone we are to defend ourselves and to blame others. In the parable of the sower, we need to understand that in those days seed was sown by being scattered broadcast and allowed to come up where it would.

What is the seed?
What are meant by the different kinds of ground?
What is the fruit which the seed should produce?

The next little parable (verses 21-22) does not seem to have much relation to the sower, does it? But read verses 23-25. You know that light is a symbol of truth. The Word of God is like seed planted in our minds, but when we "see" its meaning, it becomes like a light which "enlightens" our minds. You see, we use this same symbol language all the time. Now let us say to ourselves, "Thou art the man." This very lesson which we are studying today in Sunday school is seed which the Lord is sowing in our minds. Are our minds like the wayside, the hard-trodden path of selfish inattention into which nothing can sink, so that thoughts about ourselves, like the evil birds, carry off the seeds before they have time to sink in? Or do we listen and enjoy the lesson and then immediately get to thinking about something else and forget all about it? Or do we truly mean to do as the lesson teaches us, but give in to the first temptation which comes along? Or are we like the good ground? And then, if we do understand the lesson, do we let it shine into all the dark corners of our souls, or do we try to keep it hidden?

Some people think that verse 25 is very puzzling. Does the Lord really favor people who have plenty already? This shows how important it is always to study a verse in its "context," that is, with reference to what goes before it and what follows it. If we do this with this verse, we see immediately that by "he that hath" the Lord means the person who has not only received the good seed into his mind but has made it his own by using it in his life, the man who has used his lamp or candle of truth to "bring to light" and drive out the hidden faults and weaknesses of his character. But we know that seed which does not bring forth healthy growth dies, and a candle which is put under a closed container goes out. This is the man who "hath not"—who is bound to lose what he has.

There are two other parables in our chapter, both about seed. We do not any of us use immediately all the truth the Lord gives us. We are like the man who sleeps and rises night and day. We have our times when the good in us is awake and active, and our times when it seems to be asleep. But if we use our daytimes rightly, the Lord takes care of the seeds of truth that have been planted in our minds and without our realizing how it has happened, makes each one grow and bear fruit.

And each tiny seed is capable, like the mustard seed, of growing into a great tree. We all have what we call "principles" that we live by which become stronger and more enduring all the time. They are the trees. Where did we get our principles? Each one grew up from a tiny seed—a little idea—planted in our minds at some time or other. If the seeds were truths from the Lord, our principles are good trees. But there are also weed seeds. Some of the ideas that come into our minds are not good. If we receive them and accept them as true, our principles will be bad. So we need to remember the Lord's advice in verse 24: "Take heed what ye hear."

---

### Intermediate

Use this lesson as a study in correspondence under the Lord's own instruction. Show the young people how basic and how far-reaching the Lord's explanation of the parable of the sower is. The other two parables are illustrations of this. Be sure also to call attention to the lesson taught in verses 21-25.

The parable of the sower is one of the best known of the Lord's parables, and one which all who read their Bibles can understand in some degree at least, because the Lord Himself explains it. We know that a parable is a story which has a meaning hidden within it. There are a number of stories in both the Old Testament and the New Testament which are recognized as parables,* but in the New Church we know that all of the Word is a parable, even though most of it is also true history.

There is a reason why the Lord always speaks to us in parables (verse 34), and this reason is explained in verses 11 and 12 of our chapter. People often think that the Lord should have told us plainly all that He wants us to think and do. But suppose He had: would we all be able to understand it or be willing to believe it? And if, knowing that it came from the Lord, we refused to obey the truth, we should condemn ourselves and there would be no hope of our ever getting to heaven. The Lord has to teach us first

---

*The New Church collaterals of Edward Craig Mitchell treat forty-eight stories in *Parables of the Old Testament*, and forty in *Parables of the New Testament*. —Ed.

in simple ways and lead us a step at a time. We can all understand the stories of the Word as stories, and they are interesting and stay in our minds, and then little by little their meaning grows on us and we begin to see how they apply to us.

The Lord could explain the parable of the sower because its application is general and no one would be disposed to deny it and so be hurt by it. We all know that people differ in the way in which they receive truth. Every teacher knows that he has some pupils who are like the hard-trodden path, or wayside, so set in certain ways of thinking that no new truth can sink in. He has some who like to listen but forget almost as soon as they hear— we call such people "scatterbrains." Then there are some who do listen and understand and mean to do their work, but when they get out of class, the temptation to play instead of work is too much for them. And then there are others who really profit by what they are taught in different degrees according to their apti- tude. It is just the same with the way in which different people receive the truths the Lord gives us in the Word.

Then our chapter likens the truth we receive to the light of a lamp. It is meant to shine into every corner of our house (see Mat- thew 5:15)—you remember that our house is our character—and show us the things in us that need to be swept out. If we don't want to see our faults, we try to cover this lamp. We may cover it while we live in this world, but we can't hide our faults from the Lord, and when we come into the other world, everyone there will see them clearly. Our lamp is given us on purpose so that we may get rid of our faults before we die. Verses 24-25 are a parable which teaches us that if we do not learn to be good here, the knowledge of truth which we have refused to use will be taken away from us. Read Matthew 6:19-21.

Like the parable of the sower, the other two parables are about seed. The first teaches us that the truths we learn when we are children, even when we do not understand them, are cared for by the Lord, and that the Lord brings them up in our memory again when we need them and are ready to use them. Sometimes, we know, when some useful piece of information suddenly comes into our minds, we can't even remember where or how we learned it.

But we need to try to take in as much as possible of the Lord's truth and as little as possible of what is false. The Lord says, "Take heed what ye hear." We hear a great many wrong things in our daily lives; and sometimes we accept them without thinking, and they grow up in our minds all mixed up with the good, and we can't get rid of them until we begin to feel the harm they have done us. This is pictured by the Lord in another parable—read Matthew 13:24-30.

Every truth we learn is like the tiny mustard seed. It doesn't seem to amount to much to begin with, but it is capable of growing and putting out branches and becoming a great principle in which our wandering thoughts—like the birds—can find rest and shelter. For example, do you remember the first time you heard that the Bible is the Word of God? The knowledge was put into your mind like a little seed, and you accepted it because your parents or your Sunday school teacher said so, but it didn't mean much to you. But all the knowledge you now have of the Bible really grew out of that little seed, and think how many branches the tree has now, and it will keep on growing always.

*Basic Correspondences*

seed  =  truths from the Word

### Senior

With this class emphasize the lesson that all knowledge is for use in the service of the Lord and the neighbor, and that only if we have this desire in our hearts can we see the truth within the parables which form the letter of the Word. Then take up the individual parables with a brief explanation of the meaning and application of each. Be sure they understand what verse 25 means.

In our chapter for today we have the statement concerning the Lord that "without a parable spake he not unto them." This is true not only of the Lord when He was in the world but of all that He says to us in the Word. The whole Word is a parable. We are also told in this chapter why the Lord spoke in parables (verses 10-12) and that He explained some of His parables to the disciples when He was alone with them. The Lord was able to open something of the inner meaning of the Word to His close disciples because they had been willing to turn from their own concerns and their own ways of life in order to follow Him. Read also Luke 24:44-45. He can do the same for us if we are true disciples.

We read in the *Doctrine of the Sacred Scripture*, n. 57: "Enlightenment is from the Lord alone, and exists with those who love truths because they are truths and make them of use for life." All our knowledge of God and spiritual things comes to us by means of the letter of the Word, but without enlightenment we do not see the truth within the letter. And the Lord does not enlighten those who do not want the truth for the sake of living better lives. We can understand verse 12 if we remember that it is much worse for a person to have acknowledged the truth and then refused to try to live according to it than never to have acknowledged it at all. The Lord told Nicodemus (John 3:19): "This is the condemnation, that light is come into the world, and men loved darkness rather than light, because their deeds were evil." So the Word is given in such a way that everyone may read it and understand the words and get from it some rules for their external conduct, but its deeper truth is hidden from those who would not profit by it.

There is another reason why the Lord speaks to us in parables. Our understanding grows only with our development and experience, and yet we need to be prepared for the problems which we shall have to face. As we read the Word, we understand only as much as we are capable of understanding and using at the time, but the facts and stories which are in the letter stay in our minds and later, as we need them, the Lord can recall them to us and give us the understanding of their meaing. You remember, for example, that the Lord told the disciples many things which they did not understand and apparently forgot, but which they afterward recalled.

The parables in our chapter show us clearly the psychology of this method of instruction. Three of them concern seed, and the

Lord Himself tells us that seed represents truths from the Word. In the parable of the sower the seed is scattered broadcast—the manner of sowing in those days—just as the letter of the Word is available to everybody. The different kinds of ground are the minds of different kinds of people who read or hear the Word. Some are like the hard-trodden wayside, so settled in selfish and worldly habits of thought that their false ideas destroy the truth as fast as they hear it. Some are like the stony ground, apparently receptive but so hard underneath that the truth cannot go deep enough to take root. Some receive the truth but, when it begins to develop in their lives, allow it to be choked out by worldly things. Others are like the good ground and in them the truth is received and carried out into life.

This is a simple parable and one we can all understand, and we all need to understand and think about it. That is why the Lord saw to it that His explanation of it was recorded in the Word. It is one of the seven parables which are found in three of the four Gospels. Verses 21 to 25 show us—again in parable—the importance of our thinking about it. Such knowledge is given us to use, and its use is like the use of a light, to bring into view the things in us which we might prefer to keep hidden, our weaknesses and faults. We remember that our house is our character. Matthew (5:15) says that when the lamp is set on a stand, as it should be, "it giveth light unto all that are in the house." We are reminded in verse 22 that someday we shall no longer be able to hide our faults. Our years in this world are the time for us to recognize and get rid of them. We cannot continue to hide them after we die, and by that time our eternal character is determined. If good predominates, the things which hinder our development will drop away and we can progress more and more. But if selfishness predominates, all that we have known of the truth will be taken away. This is what is meant by verse 25. "He that hath" is the one who has made the truth his own by using it to correct and develop his character.

The other two parables show how the truth is developed in us if we do use it. We do not cause it to grow ourselves any more than the farmer makes the seed grow. We merely clear away the obstructions. All life and growth are from the Lord. And every little seed of truth which we have really planted in our minds can be developed by the Lord into a great tree.

## Adult

The teacher would do well to read carefully the *Doctrine of the Sacred Scripture*, nn. 50-61 and try to present this teaching as a whole in its bearing on our reading and study of the Word. In the New Church people have tended to swing to one extreme or the other—to neglect the study of the letter of the Word, or to neglect the study of the writings. The letter of the Word is the basic study and should be pursued systematically throughout our life, but if we, in this new age, did not also need the knowledge which the writings give us, it would not have been given us. And our study of the letter of the Word should be governed and directed by our knowledge that it is divinely inspired, and not by the pronouncements of those who study the Word as the product of human intelligence. We should see clearly the difference between these two approaches and study the Word in light rather than in darkness.

Three of the universally recognized parables of the Lord are in this chapter of Mark. The parable of the sower and the parable of the mustard seed are found also in the Gospels of Matthew and Luke, but that of the seed growing secretly is found only in Mark. There are in all some ten parables in the Old Testament and thirty-six in the New which are recognized as parables by all Christians [see note, p. 54]. But our chapter tells us that "without a parable spake he not unto them," and in the New Church we know that this statement has a far wider application than is generally understood. The whole Word is parable.

The principal reason why the Lord speaks to men always in parable is given in verses 11 and 12 of our chapter. To understand these verses we need to know who are meant by those to whom "it is given to know the mystery of the kingdom of God" and by those who are said to be "without." They are the same two groups who are meant in verse 25 by "he that hath" and "he that hath not." In the *Doctrine of the Sacred Scripture*, nn. 50-61, Swedenborg tells us how we are taught in the Word. These sections need to be studied very thoughtfully because certain statements in them, taken out of their context, have been used to support exactly opposite positions as to our proper study of the Word. Number 57 tells us that "enlightenment is from the Lord alone, and exists with those who love truths because they are truths and make them of use for life." These are those who—in verse 25 of our chapter—are said to "have." We do not have anything which we have not made our own by receiving it in the heart. Those who "have not" are described in number 60: "The contrary takes place with those who read the Word from the doctrine of a false religion, and still more with those who confirm that doctrine from the Word, having in view their own glory or this world's riches. . . . For nothing blinds a man but his proprium and the confirmation of what is false. Man's proprium is the love of self and the derivative conceit of self-intelligence." The Lord, we know, never forces anyone to believe in Him or in His Word, and so far as possible He guards us against seeing truth which we are not prepared to apply to life. This is what is meant by verse 12, and is the principal reason why the Word is given in parable.

There is another reason which is suggested in SS 51: "Many truths also are accommodated to the capacity of simple folk, who do not uplift their thoughts above such things as they see before their eyes." This was true of most of the multitude to whom the Lord spoke when He was in the world. It is true of all young children and of those adults whom Swedenborg often refers to as "the simple good." But it is also true of all of us at the beginning of our acquaintance with any new truth. It has to be presented to us first in a form in which it can be easily grasped and which can serve as a permanent basis for growing understanding.

But that we should not stop with this simple understanding of the letter, the Lord showed by explaining not only to His chosen disciples but to all of us through the recorded Word the meaning of the parable of the sower, as an indication of what lies within the letter and as a clue to the meaning of many other passages in which sowing, seed, ground, etc., are mentioned. He showed it later by opening the understanding of the apostles to see "in the law of Moses, and in the prophets, and in the psalms" the things concerning Himself (Luke 24:44-45). And especially He showed it by opening the Word in His second coming through the instrumentality of Swedenborg. The Lord does nothing useless.

We may take the parable of the sower as an example of the process by which we learn from the Lord. We all heard this parable when we were children. It came to us in simple words which we could understand, presenting a vivid picture which our imaginations could grasp. So it stayed with us. The fate of the seeds in the different kinds of ground touched our tender hearts. When we were a little older, the Lord's explanation of the parable was given us, and we realized suddenly that we might be one of those kinds of ground which did not bring forth fruit; we might be letting the Lord's truth be carried out of our minds by the birds of false thought, or scorched by our selfishness, or choked out by worldly pleasures and temptations. Our childhood concern for the poor seeds is transmuted into more mature shame for our own faults. Today, when life experience has illustrated the parable to us again and again, reading it leads us into many paths of thought concerning our own state and the state of the world. But we should note that it is as we read the parable in the letter that these thoughts come to us. The letter still stands in our minds as the "basis, containant, and support" of the meaning we have found and of new meaning which we shall continue to find to eternity.

In our chapter there are two other parables concerning seed, but before they are introduced, we have the warning of verses 21 to 24. If we have received the seeds of truth into our minds with a desire to apply them to life which has enabled them to grow and bring forth fruit, we must leave no dark corners in our character into which we will not let the light of truth penetrate. We must be willing to go all the way in self-examination and correction. This world is our opportunity to get rid of our evils. When we pass into the other, all those things in ourselves which we have been unwilling to see will be brought to light in spite of us, and in that world we shall find that they have become a permanent part of our character. We can no longer get rid of them.

If, however, we are honestly trying to follow the Lord "in the regeneration" (Matthew 19:28) we shall find that wonderful things have happened to the seed which has been sown in this world. We all fortunately are able to see some progress in understanding as we go through life. The seed springs up, we know not how. No truth that is sown in the good ground of a sincere heart will fail to produce its harvest—if not here, then in the world to come. Read here AE 1153[6].

Then the thought presented in these verses is carried further by the parable of the mustard seed,which tells us that even the least truth received from the Word has in it tremendous capacity not only for growth but for future helpfulness. It can become "greater than all herbs," and we remember that the herbs in the Creation story, the first vegetation brought forth by the earth, represent the small beginnings of good and truth which man ascribes to himself.

The chapter ends with the stilling of the storm by the Lord, and the whole thought of the chapter is focused in verse 38: "And he was in the hinder part of the ship, asleep on a pillow: and they awake him, and say unto him, Master, carest thou not that we perish?" Compare this with Psalm 107:23-30. As long as we have the letter of the Word in our minds, the Lord is present with us, and although we may imagine that the Lord is not caring for us when trouble and anxiety distress us, it is only because to us at that time He is, as it were, asleep in the hinder part of our ship. We really know that the Lord neither slumbers nor sleeps and that He cares for us always. It is we who are asleep to His presence and power, and we have only to call Him to remembrance in order to have our troubled sea become calm.

## From the Writings of Swedenborg

*Arcana Coelestia*, n. 2449[2]: "They who come into the other life are all brought again into a life similar to that which they had in the body; and then with the good evils and falsities are separated, in order that by means of goods and truths they may be elevated by the Lord into heaven; but with the evil, goods and truths are separated in order that by evils and falsities they may be borne into hell."

*Arcana Coelestia*, n. 5922[6]: "The Word as to the external sense is in a cloud, for the reason that human minds are in darkness; and therefore unless the Word were in a cloud, it would be understood by scarcely anyone, and moreover the holy things which belong to the internal sense would be profaned by evil people in the world."

## Suggested Questions on the Lesson

P. What is a parable? *a story with a hidden meaning*

J. How many parables are there in the Word? *see footnote, p. 54*

I. Why does the Lord teach us in parables? *we can see truth better if it doesn't seem at first to apply to us*

J. What are three of the parables in our lesson about? *seed*

J. What is the seed? *truth from God's Word*

J. What are the different kinds of ground? *different kinds of minds*

P. What does the Lord say about a lamp? *should be put on a stand*

I. What does light symbolize? *truth which enlightens*

S. How should we use the truth? *to help see our own faults*

J. What happens if we do not use it? *we lose it (lamp goes out)*

J. By what degrees does grain develop? *first blade, then ear, then full grain*

P. Who makes it grow? *God*

P. What does the Lord say of a grain of mustard seed? *smallest of seeds*

J. What does it become? *great bush or tree*

S. How is this like the development of the truths we learn from the Word? *at first some truths don't mean much to us, but later we may see real meaning*

# MIRACLES
*Mark 5*

With all the younger children the emphasis in this lesson may
well be on the Lord's statement, "The damsel is not dead, but
sleepeth." The fact that all our life is from the Lord, that it does
not depend on our bodies, but goes on forever, no matter what
happens to the body, should be impressed upon a child as early as
he is able to think about death at all. In all the miracles of our
lesson also it is very clear that the one for whom the miracle was
performed had full faith in the Lord's power to heal. In one case
it was an outcast, in another a rich and powerful man who had this
faith; in the third it was a poor woman. So belief in the Lord is
not a matter of outward conditions, and it was not the miracle
which produced faith. This applies to all our efforts to overcome
our faults. We must believe that with the Lord's help we can overcome them, or we shall not make the necessary effort. Parents find
even very young children falling back on "I can't" when they are
asked to pick up their toys or do some other orderly or helpful
thing.

―――

## Doctrinal Points
*The Lord is truly "the resurrection and the life."*
*We cannot now be "possessed" by evil spirits against our will.*

―――

## Notes for Parents
Have you ever said to one of your children, "I don't know what
is the matter with you today; you just seem possessed"? We say it
of ourselves, too, sometimes, when we have let temper or resentment get the better of us: "I don't know what possessed me to act
that way." We know really what possessed our child, or us: it was
the devil, which is just another name for the influence of evil in

our hearts and minds. Have you ever felt that someone you loved very much who had passed into the other life was near you giving you a feeling of comfort and help? The spiritual world is not somewhere far off. It is around us all the time and close to our minds and hearts. But there are both good and bad people there, and both try to influence us. We are free to choose our spiritual companions, sometimes much freer than we are to choose our earthly ones. This is because the Lord, when He was in the world, conquered the hells and set them in order under His control, and He does not let them tempt us beyond our power to resist if we choose to resist. He keeps us free. But at the time when He came into the world, it was possible for evil spirits to possess a person against his will. Part of the lesson the children have for today is about such a person. It is a powerful story which gives us a great deal to think about.

The rest of the lesson tells of two other miracles: of a woman who was healed by just touching the Lord's garments, and of a child—the daughter of one of the rulers of the Jews—whom the Lord raised from the dead. The Lord is life itself, and all life and health are from Him. And none of us ever really dies. He said of the child, "The damsel is not dead, but sleepeth." He woke her again in this world. When we go to sleep for the last time, He wakes us in the other world.

The Lord performed all His miracles to teach us of things He is able to do for our souls if we are willing to believe in Him and obey Him. The choice is ours.

## Primary

The older children should be able to take all three stories, although the most time should be spent on the raising of Jairus' daughter. The Lord's power to help and the necessity of faith in it and of going to Him for help will coordinate the lesson. The lesson contained in verse 39 is the most important one.

What were the three parts of the Lord's ministry?
Who were the scribes and Pharisees?
Which disciple was a publican or tax gatherer?

What did the Lord say about new wine?
What did He mean?
What did He say about the sabbath?
Our lesson today is about miracles.

Do you remember what a miracle is? It is a wonderful thing done by the Lord to teach us a lesson. The Lord, when He was in the world, did many miracles, and they were of different kinds. See if you can remember some of them we have read about. Do you remember how the Lord healed the man who had the palsy, and the man whose hand was withered? Besides these, He made blind people see and cured leprosy—a terrible disease that many people had in those times—and he multiplied a few loaves and fishes so that they fed five thousand people, and He calmed a storm at sea.

In our lesson for today He does still more wonderful things.
He cast out evil spirits from a man whom they had possessed.
And He brought back to life a little girl who had died.
Who was the little girl's father?
When they came to the house of Jairus, what did the Lord tell the mourners?
Did they believe Him?
How did He bring her back to life?
This miracle teaches us that all life is from the Lord and He controls it.
And we never really die.

The world we see around us now is just our beginning—a world given us to live in for a few years so that we may learn what is right and get rid of some of our selfish ways in order that we may be happy in heaven.

————

## Junior

In taking up the story of the demoniac, try to impress the children with the fact that the bad thoughts and impulses they have are actually inspired by evil spirits and that they do not need to be slaves as the demoniac was. It takes real courage to say "no." Relate this thought to their association with playmates. Stress the Lord's courage and our need of His help. One of the temptations which is beginning to be very active at the Juniors' age is the temptation to excuse one's shortcomings on the ground of hindering external circumstances. It cannot be too often brought home to the children of this age that we are all able to do right with the Lord's help, if we will. A full discussion of the subject of death is also in order with this group.

What is a miracle?
In our lesson for today, where had the Lord gone?

The Gospel of Matthew in telling this story says the Lord went to the country of the Gergesenes. Gergesa is a little village near the shore of the Sea of Galilee and is probably the place where the miracle actually took place, but the people could be called either Gergesenes or Gadarenes because Gadara was the principal city of the region. Find Gergesa and Gadara on a map.

The tombs were places, usually outside of the cities, where the bodies of the dead were brought for burial. According to the Israelitish law, dead bodies were "unclean," and those who had touched one could not enter the tabernacle until they had gone through a process of purification which took seven days (Numbers 19:11-13). The tombs were considered unclean because of the dead bodies in them. So the poor man of our story was an outcast, cut off even from religious worship. Yet he was really a good man. How do we know this? Read Mark 5:6.

What was the matter with the man?
How did this affect him?
How had people tried to control him?

Did you ever hear anyone say, "I don't know what possessed me to do that"? Or did your mother ever say to you when you were being particularly naughty, "You just seem to be possessed today"? There is a real fact behind such statements. Devils are people in the other world who, while they lived on earth, allowed selfishness to rule in their hearts and so came to hate everyone who did not do just what they wanted. They love to stir up our own selfishness and to suggest bad thoughts to our minds. The Lord allows them to do this because we have to see our selfishness and conquer it of our own free will before we can learn to do what the Lord wants us to do. You remember that this was why John the Baptist had to go before the Lord telling people to repent. Even in this world we sometimes do as the devils do. Did any other child ever try to persuade or to tease you into doing wrong? Perhaps you have even done this yourself to someone else, for we all have such bad tendencies in us.

We know, however, that we can always say "no" to the devils, if we will. This is because the Lord, when He came into the world, overcame all these temptations and showed us how to overcome them with His help. But in the Lord's day people had lost the way and could really become "possessed with the devil" even when they wanted to be good.

When the Lord asked the devil his name, what did he say?

This is always true, as we know when we think about it. If you are bent on doing something that you know is wrong, you are tempted to do a good many other wrong things in order to get your way, such as lying and cheating and even hurting someone you really love. No temptation ever comes alone. The devil's name is *Legion*.

When the Lord commanded the devil to come out of the man, what permission did the devil ask?

What do we mean when we say that a person is a pig?

The pig represents our desire to satisy our bodily appetites without thought of anything else.

What happened to the swine when the devils entered into them?

Perhaps our first thought is to be sorry for the poor pigs, but the Lord allowed this to happen to teach us that selfishness, when it is allowed to have its way, will in the end destroy even our ability to enjoy the good things of this world.

What was the man doing at the end of the story?

The Lord then came back across the Sea of Galilee. Many people were gathered around Him.

Who came to Him for help?
What did he want?
How do we know that he had faith in the Lord?

As the Lord was going with the ruler of the synagogue, another miracle of healing took place.

How was the woman healed?
What did the Lord tell her was the reason for her healing?

The garments which clothe our bodies are a picture of the truths which clothe our affections. The Lord's garments always picture the Word, because the Word is the expression to us of the Lord's love and wisdom. Touching the Lord's garment, and especially the border of His garment (see Luke 8:44) is trying to live according to the commandments. If we will do this, our weaknesses and faults will be overcome. But we must believe that there is this power in the commandments, just as the woman believed the Lord could heal her.

As they went along, people came from the house to Jairus to tell him that his daughter was dead, but the Lord reassured him and went on.

Whom did He take with Him?
When He came to the house, what did He tell the mourners?
Did they believe Him?
How did He raise the little girl?
How old was she?
What did He tell the people to do for her?

We learn from this story not only that the Lord has power over death, but that death is really only a short sleep. The Lord loves to help all people who are in trouble or sorrow, and He was glad to help the people for whom He performed the miracles. But He was really teaching all of us that all life and power come from Him, and that, if we have faith in Him, He can make our souls well and strong and give us eternal life.

═══════

## Intermediate

The real reason why the Lord performed miracles is the first important lesson in this class. Then call attention to the different kinds of miracles and their spiritual meaning, and spend the rest of the lesson time on the three miracles in our chapter. Be sure to make clear the difference between possession by devils in the Lord's time, and possession today.

The Gospel of Mark contains the account of many of the Lord's

miracles. We have studied some of them—the healing of the man
with the palsy, and of the man whose hand was withered. The
Lord also opened the eyes of the blind, fed the multitude with five
loaves and two fishes, walked on the sea, and stilled the storm. In
addition to these, our chapter today teaches of two other types of
miracle—the casting out of devils and the raising of the dead to life.
All the miracles which the Lord wrought truly happened, but they
were done not merely to help a few people in the Lord's time, but
to teach us, through their inner meaning, what the Lord can do for
our souls, if we believe in Him and obey Him. The condition of
each miracle was faith and obedience.

In the beginning of our chapter, the Lord crosses the Sea of
Galilee to the eastern side. We know that the Holy Land represents
heavenly life, or that part of our life which is lived in acknowledgment of the Lord as a result of learning the truths of the Word.
The cross-Jordan country pictures the part of us that has not yet
been brought under the Lord's control in this way. So the man in
this story is one who has not before been brought into contact
with the Lord.

The man was possessed by devils. You remember that when the
Lord came into the world, the power of evil had grown so strong
and the knowledge of truth from the Word had been so perverted
by the scribes and Pharisees, that people were at the mercy of evil.
Evil spirits could really possess them against their will. The Lord
in His inherited humanity took on all these temptations and overcame them, putting the hells in order under His control. It is possible for us now to be "possessed," but only with our own consent—
that is, only as we choose to let evil desires and false thoughts
control us.

The casting out of the devils shows us the Lord's power to drive
out evil from our hearts if we go to Him as the man in the story
did. The poor man was in terrible condition. So is everyone whom
evil controls. He lived in the tombs among the dead bodies, just as
an evil person is cut off from everything which is spiritually living.
He broke all the chains with which people tried to control him,

just as an evil person breaks the laws which are meant to keep him and other people safe. And this man, who was possessed against his will, was crying night and day and cutting himself with stones, which is a picture of how he suffered and tormented himself because he could not do what he knew was right.

We know that he was a good man at heart because "when he saw Jesus afar off, he ran and worshipped him." And the Lord healed him. Notice that there were many devils all working together in him. Although we see our evils one at a time, there are many associated with each one—we know, for example, that one sin can quickly lead to another. The swine into which the devils were allowed to go picture our greedy enjoyments. The devils destroyed even these. If we eat too much, we become sick and can no longer enjoy our food.

After this miracle the Lord returned into Galilee, and we have two more miracles. The poor woman was healed by merely touching the Lord's garment. Garments, as we have seen, picture the truths which clothe our affections, and the Lord's garments picture the Word. Luke says that the woman touched just the border of the Lord's garment, which represents the ten commandments in which the divine law is summed up in its lowest or most external form. Our blood is another correspondent of truth—truth as it circulates through our minds and brings strength to every part of us—so you can see that the woman is a picture of one who is constantly being weakened because the truth slips out of his mind. We are all in this state a good deal of the time. And when we are, the miracle says to us: "Keep the commandments." If we are careful to do that, then truth will not slip away from us.

Finally we have the great miracle of the restoring of life to the little girl who had died. Several times in the Gospel story we read of the Lord's raising someone from death, and we know that in the end of the story He Himself rose from the dead as the final proof that all life is in and from Him. In the story of the resurrection of Lazarus (John 11:1-44) He says: "I am the resurrection and the life: he that believeth in me, though he were dead, yet shall he live: And whosoever liveth and believeth in me shall never die." He had told His apostles that Lazarus was asleep. In our story He tells the mourners in the home of Jairus, "the damsel is not dead, but sleepeth." The lesson the Lord is teaching us is that we should understand that dying is just like going to sleep, and we know how welcome sleep is when we are tired. The Lord woke Lazarus and Jairus' daughter again in this world because He had this lesson to teach us. When we die, He wakes us in the spiritual world, a far more beautiful and happy world than this. When we wake there we shall all realize that that world and not this one is the real, living world where all true happiness is to be found.

### Basic Correspondences

the cross-Jordan country = the part of us which has not accepted the Lord's authority

swine (pigs) = greedy sense enjoyments

the hem of the Lord's garment = the ten commandments

---

### Senior

Call attention to the different types of people and different types of affliction dealt with in this chapter. The Seniors need to understand the Lord's purpose in performing the miracles, and that each miracle is a study in itself, and they need to see that all the afflictions are found in each of us in greater or lesser degree. We are to recognize and fight our evils in the Lord's strength, believing fully in His power to overcome them in us if we are faithful.

While He was on earth the Lord healed not only the bodies but the minds and souls of men. He does the same for us, if we follow Him wholly.

The first miracle of our lesson is one primarily of the healing of the mind. We need to notice that it took place in the cross-Jordan country, outside the Holy Land proper. So it pictures something in the Lord's approach to those who have not been "brought up in the church," and to those things in ourselves which we have not previously brought under the influence of religion.

We need to note also that the man in the story was essentially a good man, since "when he saw Jesus afar off, he ran and worshipped him." But he was possessed by devils and lived among the tombs; he could not be controlled by men, even with chains, and he went about unhappily, sometimes in the mountains and sometimes in the tombs, "crying, and cutting himself with stones." What a vivid picture this is of a person who desires to be good and who has his high moments, yet who, because he has not yet been brought into touch with the Lord's power to save, is a slave to strong passions and, falling into evils, torments himself constantly with the knowledge of his unhappy state. It is also a picture of each one of us in the face of some besetting sin which we are trying to overcome in our own strength and which we have not yet taken to the Lord for help.

We are told in the writings that in the Lord's day people were actually subject to becoming possessed by devils against their wills because the religious leaders had so perverted the Word that men no longer had access to the truth necessary to the preservation of their spiritual freedom. That was why the Lord came just when He did to take on our finite human nature at its worst, fight and overcome the evils in it, and so to reduce the hells to order and bring them forever under His own rule. People today can still be possessed by devils, but only if they have freely chosen the evils and falsities which are urged upon them.

The fact that the devil's name was "Legion" reminds us that every evil to which we yield involves us in many other evils. Even a small child can recognize that when he does what he knows to be wrong, he is immediately tempted to conceal it by lies.

Swine picture the affection for satisfying our physical appetites; so it was wholly appropriate that the devils should be allowed to enter into the herd of swine. But then they violently rushed the swine to destruction. When we allow our physical appetites to control us, they finally destroy all satisfaction in physical pleasures; whereas, if we keep our physical appetites under control of our spiritual reason, and exercise them only as the Lord would have us, we maintain not only our physical health but also our keen enjoyment of the good and beautiful things of the physical world.

It is perhaps characteristic of our materialistic society that so many people in reading this story are more concerned over the fate of the swine than over the healing of the demoniac.

After the healing of the demoniac the Lord came back across the Sea of Galilee and we read (verse 21) that "much people gathered unto him." Back in the Holy Land again, the miracles concern those who have the Word. The two classes of the good among those who have the Word are pictured by the two principal figures in the story, the ruler of the synagogue and the poor woman. They are like the Wise Men and the shepherds in the Christmas story. The ruler represents the learned among the people and the woman the simple good. We know that there were not many among the learned who accepted the Lord, but there were a few, of whom Jairus was one. When he saw that his daughter was at the point of death, he immediately sought the Lord, declaring his sure belief in the Lord's power to save her. On the way to the home of Jairus— in the process of giving the new truth needed—the Lord healed the woman with the issue of blood who pictures the simple good people who knew that their life blood was ebbing away but did not understand how or why, and had tried all sorts of means of healing without success (see verse 26). Jairus pictures those who knew that their nation had lost its vitality and who watched for the coming of the Messiah to save it. His daughter pictures this spiritual affection.

The woman was healed by touching the Lord's garment—Luke says the border of His garment. The Lord's garment is the letter of the Word and its hem the ten commandments. For simple good people, represented by the woman, obedience to the command-ments from the recognition that they are from the Lord restores ebbing spiritual life and re-establishes health. The ruler of the synagogue needed something more. He needed the full communion represented by the laying on of the Lord's hands. He had the Law and presumably had observed it outwardly, but he needed to feel the Lord's power within it, and once he had felt this power, he needed new nourishment to sustain his new life (verse 43).

In the Scriptures death, paradoxically, usually signifies resurrection. This is because what to us seems to be the end is to the angels the beginning of life. The spiritual world is the real world and the spiritual life is the real life. Those who live only for this world are really dead, for everything living is of the spiritual world. The Lord gave the Word and came into the world Himself to fulfill the Word, just so that we should not spend our lives here in vain. Our lives are given us for the sole purpose of developing heavenly character.

The three steps toward regeneration are clearly pictured in these last two miracles: belief in the Lord, obedience to the commandments, and the effort to receive spiritual life at the Lord's hands.

———————

### Adult

Good topics for discussion are the reason why outward miracles were performed by the Lord and why they are not performed today, what "magical miracles" are, the difference between "possession" then and now, and the various statements of the Lord concerning death and resurrection.

This chapter gives us an opportunity to consider three different types of miracles. We know that the Lord performed the miracles primarily for the sake of the Word, that through their spiritual meaning they might reveal His power to heal and restore to spiritual health and life all who look to Him.

In the beginning of our chapter the Lord has crossed the Sea of Galilee to "the country of the Gadarenes." The cross-Jordan country pictures the life which has not been developed under instruction from the Word. Possession by devils was a very real thing in the Lord's day and could happen even to one who wanted to be good. We know that there are always with us both angels and evil spirits. The evil spirits suggest wrong thoughts and stir up our natural, selfish desires; and the angels at the same time recall to our minds and hearts the knowledge of truth which is in our memories and the good desires we have felt in the past. So we are kept in freedom to choose between what is true and what is false, and between what is good and what is evil, and to do either the right or the wrong. In this way we build our characters by our own free choice. In the Lord's day, however, the truth had been so mixed with falsity by the religious leaders that there was not enough good and truth in the people's minds to balance the falsity and evil. So the evil spirits could get possession of anyone.

We know that the demoniac was essentially a good man because "when he saw Jesus afar off, he ran and worshipped him." The life he had been living is a picture of the life of a good man possessed by evil spirits. He lived sometimes in the mountains and sometimes in the tombs. That is, he had his times of high thought and resolve, but at other times his lowest nature controlled him. Swedenborg says that sepulchres "because of the dead bodies and bones in them, signify things unclean, and thus things infernal." The people of the city had tried to bind him with chains, but he had broken them. Such a man tries hard to control his passions so that he may live an orderly life like that of other men, but the evils always break out again. And so he goes about unhappily, condemning himself by such standards as he has—"cutting himself with stones."

When the demoniac finally recognized the Lord and came to Him for help, the Lord commanded the evil spirits to come out of him and afterward he was found by the people "sitting, and clothed, and in his right mind." The Lord overcame all the temptations from the hells which attacked Him in His assumed human nature, and holds the hells subject; so if we sincerely wish to get rid of our evils and look to Him for help, He will cast them out for us. It is not by accident that the man was afterward found "sitting." Sitting pictures a settled condition, here a state of security and peace. That it may also represent a state of confirmed evil we learn in the first verse of the first Psalm. "Clothed" we recognize as meaning furnished with truth appropriate to his state, and "in his right mind" means restored to the use of his reason and free choice. Whenever we are unwilling to trust in the Lord and accept His guidance, we are for the time being spiritually insane.

Swedenborg tells us that devils are those who have allowed

themselves to believe that the whole of life is in the satisfaction of their physical appetites. So they believe that if this satisfaction is taken away, they will perish utterly, and this was why the devils asked to be allowed to go into the swine, for swine picture just this kind of low, selfish desire. But actually the devils destroyed the swine, for our physical appetites, if indulged as the whole object of life, in the end destroy the very satisfaction they crave. When we overeat, for example, we may become too sick to enjoy food. The picture of the whole herd of swine running "violently down a steep place into the sea" is given us as a warning against allowing any physical appetite to get control of us.

The other two miracles in our lesson took place in Galilee, after the Lord had re-crossed the Sea of Galilee. They are both recorded in the same order in Matthew and Luke also; so we may be sure that there is a very close connection between them in the spiritual sense.

We should first note that Jairus was a "ruler of the synagogue." We know that very few of the prominent Jews accepted the Lord's claim to be the Messiah. Besides Jairus, we know of Nicodemus and of Joseph of Arimathea, who after the crucifixion begged the Lord's body of Pilate and laid it in his own new tomb. It is not easy for those in prominent places to make a radical change in their lives which they know will not prove popular. The state of Jairus is pictured by the type of his need. His daughter—Luke says his only daughter—lay at the point of death, and she was a child of twelve years of age. Daughters picture affections, and the number twelve throughout the Scriptures is the symbol of all good and truth in one complex. So Jairus pictures those of the orthodox and well-instructed who still had concern for genuine goodness and truth and recognized that they were on the point of losing it altogether.

The woman of the multitude who had the issue of blood represents the uninstructed people who were in a like recognition, the loss of blood signifying constant ebbing of truth necessary to a good life.

Both had faith in the Lord's power to heal, and some knowledge of how this healing could be effected. Jairus asked the Lord to come and lay His hands on his daughter. Swedenborg tells us that the laying on of hands signifies the transmission of power through the fullest conjunction. Jairus possessed the knowledge necessary for such conjunction, and the Lord fulfilled his desire. The woman took the simplest and most humble means. She did not even speak to the Lord. We are reminded of the publican in the temple who "would not lift up so much as his eyes unto heaven." She had such faith that she felt that if she but touched the Lord's garment—Luke says "the border of his garment"—she would be made whole. The Lord's garment of course pictures the letter of the Word and the border or hem the ten commandments in which the law of life is summed up. The power which healed the woman was the power of simple obedience to the commandments with recognition of their divine origin. We recall the Lord's teaching in Matthew 19:17, ". . . there is none good but one, that is God: but if thou wilt enter into life, keep the commandments."

The power of the Lord to revive the spiritual life even of the religious leaders is pictured in the simple account of the raising of the little girl. The Lord's words, "The damsel is not dead, but sleepeth," accurately expressed the spiritual state of Jairus, in which the remains of goodness and truth had not been completely destroyed. And the Lord's command after the miracle that something be given the girl to eat, pictures the necessity of feeding the spiritual life once it was awakened.

There is a clear progression in the four miracles of raising from the dead recorded in the Gospels. The first was the son of the widow of Nain, the picture of the restoration of truth to one who has lost it; the second is this of our story today, the reviving of good affections in those who have the truth; the third is the raising of Lazarus, the restoration of one who has had both goodness and knowledge and has apparently lost them; and the final one is the resurrection of the Lord Himself, the full manifestation of divine life and power.

## From the Writings of Swedenborg

*Doctrine of the Sacred Scripture,* n. 17: "It is the same with all the Lord's miracles which were Divine because they signified the various states of those with whom the church was to be set up anew by the Lord. Thus when the blind received sight, it signified that they who had been in ignorance of truth should receive intelligence; when the deaf received hearing, it signified that they who had previously heard nothing about the Lord and the Word should hearken and obey; when the dead were raised, it signified that they who otherwise would spiritually perish would become living; and so on. . . . Moreover, all the miracles related in the Word contain in them such things as belong to the Lord, to heaven, and to the church. This makes these miracles Divine, and distinguishes them from those which are not Divine. These few examples are given in order to illustrate what the spiritual sense is, and to show that it is in all things of the Word and in every particular of it."

## Suggested Questions on the Lesson

P. What is a miracle? *a wonderful act of the Lord's to teach us a lesson*

J. What miracles can you remember that we have studied in Mark? *palsied man, man with withered hand*

P. How many miracles are described in our lesson for today? *three*

J. Where was the first one done? *across the Jordan*

J. What was the matter with the man? *possessed by demons*

J. How did he show his faith in the Lord? *ran and worshiped Him*

J. What did the devil say his name was? *Legion (many)*

I. What does this mean? *no temptation ever comes alone*

P. What favor did the devil ask? *to go into herd of swine*

P. What happened to the swine? *ran down deep bank into sea and drowned*

J. After the Lord went back to Galilee, who came to Him for help? *Jairus*

P. What did Jairus want? *healing of his daughter who was near death*

P. What did the messengers from his home tell him? *she is dead*

J. What miracle was performed on the way to the home of Jairus? *woman healed*

J. How was the woman healed? *touched Jesus' garment*

P. At the home of Jairus what did the Lord tell the mourners? *she is sleeping*

P. How did He heal the child? *took hand, said, "Arise!"*

P. What did He tell her parents to do for her? *give her something to eat*

S. Why did the Lord perform miracles? *to teach us what he can do for our souls*

# THE LOAVES AND FISHES
*Mark 6*

Remind the classes of the varying attitudes toward the Lord exhibited by the multitudes, the disciples, and the scribes and Pharisees. Our lesson today adds further varieties: the people of Nazareth, Herod, and Herodias. Even the Primary children can see this as a picture of the different ways in which we may respond to the truth when it is presented to us by our parents and teachers and later as we read the Word for ourselves.

---

## Doctrinal Points

*The Lord has power over all things of nature.*
*Our true "daily bread" is found in the Word.*
*Hardness of heart prevents the Lord from working miracles in our lives.*
*The Word contains all the guidance we need in order to live good and happy lives.*

---

## Notes for Parents

When the Lord was in the world, He showed His divine power in many ways: He healed the sick, restored sight to the blind, cast out devils, raised the dead, stilled the storm. These were all pictures or parables of what He can do for our souls: He can give us power to overcome our weaknesses and sins, to see the truth, to drive out the evil thoughts and feelings which sometimes seem to "possess" us, to rise out of the dead level of earthly things into heavenly states, to find peace from all our worries, fears, and rebellious strugglings. People in all times have sought the Lord in their troubles and bereavements and found healing and comfort, as the multitudes sought Him long ago in Palestine and were satisfied.

But in our story for today the multitude did not come for physical healing. They came to learn from Him how to keep whole and sane and happy. Our chapter tells us that Jesus "was moved with compassion toward them, because they were as sheep not having a shepherd: and he began to teach them many things." Then at the end of the day, instead of sending the people away to buy food for themselves, He showed His power in a new way. He had them all sit down on the green grass and He took what little food they had on hand—five loaves and two fishes—and blessing it divided it among them, and it was multiplied so that the whole five thousand persons had enough to eat, and there were twelve baskets of fragments left over.

This miracle was a parable, too. The Lord does have power over all things in nature—He created them in the beginning. But natural food is not the only food we need. Our minds and souls have to be nourished, and the Lord gives us this kind of food too, if we look to Him for it. He said, "Blessed are they which do hunger and thirst after righteousness: for they shall be filled." We pray every day, "Give us this day our daily bread." Each day we have to have food for our bodies, but each day we need still more the understanding and strength to meet the tasks and problems of the day in the right way. This is our spiritual daily bread. We find this "bread" in the Word of God. Perhaps we think at first that we get very little out of our reading of the Bible—only five loaves and two small fishes—but if we look to the Lord to bless it, He can make our understanding grow so that it will be enough for all the needs of our souls.

## Primary

Begin by reminding the children of our lesson about the apostles and what the word *apostle* means. This leads directly into the actual sending out of the twelve and so into the story for today. Be sure they know what the Word *miracle* means. For this class the story of the death of John the Baptist may be omitted; if included, tell the children how and why he was put to death. Then take up the sending out of the apostles as an introduction to the miracle. If you have time at the end of the period tell them how soon the apostles forgot the wonderful power they had seen exercised, and read them the last part of the chapter, emphasizing verse 52.

You remember that out of all the people who followed the Lord and listened to His teaching—all His *disciples*, or "learners"—He chose twelve men who came to be called *apostles*, which means those "sent forth," because they were sent forth by the Lord to preach and to heal in His name. He sent them out by twos, telling them not to take any money or extra clothing, but to go from village to village and stay in the home of anyone who would welcome them and listen to them. They obeyed Him and found that all He had promised them came true.

Read the instructions He gave them in verses 8-11.
Then we are told how King Herod put John the Baptist to death.
What can you remember about John the Baptist?
Herod did not want to kill him because he believed him to be a prophet.
But Herod had made a foolish promise. Read about it in verses 21-28.
We should never make careless promises.
What did Herod think when he heard about the Lord's miracles? Read verse 16.
When the apostles came back to the Lord to report their success, He took them into a desert place to rest.
Who followed them there?
When the day was over, what did the apostles want the Lord to do with the people?
What did the Lord tell the disciples to do?
What food did they have on hand?
How many people were there to be fed?
What did the Lord have the people do?
What did He do with the five loaves and two fishes?
After everyone had eaten, how many baskets of fragments did they take up?

This was a miracle. A *miracle* is a wonderful thing done by the Lord's power. You know that the Lord made everything. He made the grain out of which the five loaves of bread were baked, and He made the fishes. So of course He could make more and more as fast as they were needed by the people. We should always remember that it is really the Lord who gives us our food. That is why we thank Him whenever we sit down to a meal. And when you are older, you will understand that there are other kinds of food which the Lord gives us—food for our minds and food for our souls—which are much more important than the food for our bodies.

Remember this when you say every day in the Lord's Prayer, "Give us this day our daily bread."

_____

## Junior

Make the connection with previous lessons through the sending out of the apostles. Review the children's knowledge of John the Baptist and tell the story of his death, stressing the lesson of Herod's weakness and its counterpart in our own experience. Then take up the miracle and its general meaning, and finally the last incident in the chapter.

What does the word *disciple* mean?
How many did the Lord choose to be apostles?
What does the word *apostle* mean?

In our lesson for today we learn that the Lord sent the apostles out by twos.

What did He tell them to take with them?
How were they to live?
What were they to do if the people of a city would not listen to them?
What did king Herod think when he heard of the wonderful things the Lord did?

The story of the death of John the Baptist is one we should know and think about. You remember that all the people believed John to be a prophet. Now we learn that king Herod believed it too. This Herod was the son of the Herod who tried to destroy the Lord in His infancy. Verse 20 says that he heard John gladly and did many things as a result of hearing him. But when John rebuked him for a particular sin of his own, he did not want to hear and so he put John in prison. Then he made a careless promise and because many of his court had heard him make it, he was afraid to break it and he put John to death. That is, he cared more for what people would say about him than he did for doing right. We are apt to wonder how anyone could do such a thing as putting an innocent man to death, but sometimes we do similar things. We are willing to be good up to a point, but when someone points out a pet fault of ours and tells us of it, we turn against him even though we know he is right; and we are also, like Herod, apt to get ourselves into difficulties by making careless promises, not stopping to think to what they may lead.

When the apostles came back to the Lord to report on the success of the journey on which He had sent them, He took them aside into a desert place to rest. But the people saw and followed them. This time evidently they came to listen to Him and not just to be healed; so He taught them all day.

When evening came, what did the disciples want Him to do with the people?
What did He say to the disciples?
What food did they have on hand?
What did He have the people do?
What did He do with the loaves and fishes?
What happened when the disciples passed them out?
How many people were fed?
How many baskets of fragments did they take up afterward?

Since the Lord creates everything in nature, we can see how, when He was living in the world, He could multiply the loaves and fishes. We should always recognize that our daily food really comes to us from the Lord, and we should not forget to thank Him for it. But there is another kind of food which is more important to us than food for our bodies. This is spiritual food, goodness and truth to nourish and develop our minds and souls. In the sermon on the mount the Lord said, "Blessed are they which do hunger and thirst after righteousness: for they shall be filled." And He said of Himself, "I am the bread of life." Sometimes people feed their bodies and starve their souls, and this is very foolish because when we die, we leave our bodies behind us but our souls go on forever and they are just what we have made them by our life in this world. So when we repeat the Lord's Prayer and say, "Give us this day our daily bread," we should think not only of the food our bodies need but also of the knowledge and strength we need to receive from the Lord in order to live that day as we ought to live.

Our chapter tells us of another way in which the Lord showed His disciples that He controls the things in nature.

How did He come to them when they were in the boat?

What did they think?
What happened when He got into the boat with them?

Then we are told that the disciples were amazed, "for they considered not the miracle of the loaves: for their heart was hardened." That is, even the disciples closest to the Lord, who had seen Him perform miracle after miracle, still did not recognize that His power was the power of God Himself. Often our hearts are hardened in the same way. We have learned in Sunday school that the Lord is the creator of everything, that He sees and knows everything, and that everything is under His control, and yet when we are in any trouble or having a hard time—as the disciples were in the boat, trying to row against contrary winds—we forget that the Lord is near and in control of things, and that all we need in order to smooth out our lives is His presence in our hearts. When we take the Lord into our boat, the troubled sea becomes calm.

## Intermediate

The principal lesson for this class is in the correspondence of the miracle itself, but it will also be helpful to children of this age to point out to them how the various forms of rejection or acceptance of the Lord repeat themselves in our own attitudes toward instruction. Stress also the "hardness of heart" which made even the apostles continually forget the miracles they had witnessed.

Before we take up the meaning of the miracle which is our special lesson for today, we should notice some important facts which are given us in the first part of our chapter. Did you ever have the temptation to scoff at some success which came to one of your brothers and sisters or to one of your schoolmates? You couldn't quite believe that he was really smarter or better than you. We all can see that this is not a right attitude to take, but it is a very natural one to our self-conceit. The people of Nazareth had this feeling about the Lord and we are told that "he could do no mighty work there." The Lord's power was there, but the people's minds were closed against it; so they could not be helped by it.

Then we have the story of the death of John the Baptist. You remember that John was accepted by everyone as a prophet. Even king Herod (a son of the Herod who was in power when the Lord was born) believed in him. But Herod had broken the religious law by taking his brother's wife away from him and marrying her himself. Herod was not a big enough person spiritually to accept correction for himself even from a prophet, and when John pointed out his sin, he had John put in prison. He did not hate John, but he did not want to listen to him anymore. Herodias, however, the wife Herod had taken, did hate John, and tricked Herod into a careless promise which resulted in John's death. One of the lessons we learn from this story is that it is very foolish to make a general promise without knowing to what we are binding ourselves. And we should not ask anyone else to make such a promise either. Herod was not only sorry afterward; he was afraid, and even imagined that the Lord was John the Baptist come back to punish him. Herod pictures the principle of self-interest ruling in our minds, the self-esteem which leads us to do some good things because people will respect us for it, but does not give us the strength to do right when doing right is hard. Herodias pictures the love of self in our hearts which wants only its own way always.

Now we come to our special lesson. The Lord had sent the twelve apostles out by twos to go through the villages and preach and heal in His name. In order that they might understand that their power did not in any way come from themselves, He told them to take no money with them and no food and no extra clothing. They did go out, and everywhere they found some people who were eager to hear them and to give them lodging and food, and they found that they could heal people as the Lord had promised them. But the Lord knew how hard it is for any of us to acknowledge in our hearts that we are not good and wise ourselves but that all our true thoughts and good desires and deeds really come from Him. We may know that this is so, but our first impulse is always to think we are a little better than other people.

So when the apostles came back to report their success, they needed more teaching and more evidence. Notice that when the multitude who had been listening to the Lord's teaching all day needed food, the first thought of the apostles was that they should be sent away to buy it for themselves. The Lord was testing the apostles when He said, "Give ye them to eat"; and they did not pass the test. They forgot that the Lord had never asked them to do anything without giving them the power to do it. How often we think the tasks which the Lord sets before us in our everyday life are too hard for us! We say, "I can't," without even trying. So the Lord gave the apostles another lesson.

As we go through the story, remember that the Lord is teaching us as well as the apostles. The twelve apostles picture all the faculties in us that make it possible for us to serve the Lord. The five thousand people stand for all our everyday thoughts and feelings. The hunger they felt represents the need we feel for enough knowledge and strength to do right from day to day. You remember that one of the Blessings is, "Blessed are they which do hunger and thirst after righteousness: for they shall be filled." The food our souls are looking for is goodness and truth from the Lord.

First the Lord asked the apostles what food they had on hand and they said five loaves and two fishes. Bread pictures goodness and fish the desire for knowledge. We must ask ourselves first how much of these we already have. If we do, we shall find that it is very little. In the Word every number has a meaning. It is not by accident that there were five loaves and two fishes. Five always means a little, but a little that is capable of becoming much; and two means that our hearts as well as our minds are in the matter— two fish, therefore, mean a desire for knowledge because we want to use it in our lives. If we have even this little amount of real goodness and desire to learn, and come to the Lord with it by recognizing that it belongs to Him and not really just to ourselves, He can bless it and multiply it until it more than satisfies all our needs. And you notice that He gave it to the disciples to give to the people. We have to do something ourselves—we have to set our best faculties to work to bring into every part of our lives the truth and goodness we receive from the Lord. The simple lesson is that the Lord has given each one of us all we need to start with, and that if we will look to Him for blessing and help and make the effort to use what we have as it should be used, our little will grow as we use it, and we shall have enough wisdom and strength to do whatever the Lord asks us to do.

Did the apostles learn their lesson? Read verses 45 to 52. The trouble is that each new problem we face seems different from any we have had before and we forget so easily. It takes us a long time, as it did the apostles, to become really convinced that we have no wisdom of our own and no strength of our own, but that the Lord is always at hand to give us power and to calm the storms which beset our path if only we will believe in Him and trust Him and let Him go with us every day.

### Basic Correspondences

|          |   |                                                |
|---------:|---|------------------------------------------------|
| Herod    | = | the principle of self-interest ruling in the mind |
| Herodias | = | self-love in the heart                         |
| five     | = | a little which can grow to be much             |
| two      | = | knowledge for the sake of use                  |

## Senior

You will perhaps help the young people in this age group most if you can lead them to study this chapter as a picture of their own mental states and reactions and of how the Lord provides that they shall have all the help they are willing to receive all along the way. If they can be led to look to the Lord in the Word for guidance rather than to the theories of secular psychologists, a real spiritual defense will be given them.

Do you ever take time out to study your own thoughts and feelings? When you go to college, you will probably study psychology, and if you do not go to college, the chances are that in any occupation you enter you will find it necessary to learn something about your own and other people's mental processes. You will need to think about these things if you are to be successful in your business relations and in your social relations, but especially if you are to have a happy home and family life. We all make a great many mistakes in life because we do not sufficiently understand ourselves and other people.

The Lord never made mistakes because He knew the heart and mind of everyone, and He was infinitely kind and patient. If we can read the lessons which lie within the letter of the Word, we shall find it the most perfect textbook of psychology ever written. All the people in the Word are in every one of us. What they do, we do; and what the Lord says to them, He says to us.

The principal figures in our chapter for today are the people of Nazareth, the apostles, Herod, Herodias, John the Baptist, and the multitude. The multitude are all our everyday feelings and thoughts and the twelve apostles the particular faculties of thought and affection which are devoted to the service of the Lord. The people of Nazareth are the mental and emotional habits which we have developed in childhood as the result of our natural heredity. John the Baptist is the prompting to self-examination and correction which the Lord provides in each one of us. Herod is the principle of self-interest ruling in the mind, and Herodias is self-love ruling in the heart.

Our chapter begins with the Lord's rejection by the people of Nazareth because they were unwilling to believe that anyone who had lived among them as one of themselves could really be divine. Many people today, in spite of all the testimony of the Gospels and of Christian history, refuse to believe that Jesus was more than an unusually good man. Our natural inclination is to be skeptical of any power to which we ourselves cannot aspire. Then the Lord sends out the twelve by twos—will and thought must always work together—to teach and to heal in His name. We are taught from the Word in Sunday school and church, and our higher faculties respond and begin the work of bringing our lives under the Lord's direction. John the Baptist has already been at work in our lives. Our parents and school teachers have taught us to control our conduct so that we may be acceptable members of our social group. Even Herod—self-interest—recognized the value of orderly conduct; the "Herod" in us knows, for example, that "honesty is the best policy." But self-interest stops short of willingness to give up self-love. When the idea is presented to us that we should really stop thinking about ourselves and what we want, we "put John in prison"—you remember the meaning of Joseph's being put in prison. And our self-love itself is not satisfied until John has been beheaded. The study of this part of the chapter could be a whole lesson in itself. For today we can think of it only in general as describing a condition which exists in the mind and heart of every one of us when we start out in life. We are conscious of Herod as the tendency to accept as valid such statements as, "If you don't look out for yourself, who will?" and, "If you don't take what you want while you can get it, you'll lose out." And we are conscious of Herodias in our love of pleasure and flattery and our resentment against anyone who fails to admire us. These are the states which are ruling in our mental country when our apostles begin to preach. You, who are on the brink of your independent adult life, need to recognize these tendencies in yourselves, tendencies which are present largely as the result of heredity and environment. For the most part they are not your fault, but they are very real and they have to be reckoned with.

The Lord, however, is also present and active and He has provided faculties in us which respond to His presence. You know that often you do see the truth of what you learn about the Lord and spiritual things and you feel an immediate response to it in your heart. But doubts and temptations constantly interfere, and the way is not all easy and successful.

The story of the feeding of the five thousand is a picture of how spiritual nourishment comes to our lives from the Lord. We pray, "Give us this day our daily bread." This is the "multitude" in us—all our complex thoughts and feelings—asking the Lord for wisdom and strength to meet our daily problems and tasks. The multitude listens to the Lord's teaching all day but does not "take it in," at least in any practical sense. The disciples—our higher faculties—would send the multitude out into the villages round about to buy food. People today sometimes look everywhere for guidance except to the Lord in the Word. But the Lord says to the disciples, "Give ye them to eat." The Lord has seen to it that each of us has enough real knowledge from the Word to form the basis of right conduct. We all have our five loaves and two fishes, enough goodness and enough knowledge of the truth to make a start if we will only use it, recognizing that it comes from the Lord and can be increased only by His divine power. If we will make our "multitude" sit down by companies on the "green grass," that is, take time to put our scattered thoughts and desires into some kind of order according to reason, and look to the Lord for the knowledge and strength for which we hunger, we shall find enough and to spare.

The last part of the chapter reminds us that the problems we have to face in life are of many different kinds. Often when we have been spiritually fed, we go out and meet contrary winds. Then we need the assurance of the Lord's power in a new way. We need to see His power to master temptations and to still the unruly things in us that make the going hard. We have seen before, in our study of the Old Testament, how victory is always followed by a new and deeper temptation. But that is the way in which our souls gain strength, just as our muscles develop by doing always harder and harder things.

## Adult

While the correspondence of the details of the miracle should be taken up, because some of the class may not know the meaning of even this very familiar story, the most fruitful topic for discussion may well be the reason for the sequence of events as arranged by the Lord in this chapter, because the introduction of the Herod story seems in the letter almost entirely unrelated to the rest of the chapter. The context in which any Bible story appears is always extremely interesting and important.

The miracle about which our lesson today centers—the feeding of the five thousand—is the only one of the Lord's miracles which is narrated in all four Gospels. In addition, a similar miracle, the feeding of the four thousand, is described in Matthew (15:32-39) and in Mark (8:1-9). Some commentators have considered the second miracle an interpolation on the ground of its similarity to the first, but there is no warrant for this, especially in view of the Lord's own reference to the two as separate miracles in Matthew 16:9-10. Every one of the Lord's acts which is recorded in the Word has its own special significance. In this case the difference in numbers gives an immediate clue to the difference in meaning, and a comparison of the details of the miracles makes a rewarding study.

But our thought today may be concerned with the basic meaning of this miracle and the reason for the particular sequence in which it appears in the Gospel of Mark. We recognize readily that the Lord's feeding of the multitude by the multiplication of a small supply of food pictures the Lord's power to increase whatever small store of goodness and truth each of us possesses as we look to Him for spiritual understanding and strength. The number five, which is the striking number in this miracle, signifies "a little" but also, considered as a factor in ten, a hundred, a thousand, etc., it signifies "much." That is, it expresses something, in itself small, which is capable of great development. So we have here the five loaves made to feed five thousand people. The loaves, made of ground grain, represent goodness in the life. John speaks of them as "barley loaves," which suggests that the goodness is of a natural rather than of a spiritual quality. The fishes represent affection for natural knowledges and the fact that there were two means that the knowledges are desired for the sake of use. The fact that twelve baskets of fragments were gathered up after the meal suggests that when we use in our lives the goodness and truth which we receive from the Lord in response to our prayer, "Give us this day our daily bread," we always see that there is much more there than we can immediately understand and apply to life—enough more to meet every need we can ever have, twelve meaning *all*. The seating of the multitude "by companies upon the green grass . . . in ranks, by hundreds, and by fifties" pictures our need of taking time for orderly consideration of what the Lord has to give us, with the basic thought of our everyday problems—the green grass—but recognizing that spiritual states are involved so far as we are capable of responding to His influx—the hundreds and fifties. The multitude represent all the complex and heterogeneous collection of thoughts and feelings of which each of us is conscious in himself. The disciples who brought the loaves and fishes to the Lord and passed them out as He multiplied them, are our higher faculties which have become capable of recognizing and specifically serving the Lord.

With this thought in mind of the meaning of the miracle, let us look for a moment at the background against which it appears in our chapter, and at its immediate results, for these are present in us, also.

First there is the Lord's visit to His "own country," to Nazareth, and His rejection there because of the inability of the people to believe that He could be different from themselves. In our personal experience this is perhaps best illustrated by our tendency to cling to childish concepts of the Lord: the babe in Bethlehem, the child in the carpenter shop in Nazareth, the man hanging on the cross, trying to visualize the Lord's earthly life and react to what our own imagination creates in this way. We must learn to think of the glorified Christ instead of the historical figure. The angel at the tomb said, "Why seek ye the living among the dead?" Also, we remember that when Mary Magdalene finally recognized Him, His immediate command was (John 20:17), "Touch me not; for I am not yet ascended to my Father." He had to rise in her thought as well as in fact.

Resuming now our consideration of the narrative: Then the disciples were sent out by the Lord by twos to preach and heal in His name, and were told not to take money, or food, or extra clothing, but to trust for their maintenance to those who would receive them willingly. This teaches us that even those higher faculties in us which acknowledge the Lord and serve Him are to take no credit to themselves and to put no reliance on their own powers, but to trust in the Lord for knowledge and power, and not to try to buy or force reception where it is not freely offered. Here is a lesson, too, in the manner of our missionary efforts. To go by twos is to use both love and wisdom in our approach, and we must always keep in mind that the message we bear is the Lord's, not to be tampered with by our own intelligence, and that there will be those who will welcome it and those who will reject it. This applies equally to certain areas in our own lives. We all receive the Lord's truth gladly in some fields of our thought and action, and reject it in others.

So it is not by accident that the story of the death of John the Baptist is introduced at this point, for the spiritual counterparts of Herod and Herodias are the two greatest obstacles in the way of our spiritual development. This Herod was the son of the Herod who was on the throne when the Lord was born. The Herods were Idumaeans, descendants of Esau. The Idumaeans had adopted the Jewish religion for the purpose of gaining control of the nation. Herod therefore represents the principle of self-interest at work in the mind, making use of the things of religion for selfish ends; and Herodias is the self-love in the heart which is the consort and the moving spirit behind that principle. Herod could recognize John as a prophet and hear him gladly and obey him in many things (verse 20), but when John pointed out the evil of self-love, Herod put him in prison. Self-interest recognizes the value of an orderly life and an appearance of religion, but will not listen to any deeper prompting. And self-love itself hates all restraints and is constantly trying to remove them. Herod and Herodias are in each one of us. We know how, when we are facing any decision, considerations of self-interest inevitably come into our minds, and we all struggle constantly with our natural selfish impulses. Self-interest recognizes the power of religion and fears it. Self-love merely seeks to destroy it.

Our chapter shows us how slow we are to learn even by experience. After the feeding of the five thousand, the Lord went into a mountain to pray after sending the disciples in a ship across the Sea of Galilee. We have to go back into the world of everyday affairs. The Lord seems to withdraw and leave us alone. Our minds, like the Sea of Galilee, are subject to contrary winds and we seem to be getting nowhere. Like the disciples we are prone to forget even recent experiences of the Lord's power (verse 52). The Lord has to manifest it to us all over again, walking to us across the troubled sea of our memories and entering again to calm the winds and bring us safely to shore (cf. AE 514$^{22}$). The order of regeneration is by means of one temptation after another, and it is helpful to remember that "in temptations apparently man is left to himself alone, although he is not; for God is then most nearly present in man's inmosts and sustains him; therefore when man conquers in temptation he is inmostly conjoined with God." (TCR 126)

## From the Writings of Swedenborg

*Arcana Coelestia*, n. 5291: "It is the same where the Lord mentions these numbers in other places . . . and also even in the historic facts that the Lord fed five thousand men with five loaves and two fishes, and that He commended them to sit down by hundreds and by fifties; and after they had eaten they took up twelve baskets of fragments. . . . As these passages are historic it can hardly be believed that the numbers in them are significant . . . when yet there is a secret in each number. For every detail happened of Providence, in order that Divine things might be represented."

## Suggested Questions on the Lesson

J. Why could the Lord not do many miracles in Nazareth? *lack of faith in Him there*

J. What instructions did He give the apostles when He sent them out? *take no "extras"*

J. Who did king Herod think the Lord was? *John the Baptist*

P. What had Herod done to John the Baptist? *beheaded him*

J. Who really caused John's death? *Herodias*

I. What do Herod and Herodias represent in us? *self-interest, self-love ruling*

J. When the multitudes were hungry, how did the disciples suggest that they be fed? *send away for food*

J. What did the Lord tell them to do? *you feed them*

P. What food did they have on hand? *five loaves, two fish*

P. What did the Lord have the people do? *sit down by hundreds and fifties*

P. What did He do with the loaves and fishes? *blessed, broke*

P. How many people were fed? *five thousand*

P. How many baskets of fragments were left? *twelve*

J. Where did the Lord send the disciples afterward? *Bethsaida (across the sea)*

P. What trouble did they have? *strong headwind*

J. How did the Lord reach and help them? *walked on water*

I. What kind of food do we need beside food for our bodies? *food for our souls: wisdom and love*

S. How is our spiritual food multiplied? *put scattered thoughts in order, use our available talents as best we can, look to the Lord for knowledge and strength*

## LITTLE CHILDREN
*Mark 10*

We can lead into this lesson by linking it to Palm Sunday and telling them that our story is of some things that happened on the journey to Jerusalem that last time. Point out to the Juniors and Intermediates on a map the three divisions of the Holy Land and how the Lord and His apostles came down on the east side of the Jordan this time and crossed near Jericho. We learn also in Luke that He went up from Jericho to Jerusalem.

---

### Doctrinal Points

*In all our relationships in life we should look to the Lord, trust in Him, and be guided by His Word.*

*Innocence means not trusting in ourselves or insisting on having our own way, but letting the Lord direct us.*

*"Trust in riches" means trusting in our own goodness and wisdom.*

---

### Notes for Parents

We parents are probably more conscious than others are of the seriousness of the increasing rate of divorce and of juvenile delinquency in our country, but we do not always realize that the two evils are closely allied and come from the same source. Our chapter for today shows us what that source is and the only way in which these evils can be overcome.

What does the Lord mean when He says, "Whosoever shall not receive the kingdom of God as a little child, he shall not enter therein"? The kingdom of God is the rule of the Lord in the heart and mind, not just after death, but while we are living in this world. A little child receives everything from his parents without question, believing in his parents' wisdom and trusting his parents to take care of him. The Lord is our heavenly Father, all-wise and all-powerful. We are still His children, and we should believe what

97

He tells us and trust in Him just as our children, when they are little, believe in and trust us.

In this chapter the Lord tells us several things which we need to believe and to hold in our thoughts:

1. He tells us that marriage should not be broken. If we recognize marriage as a sacred covenant which enables the husband and wife to serve the Lord together as one, developing increasing unselfishness through their love for each other and for their children, our marriage will be blessed with increasing happiness and peace.

2. He tells us that children should be brought to Him for blessing. We should see to it that our children are brought up in the knowledge of the Lord and His laws, so that they will be true citizens of the kingdom of heaven.

3. He tells us that we should not only obey the commandments but should also believe that to follow Him is more important than any possessions or position we may have in this world.

4. He tells us that to be of use to others is true greatness, as His own example showed. We can all be of use, whether we are rich or poor, learned or ignorant; so we can all be truly great if we choose. The only thing that stands in the way of our success in marriage, in bringing up our children, in living a useful life, is selfishness. If we can put away our thoughts of self-interest and self-importance and look to the Lord for guidance and strength, as little children look to their parents, we shall be blessed and happy receivers of the kingdom of heaven.

---

## Primary

It will be best to begin this time with the reading of the lesson, and then discuss it with a view to impressing on the children the meaning of love to the Lord and to the neighbor, and the necessity of overcoming some of the little faults which they have which make their parents and others unhappy. The tendencies to selfishness and feelings of superiority are sometimes becoming strong at this age, and the children should be shown clearly what they lead to.

What is our lesson for today about?

The Lord loves everyone, but everyone is not willing to receive His help.

He loves little children because they are innocent and trustful.
Innocent means not wanting to hurt anyone.
Little children do not depend on themselves.
We should all trust the Lord just as little children trust their parents.

You see, the Lord loves little children. You know that your father and mother love you. They take care of you, give you a home to live in, provide food for you to eat and clothes for you to wear. But behind your parents is the Lord, who gives us the world to live in, with trees and stones to make our houses, and the seeds and the animals from which our food and clothing come. So we should all love the Lord and thank Him, just as we love and thank our fathers and mothers.

Our parents have another duty toward us. They teach us what is right and wrong, and do all they can to see that we grow up to be good men and women. And we know that we ought to listen to our parents and obey them. But where do our parents get their knowledge of what is right and wrong? They get it from the Lord in the Word.

When the Lord was in the world, He spoke His teaching to all who would listen.

What did the rich young man ask the Lord?
What did the Lord tell him was the first thing necessary?
When the young man said he had kept the commandments, what more did the Lord ask?
Why did the young man turn away from the Lord?
What did the Lord tell the disciples?
The Lord did not say that people ought never to be rich, but that they should not trust in riches.
Whether we are rich or poor, we can obey the Lord and trust in Him.
If we trust in the Lord and obey Him, the Lord will make us happy whatever our outward circumstances may be.

The Lord gives us many wonderful things and wants us to enjoy them, but He knows that we cannot really enjoy them unless we share them with other people and use them to give happiness to others rather than just for ourselves. We should love and help other people just as the Lord always loves and helps us. Following the

Lord means following His example. We are all the Lord's children if we love and obey Him.

―――――

## Junior

It is well to put into the minds of children even as young as these the thought of what marriage ought to be and of what can spoil it, for the younger a child grasps the ideal, the less likely he is to absorb the wrong ideas of marriage which are so prevalent in the world. All through the chapter there are practical lessons for the Juniors and they can also understand the correspondence of rich and poor, and of blindness.

We are giving our lesson for today the title "Little Children" because verses 14 and 15 are really the key to the meaning of the whole chapter. If you read the chapter carefully, you find that in every incident through verse 45 the Lord is teaching us that we should not be always thinking about what we own and what we want, but should try first of all to do right and trust in Him to give us all the things we really need.

Little children in our lesson mean children so young that they have not yet begun to disobey and to try to get their own way. That means that they have two virtues which are the most important of all: innocence and trust. The things that turn us away from the Lord and heaven, as we all know, are selfishness and disobedience. They cause all the trouble in the world. To "receive the kingdom of God as a little child" is to believe in the Lord and obey and trust Him instead of thinking ourselves the most important thing in the world and imagining we do not need to learn from the Lord.

Let us see how this is illustrated in our chapter. It begins with the teaching about marriage. You know that even today in Christian families many marriages are broken up and the husband and wife are divorced. This is almost always the result of selfishness, of the fact that each partner in the marriage wants to have things his or her own way. True love is always unselfish, and if the husband and wife do as the Lord wants them to do, each will be thinking of the other's happiness instead of his or her own, and they will love each other more all the time as the years go on.

Then think of the story of the rich young man.

What did he ask of the Lord?
What did the Lord first tell him to do?

The young man had kept the commandments and we read that the Lord loved him for this. But the Lord saw that there was something else wrong with him, and it was a very important thing. He was proud of himself for doing right and trusted in himself and his riches and not in the Lord. He had the obedience but not the humility of a little child.

What did the Lord tell him to do?

Some people have thought that this verse means that everyone should give away whatever he happens to possess and try to be poor. Some religious people believe this and make a virtue of not owning property as individuals, considering themselves better than ordinary people for this reason. But if you read verses 23 and 24 [KJV] carefully, you will see that the Lord is not condemning the possession of wealth, but trust in wealth, that is, thinking that it is more important to be rich than to be good. [Cf. I Tim. 6:17-19.] In this world people are often judged by what they have instead of by what they are, but in the eternal life in the other world what we are is all that counts. The rich young man went away grieved because, although he lived an orderly life and wanted to get to heaven, he really cared more for his money than for goodness.

Following this we see how little the disciples understood the Lord's meaning.

What did James and John want?
What did the Lord tell them?
What does He say is the way to true greatness?
What does He say was His purpose in coming into the world?

Following the Lord means following His example. He told the young man to "take up the cross." Because of this command, which the Lord gives several times in the Word, and because the Lord died on a cross, people have come to think that taking up the cross means suffering. But verses 44 and 45 show us what it really means: it means trying always to think of what we can do to help other people instead of putting our own desires first. This does not mean doing some big thing for somebody once in a while, but doing the little things every day that make life easier and happier for our parents, our brothers and sisters, our teachers, and our friends. Sometimes people think it is fun to make trouble. We all probably have this temptation when we are children, and some people never overcome and outgrow it. These are the people who cause unhappiness and suffering, and some of them become those we call criminals. We should recognize this love of making trouble as the opposite of innocence, for innocence means "not harming" and not wanting to harm anyone. If we have this temptation even in a small way, fighting against it is the "cross" we must take up in order to be true followers of the Lord. Gentleness, kindness, and helpfulness are the qualities the Lord showed in His life and loves to find in us.

The miracle which the Lord performed immediately afterward (verses 46-52) has something to do with our lesson, too.

What did He do for Bartimaeus?

See if you can think of another kind of sight we have besides the sight of our physical eyes. It is the kind we mean when we say, "Oh, I see." We mean that our minds see the truth of something which we have not understood before. The Lord can give us this kind of sight, too, if we look to Him for it and believe in Him. Perhaps you were blind to the meaning of this chapter in the Bible before you began to study your lesson and now the Lord has made you see. If so, read carefully the last verse of the chapter. The Lord told Bartimaeus to go his way, but when he received his sight, the way he chose was to follow the Lord.

═══

### Intermediate

Here again the teaching concerning marriage should be stressed as a preparation for later instruction. The general lesson of the chapter can be brought out through the correspondence of Judea and of little children. Also, one of the unpleasant traits characteristic of the Intermediate age is the tendency to "know it all," and this is a good lesson in which to point out and suggest the foolishness of that fault.

We should note at the beginning of our chapter that the Lord has come down into Judea. In the Lord's time, we remember, the Holy Land was divided into three general regions: Galilee in the north, Judea in the south, and Samaria between them in the center. Just as in the time of the divided kingdom in the Old Testament story, Judah represents the will and Israel the understanding in the man of the church, so now Judea represents the will and Samaria the understanding; Galilee pictures the outward life or conduct. The center of worship was in Jerusalem in Judea, and the Lord was born in Bethlehem of Judea. This pictures that in a truly good person worship must spring from the will or heart. But we have to make our outward conduct right if the Lord is really to rule in our lives, and this is a long, slow process; so the Lord was brought up in Nazareth of Galilee, and most of His ministry was in Galilee. And in everything we do we have to use our minds. We have to think if we are to worship the Lord truly in our hearts, and we have to think if we are to carry out the Lord's commandments in our conduct. So Samaria lay between Judea and Galilee and was crossed in going from one to the other.

Most of the Lord's teaching which we have studied so far was given in Galilee, especially in Capernaum near the Sea of Galilee; so it has been chiefly concerned with what we should do. Now we are in Judea and the teaching in our chapter is concerned with how we should feel—what our hearts should be like.

You know that often you do what you know you ought to do when down in your heart you want to do just the opposite. This was what the Pharisees did. They made a great show of obeying every little clause in the law when at heart they did not love goodness at all but were selfish and covetous and domineering. So as soon as the Lord entered Judea, they were right there "tempting him" again, trying to find some cause for condemning Him. This time they asked Him about marriage and divorce. They were making an excuse of a single verse of the law of Moses (Deuteronomy 24:1) to do things they wanted to do, that is, to divorce their wives when they felt like it. Even that one verse, when we read it carefully, does not say what they pretended it said, and the Lord's answer reminded them that the law of Moses also contained a statement which forbade the interpretation they were giving to the verse in Deuteronomy. Marriage is meant to be permanent. If the husband and wife both want to obey the Lord, they will not be separated but will become more and more united as the years pass.

The very next incident in our chapter shows us just what we really need in marriage as in everything else. It is to look to the Lord, trust in Him, and be guided by Him in all things just as little children depend upon their parents. In the Word little children always represent innocence. The literal meaning of innocence is "not harming" and we know that all the harmful things we do come from selfishness in our hearts. So innocence involves not trusting in ourselves or wanting our own way, but letting the Lord direct us. Swedenborg says innocence is "a willingness to be led by the Lord."

Now see how this teaching is illustrated in the next story in our chapter. When the rich young man came to the Lord and asked, "Good Master, what shall I do that I may inherit eternal life?" he thought of the Lord as merely an unusual man, probably a prophet, to whom many people were going for advice. The very first thing the Lord pointed out to him was that there is no genuine goodness except in God. The young man did not really want to acknowledge the Lord as God because he wanted to leave himself free to accept or reject His advice. The people today who refuse to believe that Christ is God do so really for this very reason. They, like the rich young man, are quite willing to lead orderly external lives, to obey the commandments. They have been brought up to do so and like to be respected and praised. But when the Lord asks something of them which will mean a real sacrifice, a real giving up of their pride in their own goodness and wisdom, they are not willing to follow Him.

The "trust in riches" which the Lord condemns is not just trust in money, but trust in one's own goodness and wisdom. This keeps people out of heaven, because in heaven everyone knows that only the Lord is good and wise, and so everyone there is like a little child depending on the Lord as his heavenly Father.

The apostles still did not understand this. Like the Pharisees, external correctness seemed important to them, and they wanted credit for themselves and rewards of an external and visible kind. We see this clearly in verses 28 to 41 of our chapter. But they, unlike the Pharisees, at heart wanted to be good. So the Lord could teach them that happiness is not in getting but in giving, not in ruling but in serving. We can know from our Easter lesson that they still did not really understand, but they saw enough to wish to follow the Lord still.

This is what is pictured by the miracle with which our chapter closes. Blindness represents ignorance of spiritual truth. Sight, which is understanding, can be given only through faith in the Lord—that same innocence of which we have been thinking. Blind Bartimaeus had that faith and so the Lord could give him sight. And we should note that he proved his faith. When the Lord said to him, "Go thy way; thy faith hath made thee whole," he chose to go the Lord's way.

### Basic Correspondence

| | | |
|---:|:---:|:---|
| Judea | = | the will or heart |
| Samaria | = | the understanding |
| Galilee | = | the outward conduct |
| little children | = | innocence, "a willingness to be led by the Lord" |
| blindness | = | ignorance of spiritual truth |

## Senior

Every step in the chapter is important for the Seniors, especially the teaching concerning marriage and the story of what innocence really means and why it is essential. It will be a long time before this age group attain the innocence of wisdom, but if they see it clearly as a goal, it will help to check self-satisfaction and self-will.

In our chapter for today the Lord says, "Whosoever shall not receive the kingdom of God as a little child, he shall not enter therein." How do little children receive things? They receive them with perfect confidence and trust, knowing that they could not get them for themselves but only from a wiser and greater person who loves them and takes care of them. They look to their parents for support and guidance in everything. This is the quality called innocence which Swedenborg tells us is the very sphere of heaven. No man or woman is in heaven who trusts in his own goodness or wisdom.

This is a sobering thought, because we realize that we all naturally want to be praised and rewarded for the good things we do and are prone to think at any given time that we know more than anyone else. We are all naturally not innocent. The innocence which we see in little children is not really their own because it comes from ignorance and we know that they soon "outgrow" it. But those innocent states from our infancy are stored up in us by the Lord as the "remains" of which Swedenborg often speaks, and they form the basis for all our later spiritual development. And the whole object of our life in this world is to grow into innocence again—into the state of perfect humility and trust in the Lord which is called "the innocence of wisdom."

This is the basic thought of our whole chapter. The Lord came down into Judea, which is the division of the Holy Land that represents the heart or will. He was tempted by the Pharisees with the question on marriage and divorce and showed them that the Law really teaches that a marriage should not be broken at all. Throughout the Word, marriage is a picture of the union of love and wisdom, of desire and understanding, of love and truth. Neither is sufficient without the other. In a marriage the husband and wife need each other and together can serve the Lord as neither could possibly serve Him alone. Marriage should be entered into "for love," but true love is always unselfish and must always come from the Lord. If the husband and wife look to the Lord for guidance and love each other unselfishly, they will grow more and more one as the years go by. The thing which separates husband and wife is almost always selfishness, the desire of one or the other or both to have his or her own way and to rule, the unwillingness at heart to be led and governed by the Lord.

This same thought is presented in another way in the story of the rich young man. In the beginning of the interview the Lord called his attention to the fact that "there is none good but one, that is, God." The Lord in this statement is not disclaiming that He is God but is trying to make the young man see that only from God can true knowledge of the right way be obtained. The young man had taken the first necessary steps toward attaining eternal life by obeying the commandments. But he was proud of his attainments and of the position he held in the world. He did not have the necessary humility in his heart. He was not ready to give up the treasures of earth for the treasures of heaven. So he went away grieved.

If we read carefully verses 23 and 24 [KJV], we see that the Lord does not condemn riches, but trust in riches. And we should understand that the riches meant are not merely money but possessions of goodness or knowledge which we believe to be our own. The rich man or the learned man who recognizes that his riches or learning really belong to the Lord and are to be used in the Lord's service enters heaven as easily as the poor or unlearned man. The rich man who cannot enter heaven is the one who is the opposite of the "poor in spirit" in the first of the Blessings, of whom it is said, "theirs is the kingdom of heaven."

The next part of the chapter shows that even the apostles, in spite of all the Lord's personal instruction, still thought in terms of personal merit and the rewards it might bring them. They were thinking and talking of these things at the very time when the Lord was trying to prepare them for His coming death and resurrection, for they were on their way to Jerusalem for the last events of His life on earth. We can see that this absent-mindedness was probably the very reason why, at the time of the crucifixion, they did not remember that He had said He would rise again. When our minds are full of ourselves, we do not hear the Lord.

Contrasted with the state of the Pharisees, the rich young man, and even the apostles, who all had every opportunity to know the truth, is the state of the blind Bartimaeus, who "sat by the high-way side begging" and cried to the Lord for mercy. We know that blindness pictures ignorance of the truth. All Bartimaeus asked was to receive his sight. He had perfect faith in the Lord's power and because of this faith the Lord was able immediately to restore his sight. And it is said that as soon as he could see, he "followed Jesus in the way." He was both poor and blind, but he had the innocence of a little child, the willingness to be led by the Lord.

---

### Adult

The various quotations from Swedenborg in connection with the text of the chapter give discussion material. Verses 18 and 25 should be taken up, as they are often questioned.

The incidents recorded in our chapter for today happened as the Lord was on His way to Jerusalem for the last time. He had come down from Galilee this time not through Samaria but on the other side of the Jordan through Perea and crossed into Judea near Jericho. As usual the series of events in the chapter presents an interesting sequence. Judea, we know, of the three divisions of the land in the Lord's time, represents the will. It is in the will that our worship centers. It is there that the Lord is born in us as a simple desire to "be good." But it is also there that the most bitter and persistent opposition to the Lord centers, in our natural self-ishness and worldliness. And it is there that men reject and crucify the Lord as a result of that selfishness. As we should expect, the whole teaching of the chapter centers in the nature of a good will. The Pharisees, the rich young man, and the apostles were all proud of their externally correct lives, but in the Pharisees and the rich young man knowledge of the truth was not united with love of or replenishing the earth. Nothing is wasted. There is a reason for everything.

...uman beings are different from all other created things in that they can think, fee...
...eason things out. What would be the use of developing these faculties if they coul...
...uddenly be cut short by accident or sudden death; or if they progressed to ripe old...
...only to be snuffed out like a candle? What a waste of effort, and what a senseless
...ion! The brain which concieved the wonders of the universe and gave you your intel...
...could surely do better than that? It is true in a sense to say that the dead contin...
...to live on in the memories of those who knew them. Also their actions may have long-
...lasting and far-reaching effects in the world. Shakespeare says "The evil that men
...lives after them - the good is often interred with their bones." However, one has o...
...to think of the innumerable works of art, music, science, literature, etc. to realis...
...this somewhat gloomy view of life is hardly accurate in all cases. But are these su...
...cient to make life worthwhile, and do they really explain its purpose and meaning?

...he truth of it is that you are not a body - you are the part which thinks, feels an...
...reasons, and that never dies. Bodies die and decay, but what matter if they do? Yo...
...the real you, will never die, and neither will anyone else.

If you want to be convinced of this, turn first to the Bible, which is the Word of G...
...ou do not accept this statement? Many don't, but be fair - give it a trial - convi...

# CORRESPONDENCES IN RHYME.

### 1. THE MOUTH

The mouth to mem'ry corresponds.
For thoughts of truth and good
Go first into the memory
As in the mouth goes food.

### 2. THE TONGUE

The Tongue relates to taste or speech
Its meaning thereby reckoned
The first denotes a love of good,
A love for truth the second.

### 3. THE EYES

Those tender visual orbs the eyes.
Such watchful care demanding;
The spirits sight they signify,
To wit, the understanding.

### 4. THE EARS

The ears to hearing correspond.
But hearers, who are they?
They only hear aright who act;
Hence, "hear" includes "obey".

### 5. THE FACE

An angels face his life reveals,
Portrays his mind and heart,
Hence, in the Word face corresponds,
To mans internal part.

### 6. THE BONES

The bones, the groundwork of our frames,
And seat of power innate,
These correspond to lowest truths,
Or truths in ultimate.

*********************************************

being led by the Lord. Marriage pictures the union of goodness and truth. Spiritually the Pharisees had divorced the true "wife"— love of the truth for the sake of life—excusing themselves in the literal story on the ground of a law of Moses (Deuteronomy 24:1) which they misinterpreted to suit their purpose. This misinterpretation is an accurate picture of what exponents of "faith alone" have always done, defining the word *faith* to suit their desire to be saved without getting rid of their evils.

Marriage, as our traditional New Church marriage service states, "has its origin in the union of the Divine love and wisdom in the Lord." The verses which the Lord quotes suggest to us the need of putting aside our natural inherited selfishness in order to come into a true spiritual union. The breaking of a marriage is almost always due to selfishness in one or both parties to the marriage. And the only way of overcoming selfishness is through looking to the Lord for guidance and strength. Swedenborg says (AC 162): "It is the celestial (or heavenly) marriage from and according to which all marriages on earth must be derived; and this marriage is such that there is one Lord and one heaven, or one church whose head is the Lord. The law of marriages thence derived is that there shall be one husband and one wife, and when this is the case they represent the celestial marriage, and are an exemplar of the celestial man." If the husband and wife both recognize the Lord as the only source of love and wisdom and are really trying to serve Him together, they will inevitably attain increasing union and increasing happiness. This is an ideal of marriage which we should not only hold in our own minds but which we should hold before our children by both our teaching and our example. If children grow up with this ideal, they have a powerful protection against the temptations presented by the low standards of marriage in the world around them.

It is not by accident that the Lord's discussion of marriage with the Pharisees is immediately followed by His blessing little children. Not only is it natural to think of children when we think of marriage, but the quality of innocence which they represent is exactly the quality which was lacking in the Pharisees. The Latin root of the word *innocence* literally means "harmlessness." The desire to hurt others is the end result of self-love. It was evident in the Pharisees and it is also one of the most noticeable attitudes in the partners in a marriage on the way to being broken.

But innocence has a deeper significance also. Swedenborg discusses it at some length in nn. 276-283 of *Heaven and Hell*. Here he shows that innocence is basically "a willingness to be led by the Lord" and that, while little children exhibit innocence in its external form and so correspond to innocence, their innocence—being from ignorance—is not genuine. Genuine innocence is that humility into which the regenerating person grows gradually as he overcomes self-love and pride in self-intelligence and learns to trust wholly in the wisdom and love of the Lord. (See the quotation from HH 278 below.)

The story of the rich young man teaches the same lesson in a different way. He wanted to lead a good life and to get to heaven, but his ideas of both were wholly external, and he had no thought of his need of or dependence on God. That was why the Lord said to him, "Why callest thou me good? there is none good but one, that is, God." The Lord was not disclaiming divinity, for He proceeded to answer the young man's questions with authority. He was pointing out to us as well as to the young man that unless we receive His words as proceeding from God, they will not be effective in our lives. That the young man did not so receive them is evident from the fact that he turned away when the Lord told him to give up his own possessions and follow Him. Verse 25 has troubled many, but the Lord's own significant change from "have riches" to "trust in riches"* should show us what He means. Throughout the Scriptures the rich in a bad sense are those who are rich in their own estimation, as opposed to the "poor in spirit" of whom

---

*Most versions after KJV omit the phrase "for those who trust in riches" on the presumption that it is a later gloss. Swedenborg nowhere quotes the verse in question. —Ed.

it is said that "theirs is the kingdom of heaven." In *Heaven and Hell* (365) we read: "By the rich man of whom the Lord says: 'It is easier for a camel to go through a needle's eye than for a rich man to enter into the kingdom of God' (Matt. xix. 24), the rich in both the natural sense and the spiritual sense are meant. In the natural sense the rich are those that have an abundance of riches and set their heart upon them; but in the spiritual sense they are those that have an abundance of knowledges and learning, which are spiritual riches, and who desire by means of these to introduce themselves into the things of heaven and the church from their own intelligence." The apostles themselves needed the same lesson. They truly desired to follow the Lord, but their minds were clouded with worldly concepts. In AC 29 Swedenborg says: "The man who is being regenerated is at first of such a quality that he supposes the good which he does, and the truth which he speaks, to be from himself, when in reality all good and all truth are from the Lord."

The healing of blind Bartimaeus forms a fitting close for the chapter. In contrast to the others with whom the Lord has been dealing this man is poor and insignificant. But he has perfect faith and looks only to the Lord's mercy for the restoration of his sight. In a number of other cases of blindness the Lord employed means for restoring sight and the miracle was gradual. But it is said that Bartimaeus, when the Lord summoned him, "casting away his garment, rose, and came to Jesus." That is, he immediately put off all thoughts of his own and lifted his mind toward the Lord, and he asked only that he receive sight. "And Jesus said unto him, "Go thy way; thy faith hath made thee whole. And immediately he received his sight." And the way he chose to go was to follow Jesus. He received the kingdom of God as a little child.

―――――――

## From the Writings of Swedenborg

*Heaven and Hell*, n. 277: "The innocence of childhood or of children is not genuine innocence, for it is innocence not in internal form but only in external form. Nevertheless one may learn from it what innocence is, since it shines forth from the face of children and from some of their movements and from their first speech, and affects those about them. It can be seen that children have no internal thought, for they do not yet know what is good and what is evil, or what is true and what is false, of which such thought consists. Consequently they have no prudence from what is their own, no purpose or deliberation, thus no end that looks to evil; neither have they anything of their own acquired from love of self and the world; they do not attribute anything to themselves, regarding all that they have as received from their parents; they are content with the few and paltry things presented to them, and find delight in them; they have no solicitude about food and clothing, and none about the future; they do not look to the world and covet many things from it; they love their parents and nurses and their child companions with whom they play in innocence; they suffer themselves to be led; they give heed and obey."

*Heaven and Hell*, n. 278: "The innocence of wisdom is genuine innocence, because it is internal, for it belongs to the mind itself, that is, to the will itself and from that to the understanding. And when there is innocence in these there is also wisdom, for wisdom belongs to the will and understanding. . . . Because innocence attributes nothing of good to itself, but ascribes all good to the Lord, and because it thus loves to be led by the Lord, and is the source of the reception of all good and truth, from which wisdom comes—because of this man is so created as to be during his childhood in external innocence, and when he becomes old in internal innocence, to the end that he may come by means of the former into the latter, and from the latter return into the former. For the same reason when a man becomes old he dwindles in body and becomes again like a child, but like a wise child, that is, an angel, for a wise child is in an eminent sense an angel. This is why in the Word, 'a little child' signifies one who is innocent, and 'an old man' signifies one who is wise in whom is innocence."

---

## Suggested Questions on the Lesson

J. Where does our lesson for today take place?   *in Judea*

J. Where is the Lord going?   *to Jerusalem*

J. What did the Pharisees ask Him?   *is it lawful to divorce?*

J. Why did He say Moses permitted divorce?   *their hardness of heart*

P. How did He say people must receive the kingdom of God?   *like a child*

I. What is innocence?   *literally, harmlessness; spiritually, willingness to be led by the Lord*

J. What did the rich young man ask the Lord?   *what must I do to inherit eternal life?*

P. What did the Lord first tell him to do?   *obey the commandments*

J. What did He tell him next?  *sell his goods, give to the poor*

J. Why did the young man turn away?  *he was very rich*

J. What did the Lord say about riches?  *make it hard to get into heaven*

I. What does trusting in riches mean?  *trusting in one's own goodness and wisdom*

J. What did James and John ask for?  *seats of honor in kingdom*

J. What did the Lord tell them?  *not mine to give*

S. What reason did the Lord give them for His coming into the world?
   *to serve, and to give His life*

## PALM SUNDAY
*Mark 11*

This second of our special lessons can easily be tied in with the course by referring to the Christmas lesson and reminding the classes of the purpose of the Lord in coming into the world. The meaning of the words *Messiah* and *Christ*—the anointed one—should be mentioned as well as the fact that anointing is putting oil on a person or object, that oil is the symbol of the Lord's unselfish love, and that this means that the Lord came into the world as the Messiah out of pure love for mankind.

========

### Doctrinal Points
*Our natural selfishness keeps us from ever fully controlling our natural reason.*

*The "temple" of our minds needs to be cleansed of any tendencies to use our religion for selfish purposes.*

*The "mountains" our faith can move are those things which stand in the way of our spiritual progress.*

========

### Notes for Parents
Today in the churches is known as Palm Sunday and as the beginning of Holy Week, commemorating the last week of the Lord's life on earth. It was the week of the Jewish Passover, and the Lord and His disciples had come up to celebrate this feast. On Sunday, the beginning of the week, the Lord entered Jerusalem riding on an ass, as was the custom for kings and judges. He was acclaimed by crowds of people who cast their garments and palm branches in His path and hailed Him as their king and savior. During the first two days of the week He taught in the temple, having first driven out the money-changers and sellers of doves who had brought their business into the very temple court itself. At night He went out to Bethany and lodged at the home of His friends Mary and

114

Martha and their brother Lazarus, whom He had raised from the dead. On Wednesday He did not go into the city because the people had begun to turn against Him. They thought that the Messiah, when He came, would set Himself up as their earthly king, overthrow the power of Rome, and make them a great nation again. That was why they hailed Him on Palm Sunday. But when they found that He had come to save them from sin instead of from Rome, from their spiritual enemies instead of from their earthly enemies, they rejected Him.

On Thursday evening He came into Jerusalem again and ate the Passover with His disciples. We have probably all seen copies of the famous painting which depicts this "Last Supper." It was then that He instituted the "Lord's Supper," the Holy Communion, which in the Christian Church takes the place of the Passover. After supper, knowing that Judas had betrayed Him, He went out into the Garden of Gethsemane to pray. There He was taken by His enemies and brought to trial, and on Friday He was crucified. His body was placed in the tomb and the tomb was sealed.

This is in brief the story of Holy Week. We should think this week as we prepare for Easter of all that the Lord's coming has meant to the world and of what it means to us. And we should ask ourselves how far we are like the people who welcomed the Lord as their king on Sunday and crucified Him on Friday. For we are all like them sometimes. We say we believe in the Lord, but when His way is not the way we want to follow, we put Him out of our minds.

---

## Primary

Start by telling the children what day this is and why it is called Palm Sunday. Then give the introductory connections in a simple way before reading the lesson from the Word. Read the children the prophecy in Zechariah 9:9 to show them why the people knew that this was the Messiah. Be sure they know the meaning of the words *Messiah*, *Christ*, and *Hosanna*. Tell them briefly what happened between Palm Sunday and Easter which leads us to call this "Holy Week."

What is the New Testament story about?
How many Gospels are there?
*Gospel* means "good news."
You remember that all through the Old Testament story the people were growing more and more wicked.
The good people who were left were unhappy about it.
They clung to the promises given them through the prophets that someday the Lord would come into the world as the Messiah to save them.
So His coming and His life were good news.
We have learned how He came into the world and how He began His ministry.
We shall have more lessons about that ministry.
But today and next Sunday are special days.
What are they called?
Of what did the Passover feast remind the Jews?
The Lord went up to Jerusalem every year for this feast.

The Lord and His disciples were on their way to Jerusalem for the feast of the Passover. The Lord, because He was God, knew that this was the very time when His enemies, who hated Him because He pointed out their wickedness, would seize Him and put Him to death. He had told His disciples this and they had begged Him not to go. But He told them that it was necessary for Him to do everything that had been prophesied about Him, and also that He would rise again from the dead.

He had to pass through death and rise again to fulfill the prophecies and to teach us what death really is, so that we would not be afraid of it.
How did He enter Jerusalem on Palm Sunday?

The other Gospels tell us that the colt was an ass's colt. Do you think it was strange that the Lord chose to ride on an ass or donkey? It was not strange to the disciples who believed Him to be the promised Messiah, for it was the custom in that country for kings and judges to ride on asses, and they knew the Messiah was to be both king and judge, and it had also been prophesied that He would come riding upon an ass's colt.

The word with which the people hailed the Lord—*Hosanna*—is a Hebrew word which means, "Save, we pray thee." The trees which the people cut branches to strew in His path were palm trees. That is why we call this Sunday "Palm Sunday."

## Junior

Have the class look up and read the Scripture references in their notes, and try to show them something of what was in the minds of the people who welcomed the Lord and why they so soon turned against Him. Make the connection between this and our own experience and urge the children to think about it during Holy Week as a preparation for Easter.

How many Gospels are there?
What are the Gospels about?

We interrupt our regular course for the special Palm Sunday and Easter lessons, and then go back to our schedule after Easter.

What do we celebrate on Easter Sunday?

We remember that there were many prophecies in the Old Testament which pointed to the coming of the Messiah. A few of them even foretold some of the details of His life on earth. Read Psalm 22:1-18 and Isaiah 53. These tell especially about the end of His life. The Lord knew that He had to pass through death to show us the whole way of life. He had to let men do their very worst to Him so that we might understand that our real life is not affected by what others do to us but depends on what we do ourselves. So when He told His disciples that He would be put to death at this time and they tried to persuade Him not to go to Jerusalem for the Passover, He merely answered that it would be wrong for Him not to complete the work He came into the world to do.

What did the Passover commemorate?
What kind of animal did the Lord ride into Jerusalem on?

We learn from the other Gospels that the colt was an ass, not a horse. It was the custom for kings and judges to ride upon mules and asses. Read Judges 5:10, 10:3-4, 12:13-14, II Samuel 16:1-2; and the specific prophecy of the Lord's entry into Jerusalem upon an ass, which is found in Zechariah 9:9. When the people saw the Lord riding upon an ass, they understood that He was declaring Himself to be the Messiah, their king and judge, and they accepted and acclaimed Him.

What had the disciples put upon the ass for the Lord to sit on?
What did the people spread before Him?

From what kind of tree did they cut the branches (John 12:13)?

What did the people cry?

*Hosanna* means, "Save, we pray thee."

This was a triumphal journey. But we learn from many things in the Gospels that most of the crowd who welcomed the Lord imagined that He was coming to set Himself up as their earthly king, to deliver them from the Roman rule and make their nation once more a leading one in the world. They very soon found that this was not the kind of king He came to be. His kingdom is in the hearts and minds of men. Read His conversation with Pilate, the Roman governor, in John 18:33-37. The people who welcomed Him on Palm Sunday did not want this kind of king. So they turned against Him only a few days later, and put Him to death.

We call the week from Palm Sunday to Easter "Holy Week." The Lord spent Monday and Tuesday teaching in the temple, but at night He went out to the little village of Bethany on the slope of the Mount of Olives not far from Jerusalem. He had friends there with whom He could lodge—Mary and Martha and their brother Lazarus, whom He had raised from the dead.

What did He do in the temple before He began to teach there?

What happened to the fig tree on which He found no fruit?

Some people cannot understand why He made the fig tree wither, but if we remember that "fruit" is the symbol of good deeds, we can see that He was merely using the fig tree to teach His disciples and us that anyone who does not do good to others is spiritually dead. Everything the Lord did while He lived in the world is a parable, teaching something that happens in our souls.

The Gospel of Mark does not tell us about the Lord's Prayer, as Matthew and Luke do, but in this chapter we are given an explanation of one of the petitions in the Lord's Prayer.

Which one is it?

The chapter also gives us an example of the way in which the Lord often answered the charges of the scribes and Pharisees—by asking them a question they could not or would not answer. They never could get the better of Him, of course, and that made them hate Him all the more.

On Thursday of that week the Lord came into the city with His disciples to eat the feast of the Passover, and it was at that feast that He instituted the Holy Supper, about which we shall have a lesson later this year. After the feast He went out to the Garden of Gethsemane to pray. There His enemies seized Him, and the next day He was crucified—only five days from the triumphal entry into Jerusalem! This seems very sudden and strange, but it really was not. The resentment of the scribes and Pharisees had been building up for three years until it suddenly ended in unreasoning violence. Does this ever happen to us? Do you ever let a feeling of dislike and resentment against someone work and work in your mind and heart until the temptation to do something bad to him becomes too strong for you? The disciples and the few good people in Jerusalem were not strong enough or brave enough to oppose the determination of the Lord's enemies. Do you know that every one of us has in his own soul ideas and feelings that correspond to both the disciples and the scribes and Pharisees? We have our good intentions and we have our selfish and worldly desires. Let us think this week about the last few days of the Lord's life on earth, and try very hard to strengthen our good intentions and to condemn and put away those selfish things which are always trying to destroy the Lord's life in our souls.

---

### Intermediate

The correspondence of the details of the entry into Jerusalem is the important lesson for this class, especially the correspondence of the ass and what our "natural reason" is. The Intermediates are at the age when the natural reason seems the arbiter of everything, and a lesson in Sunday school can very well help them to see its limitations and the necessity of subjecting it to the Lord's direction.

The special lessons for Palm Sunday and Easter seem to interrupt our orderly study of the Gospel of Mark, but we may find that they help us to understand better some of the lessons we shall have after Easter.

We all know that the Sunday before Easter—Palm Sunday—is celebrated in the church in commemoration of the Lord's entry into Jerusalem at the beginning of the last week of His life on earth, and that the week between Palm Sunday and Easter is called "Holy Week." During that last week the Lord taught in the temple, celebrated the Passover with His disciples, was betrayed, seized, tried, and crucified, lay in the tomb from Friday night to Sunday morning, and then rose from the dead. During this week we should think about all these things and try to understand a little of what the Lord did for us and of what we must do for Him if we are to be His true followers.

On Palm Sunday the Lord entered Jerusalem as king and judge. The Gospel of Mark speaks only of His riding upon a "colt," but the other Gospels make clear that it was an ass's colt. This had been prophesied in Zechariah 9:9. The people knew the prophecy and they also knew that it was the custom for kings and judges to ride upon mules and asses. Read Judges 5:9-10 and I Kings 1:33, 44. There are several other passages in the Old Testament which testify to the same custom. Such customs were not without meaning, for we know that ancient Jewish history was directed by divine providence in such a way that it could be used for the writing of the Word. In our lesson on Abraham's sacrifice of Isaac, we learned the correspondence of the ass. It pictures our natural reason, that faculty which enables us to live and accomplish our tasks in the world. It is a very necessary and useful faculty but it needs to be kept subject to a higher power, the understanding of what this life is given us for. We all tend to use our natural reason to get things for ourselves. When we are asked to do something which will take time and effort, the first thing we are likely to think of is: What will I get out of it? Will it be fun? Will it interfere with my doing other things I like to do? Our natural selfishness keeps us from ever fully controlling this tendency of our natural reason. The Lord was the only one who really mastered it. Notice that when

He sent the disciples to bring Him the ass, He said, "ye shall find a colt tied, *whereon never man sat.*" Then notice that when the disciples brought the colt, they "cast their garments on him" for the Lord to sit on. Garments picture the truths in which the mind is clothed. The Lord's garments are the letter of the Word and the various senses within it. Our garments are the ideas of truth we have in our minds. We must make these subject to the Lord. So to symbolize this the people also cast their garments before the Lord for Him to ride over. The branches of the trees picture the principles according to which we conduct our everyday life. The Lord must rule these, too. We learn from the Gospel of John that the branches were palm branches, which picture our knowledge from the letter of the Word that the Lord is our savior. If we let our daily lives be governed and directed by the thought that only obedience to the Lord's truth can lead us to a heavenly character, we are casting palm branches before the Lord. The people of the Lord's day did not know what their action really meant, but again in following an established custom they knew that they were acknowledging Jesus as the promised Messiah. The same acknowledgment was in their use of the word *Hosanna*, which means "Save, we pray thee."

The people welcomed the Lord as savior and king, but very soon they discovered that He was not the kind of king they wanted and had expected Him to be. They wanted a king who would overthrow the power of Rome and restore their nation to a place of special prominence. There are two other incidents in our chapter which teach us this. One of these is the cleansing of the temple by the Lord (verses 15-17). When He said they had made His house a "den of thieves," He meant that they were using their religion as a means to get things for themselves. We do this today if we go to church to make people think we are good or just to "get in" with someone whose acquaintance we think will be of advantage to us. The other incident—that of the fig tree (verses 12-14 and 20-21)— teaches that although the people had the knowledge of what was right, they were bringing forth no genuine goodness in their daily lives. The fig tree represents the natural plane of our lives, its leaves the truths proper to this natural plane, and its fruit natural good works. In the sermon on the mount (Matthew 7:19) the Lord says, "Every tree that bringeth not forth good fruit is hewn down, and cast into the fire."

The people who welcomed the Lord on Palm Sunday crucified Him on Good Friday. We wonder how this could have been possible. But we may do the very same thing. Did you ever hear something in Sunday school which you saw was true and right and then afterward, when you tried to obey it, found that it did not seem to "get you anything," and therefore you put it out of your mind? We welcome the Lord as our king when we acknowledge that we ought to live as He wants us to live. Then if we keep on trying faithfully to obey Him, we are like the disciples who really loved Him, but if we give up trying as soon as we find that what we ought to do is not what we want to do, we are like the crowd who turned so quickly against Him and put Him to death.

There is something else in this chapter which has puzzled many people. In verses 22-24 does the Lord really mean that if we have faith enough, we can move mountains and get anything we pray for? The trouble is that people have come to think of "faith" as something just in the mind, to think that merely saying, "I believe in the Lord," is really believing in Him. Their own practice in things other than religion should teach them better. When they have faith in a doctor, they consult him often and obey his instructions and take his medicine. When they no longer are willing to obey him, they say it is because they have lost faith in him. It is the same with faith in God. If there is no obedience, there is actually no faith. If we have true faith in the Lord, we shall try constantly to find out what He wants us to do and we shall do it, and we shall not pray for or try to do things which are contrary to His order. The mountains which we can move are the things which stand in the way of our spiritual progress, the selfish feelings and thoughts and the bad habits which we have to "get over." See how we use correspondence in our everyday language. Often if we think just what we mean by an expression like "to get over" something, it will help us to read the Bible with more lively interest and understanding.

*Basic Correspondences*

|  |  |  |
|---|---|---|
| garments | = | truths |
| trees | = | general principles |
| branches | = | principles used to govern our day-to-day life |
| mountains (as obstacles) | = | selfish feelings and thoughts we have to "get over" |

## Senior

Use this familiar lesson to introduce a discussion of what true faith is and our constant need of faith in the Lord instead of faith in ourselves.

Each of the Gospels differs just a little from the others in its account of the Lord's entry into Jerusalem on Palm Sunday and the events immediately following it. The Gospel of Mark places the incident of the cleansing of the temple on the day following, John places it near the beginning of the Lord's ministry, and Matthew and Luke make it His first act upon entering the city on Palm Sunday. We should note that the order of events is important only as it affects the internal sense, and that the recording of the sequence of events in the various Gospels was under the control of divine providence, and each sequence has its own purpose. Only Matthew and Mark record the incident of the fig tree. John does not record the question of the Pharisees concerning the Lord's authority. In Mark and Luke the animal on which the Lord rode is called merely a colt, but John calls it a young ass and Matthew says that the disciples were sent to find "an ass tied, and a colt with her." The prophecy which the Lord fulfilled in this journey is found in Zechariah 9:9: "Rejoice greatly, O daughter of Zion; shout, O daughter of Jerusalem: behold, they King cometh unto thee; he is just, and having salvation; lowly, and riding upon an ass, and upon a colt the foal of an ass." That kings and judges were accustomed to ride on mules and asses we learn from many passages of Scripture. The people knew this custom and they knew the prophecy. So they hailed the Lord on that day as the promised Messiah, the king of the line of David who was to come as their savior. *Hosanna* means, "Save, we pray thee."

The Lord was the Messiah. He did come as king and savior. But, as He told Pilate at the time of His trial, His kingdom is "not of this world" (John 18:36). The people were expecting a king who would overthrow the power of Rome and restore their nation to prominence. As soon as they realized that Jesus had not come to Jerusalem for this purpose, they turned against Him and put Him to death.

The state in which the church was in those days is pictured by the incident of the fig tree which withered away because the Lord found no fruit on it. The fig tree represents the natural man and the external church. If these do not bear the fruit of good works, there is no spiritual life in them. The same condition is pictured in the incident of the cleansing of the temple. The people then were using their religion for selfish ends, just as people sometimes use it today, joining whichever church they think will be most profitable for their business interests or for their social position or as a cover for their own un-Christian practices.

What does the Lord's entry into Jerusalem on Palm Sunday mean in our individual lives? Jerusalem and the temple always represent the inmost place in our lives where the Lord should dwell. Swedenborg tells us many times that a person's idea of God is what really governs his life. If we form our idea of God from our own selfish character, we shall be governed only by considerations of self-interest. If we believe there is no God, we shall be blown about by the shifting winds of materialistic thought. If, however, we believe the Lord Jesus Christ to be God, we shall govern our lives according to His precepts and example.

In Mark's account of this incident there is one verse (verse 4) which adds a very striking detail not found in the other Gospels. The two disciples "found the colt tied *by the door without in a place where two ways met.*" We remember that the ass pictures the natural reason, that faculty which enables us to "put two and two together," to see the connections among the things we take into our minds through the senses and their bearing on our everyday life in the world. It is a very necessary faculty, the first one we have to develop as we pass out of our infancy. It is, just as our verse says, "tied by the door without," at the very entrance of our souls. It is said to be "tied" because it is not safe to give this natural reason its freedom. The ass is a useful animal but a willful and stubborn one. It is very sure-footed, but it looks at the ground. Our natural reason, if left to follow its own direction, sees nothing above the things of the natural world. The particular ass in our story was a colt "whereon never man sat." It was in a place "where two ways met." It had never been made to go in either direction. When we are very young, our natural reason is in just this position. The two ways picture the choice which is offered us, the choice between our own selfish way and the Lord's way. The colt can be safely loosed if it is to be brought to the Lord for His service. That is, if we recognize the Lord as our God and accept His direction, our natural reason will readily perform its true function of confirming spiritual truths by means of natural ones. To the man who believes in the Lord, "The heavens declare the glory of God, and the firmament sheweth his handiwork." We all find our natural reason unruly many times during our lives. The Lord was the only one who actually rode the ass's colt into Jerusalem, i.e., completely controlled His natural reason.

The same truth is carried further in the other details of the story. The disciples put their garments on the colt for the Lord to sit on, and the people threw their garments in the road on which the Lord was riding. Our garments are the ideas which clothe our minds. These must be submitted to the judgment of the Lord's truth. And the palm branches were also cast before the Lord. Trees represent our general principles and their branches the more specific principles which grow out of them. These must likewise be submitted to the Lord. The palm tree in particular represents the principle that all goodness and truth come from the Lord alone.

There is a beautiful coherence in this chapter in the internal sense. First we are shown what it means to acknowledge the Lord as our king and savior and we are warned against the danger of hypocrisy. Then suddenly in verse 2:2 the Lord says: "Have faith in God," and tells His disciples that if they have faith, anything they ask will be granted. This has puzzled many people, but we should see that the Lord has been showing us that faith is not an empty statement of belief but is the kind of belief which includes obedience. If we really have faith in God, we shall believe that His ways are right, and the things we ask for will be things which He can grant because they will be good for us and for others. The mountains we shall be able to remove are the "high places" of self-will and self-intelligence which stand in the way of our spiritual progress.

---

## Adult

The story and its meaning should be so familiar to the Adults that it needs only a brief review, and most of the time can be spent on the controversial incident of the fig tree and the statement about faith and prayer. The reason for the variation in the order of events in the four Gospels should be mentioned.

We are all familiar with the story of the Lord's entry into Jerusalem at the beginning of the last week of His life on earth, and probably with its general correspondence. He fulfilled the prophecy in Zechariah 9:9. The people knew the prophecy and also that it was the custom for kings and judges to ride on mules and asses. Read Judges 5:10, 10:3-4, 12:13-14, II Samuel 16:1-2, 13:29, and I Kings 1:33, 38, 44. They had no doubt that they were welcoming the Messiah who was come to be their king and savior. Palm leaves have always been the victor's award. The palm tree represents the principle that the Lord alone saves. The cry of the people—*Hosanna!*—means, "Save, we pray thee!" This word, which in our English translations of the Bible appears only in the New Testament, was in common use in the musical service of the temple.

The translators of the Old Testament translated instead of trans-literating it.

The ass's colt "whereon never man sat" pictures the natural reason, which only the Lord fully mastered from beginning to end in His earthly life. Our natural reason, like the ass, is very sure-footed but looks always at the ground and is stubborn and willful. It is a very necessary and useful faculty, but it must be kept under control. We remember that Abraham, when he was moved to sacrifice Isaac, "rose up early in the morning, and saddled his ass." His natural reason, which would have rebelled against such a sacrifice, had to be prepared to obey. Our natural reason is the first reason we develop as we come out of infancy. Mark—alone of the four Evangelists—tells us that the two disciples "found the colt tied by the door without in a place where two ways met." The "door" is the entrance to our souls—the same door at which the Lord stands and knocks (Revelation 3:20)—and the natural reason is tied to it on the outside, the side where our senses connect us with life in the material world. In that life from the beginning two ways are set before us, the way of self-interest and the way of the Lord's service. It is safe to "loose" the ass only if he is to be brought to the Lord. We "bring the colt to the Lord" when we are willing to rethink our natural ideas in terms of the Lord's teaching concerning eternal values. We "cast our garments before the Lord" when we submit all our thinking to the test of comparison with the truths of the Word. A king is one whose laws are acknowledged and obeyed. We welcome the Lord into Jerusalem as king when we accept His precept and example as the inmost law of our life.

In the Gospel of Mark the order of events is slightly different from the order in the other Gospels, and we need to remember that the order as well as the words was preserved under divine inspiration. The development in each Gospel has its special use. There are three major events in our chapter which follow the Lord's entry into Jerusalem, and they represent the immediate effect on heart, mind, and conduct of the Lord's entry into our souls as king and judge. The cleansing of the temple is the examination of our motives; the incident of the fig tree pictures the judgment of our conduct; and the question posed by the chief priests, scribes and elders, and the Lord's answer to it, search our thoughts.

In this Gospel the first two incidents are interwoven. As in Matthew and Luke, the Lord is said to have gone directly to the temple, but in Mark it says He merely looked about and then, because evening was come, went out to Bethany. In the morning, as He came toward Jerusalem again, He looked for figs on the fig tree and finding none said, "No man eat fruit of thee henceforth forever." Then He entered the temple, cast out the money-changers and dove-vendors, and told them they had made His house a den of thieves. Again He went back to Bethany for the night, and in the morning on the way to Jerusalem the disciples noticed that the fig tree was withered away.

The incident of the fig tree has been a favorite point of attack on the authority of the Bible story, the argument being that certainly the Lord would not have been so petulant as to curse a tree for having no fruit on it when it was not the season for fruit. That there is something more in the story than this we should know from the parable of the barren fig tree in Luke 13:6-9. Swedenborg tells us that the Lord had to open the Word in order that belief in it might not perish. See the quotation from AC 885 below regarding the incident of the fig tree.

The direct cause of the barrenness of the church was the perversion of their worship through self-love. So the cleansing of the temple—the exposure of this self-love—followed immediately. Then the result became apparent in the withering of the fig tree. That the cursing of the fig tree was no careless outburst should be evident from verses 21 and 22, for when Peter called attention to the fact that the fig tree was withered, the Lord's answer was, "Have faith in God." The verses which follow have also often been brought into question, but this is because of a wrong idea of what religious faith is. We understand well enough what faith is in every other field. If we have faith in a doctor, we follow his advice. If we have faith in a friend's honesty, we believe what he says and act accordingly. But men seem to think that a man has faith in God if he merely says, "I believe in God," whether he knows and obeys God's teachings or not. We should know better. True faith—which involves the belief that the Lord is all-wise as well as all-powerful—is a prerequisite for the fulfillment of the promises in verse 23 and 24. Read AE 405[53].

Finally we have the question posed by the chief priests, scribes, and elders: "By what authority doest thou these things?" This is the reaction of the self-satisfied mind to the impact of the Lord's coming. Its immediate thought is, "What right has anyone to tell me what I ought to be and to do?" "Why should I believe the Bible?" And the Lord's answer is the one unanswerable one: "The baptism of John, was it from heaven, or of men?" The people believed John to be a prophet. All our common mental faculties recognize that virtue is better than vice, unselfishness better than selfishness, humility better than pride—that is, that the precepts of the Lord present the true ideal of what life ought to be. If we deny these things, we put ourselves outside the pale of common decency. But if we accept them, we are admitting their right to authority, and condemning ourselves.

So the Lord put squarely before the religious leaders the question of accepting or rejecting Him. That they rejected Him we know, and their rejection brought their dispensation to an end. If we accept the Lord as our king and savior, we must accept His laws as the laws of our life. We must "loose the ass" only to bring Him to the service of the Lord.

## From the Writings of Swedenborg

*Arcana Coelestia*, n. 9212[6]: "By the disciples putting their garments on the ass and her colt, was represented that truths in the whole complex were submitted to the Lord as the Highest Judge and King: for the disciples represented the church of the Lord in respect to its truths and goods . . . and their garments represented the truths themselves. . . . The like was represented by the multitude strewing their garments in the way, and also branches of trees."

*Arcana Coelestia*, n. 885: "Specifically, by this fig-tree there was meant the

Jewish Church, in which there was no longer anything of natural good; and the religious teaching or truth that was preserved in it, are the 'leaves'; for a vastated church is such that it knows truth, but is not willing to understand it. Similar are those who say that they know truth or the things of faith, yet have nothing of the good of charity; they are only fig-leaves, and they wither away."

## Suggested Questions on the Lesson

P. Where was the Lord born?  *Bethlehem*

P. Where did He grow up?  *Nazareth*

P. Who was sent before Him to prepare His way?  *John the Baptist*

J. How long was His public ministry?  *about three years*

P. What is today called?  *Palm Sunday*

J. What did the Lord do on that day?  *rode into Jerusalem as a king*

P. What animal did He ride into Jerusalem on?  *an ass or donkey*

J. Where did His disciples find the ass?  *tied outside a door*

P. Why do we call this *Palm Sunday*?  *people spread palm branches* (John 12:13)

J. Where did the Lord spend the night?  *Bethany*

I. What did He do in the temple?  *drove out money-changers and sellers of doves*

J. What happened to the fig tree which had no fruit on it?  *withered*

J. What did the Lord tell His disciples they could do if they had faith? *move mountains*

J. To what part of the Lord's Prayer does He refer in this chapter?  *forgive debts*

J. What question did the priests and scribes ask?  *"By what authority . . .?"*

I. How did the Lord answer them?  *asked source of John's baptism*

J. What is this week called?  *Holy Week*

J. What happened on Thursday of the week?  *Last Supper, arrest*

J. What happened on Friday?  *crucifixion*

I. What is represented by the Lord's riding on an ass on which never man sat? *His mastery of His natural reason*

S. What does the incident of the fig tree mean?  *if there are no good works there is no spiritual life*

P. What will next Sunday be?  *Easter*

# THE HOLY SUPPER
*Mark 14*

As an introduction to this lesson review briefly the Palm Sunday account, calling attention to the fact that the Lord came to Jerusalem to die and told His disciples so, but that they did not understand or remember what He said. Note that during the last week of His earthly life He spent the nights at Bethany.

---

## Doctrinal Points
*The Holy Supper is a means for us to welcome the Lord into our lives.*

*Our "upper room," our ability to think about the Lord and heavenly things, needs to be "furnished and prepared" for Him.*

*The Holy Supper commemorates our redemption by the Lord from the power of evil.*

---

## Notes for Parents
It is a very sad fact that many people never in their whole lives take part in the Lord's Supper. In Revelation 3:20 the Lord says to us, "Behold, I stand at the door and knock: if any man hear my voice, and open the door, I will come in to him, and will sup with him, and he with me." A line in an old hymn says, "Oh shame, thrice shame upon us, to keep Him standing there."

There is no one who at some time in his life has not been told about God. That knowledge is the Lord knocking at the door of his mind. But the Lord never forces His way in. He leaves us free to admit Him or to keep Him out. If we care only for ourselves and our own way, we do not want to let the Lord in. But the Lord is the light of our life, and when we shut Him out, we stumble along through life in the dark, often hurting ourselves and others, sometimes getting what we think we want but never satisfied, never happy for very long at a time, jealous of those who seem to have more than we have, resentful over any trouble that comes to us, afraid of sickness and old age and death, and always blaming others for our unhappiness and disappointments.

To hear the Lord's voice is to recognize that we should obey His commandments. Then we open the door of our minds and try to learn all we can of what He wants us to do and to be. At first it takes some self-sacrifice, some changing of our habits, but we soon find that we have let in the light with the most welcome guest of all. Our way becomes clear and we find new joy from day to day. The Lord loves each one of us. He wants to give us each all we can receive of His own goodness and truth which are His very life. This is what is pictured by the bread and wine of the Holy Supper, which in our chapter for today the Lord calls His body and blood. If we give up our own way and become His true disciples, we may sit at His table and share in His joy. As the prophet Hosea says: "Then shall we know, if we follow on to know the Lord: his going forth is prepared as the morning."

### Primary

Even the little ones can understand the story of the last Passover and that what the Lord did then was the beginning of what we call the Lord's Supper or Holy Communion. They should look forward to sharing in it when they are older. The teacher should also tell the children briefly the story of the other events in the chapter, especially of the betrayal and the trial before the high priest.

Do you remember how on Palm Sunday the Lord rode into Jerusalem on an ass and all the people cast palm branches before Him and cried "Hosanna"? This was very near the end of His life on earth. He and His disciples had come to Jerusalem for the feast of the Passover, the most important of the feasts. It was a feast celebrated every year in memory of the time when under Moses the Lord led the people out of Egypt, where they had been slaves.

The preparations for this feast lasted several days and everything had to be done according to the directions the Lord had given Moses. The food was lamb roasted with herbs, and unleavened bread—that is, bread made without yeast. They drank wine with this feast.

Where did the Lord stay at night during the last week of His life on earth?
The Passover feast was always celebrated on Thursday evening.
Whom did the Lord send into Jerusalem from Bethany to prepare for the feast?
How did He tell them to find the right place?
Where in the house was the room which they used?
While they were eating, what did the Lord tell them one of them would do?
To "betray" means to help an enemy injure someone who considers you his friend.
What did the disciples all immediately begin to ask?
We, too, should be more concerned about our own faults than about those of others.
What did the Lord do with the bread and wine as they were eating?
What did He say the bread and wine were?
When you are older, you will understand what He meant.
This was the beginning of what we call the Holy Supper or the Lord's Supper or the Holy Communion.
Ever since the time of our story the Christian Church has celebrated this feast in place of the Passover. We celebrate it several times during the year.

Perhaps you have sat with your parents in church when it was being celebrated and watched the minister give them the bread and wine. You will share in this feast, too, when you are old enough to understand what it means and to be confirmed in the church. But you may learn now that it is a very holy feast celebrated in obedience to the Lord's command in remembrance of our being saved by His life on earth from slavery to the power of evil, a slavery worse than slavery to Egypt.

---

## Junior

The Juniors should be given in outline the whole story of the chapter, but special emphasis should be placed on the connection between the Passover feast and the institution of the Lord's Supper. If necessary, spend a little time in reviewing the origin of the Passover.

What did the Lord say about little children?
How did He say we must receive the kingdom of God?

What was the rich young man unwilling to do?
What did the Lord say about those who trust in riches?
What did He tell the disciples was about to happen to Him?
Why did they not understand Him?
What did He say we must do in order to be great in heaven?
What did He do for the beggar Bartimaeus?

In our Palm Sunday lesson we learned about the Lord's entry into Jerusalem, about how He drove the money-changers and dove-vendors out of the temple court, and how He taught in the temple.

During that last week where did He go at night?
Who lived there?

Mary was the woman who is mentioned in the first part of our chapter for today (see also John 12:3). John also tells us that it was Judas who complained that the ointment should have been sold. Read John 12:4-6.

Why had the Lord come to Jerusalem?
What did the Passover commemorate?

You perhaps know that Jews today still celebrate the Passover as their greatest feast. And you know that Christians do not celebrate it. From our chapter for today we learn why this is. At the last Passover feast which He ate with His twelve apostles the Lord instituted a new feast to take its place. In the account given in Luke (22:19) it is recorded that the Lord said: "This do in remembrance of me." He called the bread His body and the wine His blood. You will perhaps have to be a little older to understand just what He meant by this, but we can all understand that the Lord, by coming into the world and fighting all the temptations we have to fight and even choosing death rather than doing anything He knew would be wrong, broke the power of evil which was getting control of men and made it possible for us to resist our temptations by His help. He saved us from slavery to the power of hell, a much worse slavery than the slavery to Egypt out of which Moses had led the children of Israel. So the Christian Church at specially appointed times celebrates the Lord's Supper in remembrance of Him.

You know that the Lord's Supper is also called Holy Communion.

To understand this name you might try to think why it is that we all enjoy eating together. We enjoy the food, of course, but it is more than that. While we eat together, we think and talk together— we "commune" with each other. We feel each other's close friend- ship and common interest. In the same way, when we eat the Holy Supper, we feel the closer presence of the Lord and the angels. You should look forward to the time when you are old enough to be confirmed and to share in this Holy Communion.

But there is more in our chapter. Once in a while our mealtime is not so happy as it should be. Someone in the family is out of harmony with the rest and, even if his "contrariness" does not come to open words, it disturbs the peace of all.

When the Lord said, "One of you will betray me, one who is eating with me," what did each of the disciples say?

This is just what each one of us should say to himself when we feel out of harmony with others. We should not place the blame on the others until we have carefully examined ourselves, and often we shall find that we ourselves are to blame.

Where did the Lord go after supper?

The prayer of the Lord at Gethsemane is an example to us when we are facing something which we know will be very hard for us. We all naturally wish that the Lord would not require hard things of us—that there may prove to be some easier ways—but we should keep in mind that the Lord never lets hard things come to us ex- cept for our good, and we should be willing to go bravely through any hard task which He sets before us.

Who betrayed the Lord?
How did Judas show the Lord's enemies whom to seize?

Read verses 51 and 52. This is the only Gospel in which this little incident is mentioned. It is possible that the young man was Mark himself. You remember that Mark's mother was one of the early Christians in Jerusalem.

Before whom was the Lord tried?
Of what did the high priest say He was guilty? Why?

What did Peter do of which he was afterward ashamed?

We may wonder how Peter could have been so weak, but we do the same thing ourselves every time we are afraid or ashamed to stand up for what we know is right. To be able to speak out for what is right when everyone about you is bent on doing wrong shows the highest kind of courage.

———————

## Intermediate

The correspondence of the Lord's Supper and what is actually accomplished through it constitute the lesson of first importance for the Intermediates. They will soon be joining the church and need particularly to feel the value of this step in its relation to the privilege of partaking of Communion.

We recall that when the Lord gave His disciples the instruction concerning the necessity of childlike acceptance of divine truth and when He told them that true greatness is in serving the Lord and the neighbor instead of in riches or in personal prominence, they were on their way to Jerusalem, the last journey the Lord would make on earth. From the Palm Sunday account you will remember that during His last week on earth the Lord at night lodged not in Jerusalem but in the village of Bethany not far away, in the home of His friends Mary and Martha and their brother Lazarus.

The first incident in our chapter for today takes place in Bethany. The Gospel of John (12:3) tells us that the woman who anointed the Lord with the precious ointment was Mary, and that it was Judas who voiced the objection to the act as a waste of money. The lesson which the Lord teaches us in this little story is the same that He teaches in another story about the same Mary in Luke 10:38-42, that there are things more important than material benefits. Love to the Lord and the desire to learn from Him are the most important of all. We should notice that here again the Lord told His disciples—if they had been willing to understand— that He was about to be put to death.

Then we have the story of the last Passover feast which the Lord ate with His disciples and of the first celebration of the Holy Supper. You remember that on Palm Sunday the Lord sent two of His disciples to find the ass on which He was to ride into Jerusalem. Now He sends two to find the right place for the Passover feast and to prepare for it. The number two, as we learned in our lesson on the loaves and fishes, always means that we want to know the truth not just for its own sake but for the sake of doing it, that is, that our will and our understanding must go together if we are to accomplish anything. The Lord did not let the two find a place of their own choosing: they were to follow a man with a pitcher of water. This means that we must follow the truth which the Lord gives us in His Word. The place that they found was a "large upper room furnished and prepared." What they were about to do was to share with the Lord a very holy feast. We remember that a house represents our character. The upper room is the part of us which is above the level of merely worldly thoughts. We all have this upper room—the ability to think about the Lord and heavenly things—but we often keep it closed and unused. And sometimes we do not even bother to furnish and prepare it for receiving the Lord—we do not try to supply it with knowledge from the Word and to prepare it by trying to understand what the Lord wants of us.

For the people of the Old Testament the Passover was the greatest feast of the year, commemorating their deliverance from bondage in Egypt so long before. Have you ever wondered why we like to eat together? People of all nations have the same feeling; it is not just a tradition of our own. It isn't just because we all enjoy good food. There is something about sharing the same food that draws people closer together. This is because food and drink for the body correspond to food and drink for the soul—goodness and truth—and both come from the Lord, and to share the same goodness and truth is to be close together in spirit. At the Passover feast the disciples were closer to the Lord than at other times. Although they did not realize it, He was about to complete His work of delivering men from a worse slavery than the slavery in Egypt—from slavery to the power of evil. So at this time He gave them a new feast which for the Christian Church was to take the place of the Passover. We call this feast the Lord's Supper or the Holy Supper or Holy Communion.

The Lord called the bread and wine His body and blood. Some Christians take this literally and believe that by some mystical change the bread and wine are actually turned into the body and blood of Christ. But we know that material things are not the most important things. The Lord is really love and wisdom, or goodness and truth, and the bread and wine are symbols of this goodness and truth.

You are reaching the age—if you have not already reached it—when you will be confirmed and will join with older people in the Lord's Supper. In Revelation 3:20 the Lord says, "Behold, I stand at the door, and knock: if any man hear my voice, and open the door, I will come in to him, and will sup with him, and he with me." We hear the Lord's voice when we obey His commandments. We open the door to Him when we put away selfish and worldly feelings and thoughts and let His unselfish love come into our hearts. Then, as we take the bread and wine, we should think that the Lord is present with us more closely than He can be in any other way, giving us with the bread and wine all that we need and can use of His goodness and truth. Remember that the Lord is always there and giving and that what we receive depends upon us.

There was one present at the Passover feast who took part in the new sacrament but was not in a state to receive goodness and truth from the Lord. This was Judas, who had already planned to betray Him. Judas represents everyone who pretends to be a follower of the Lord but is really seeking his own advantage. He also represents the selfish and worldly tendencies which are in every one of us, even when we are outwardly worshiping the Lord. If we are truly humble, we are conscious that we have these tendencies. You notice that when the Lord said to the apostles that one of them would betray Him, they did not begin to look suspiciously at each other. Each one began to be sorrowful, and to say, "Is it I?"

The story of the betrayal and of the Lord's trial before the high priest and of Peter's denial of Him is one you should read carefully, not just wondering how people could have done such things to the Lord long ago, but thinking how each of us to some extent does the same thing today, not being true and brave enough always to speak the truth and to do right.

### Basic Correspondences

the upper room  =  the higher plane of the soul
bread  =  goodness
wine  =  spiritual truth

---

### Senior

For this class the emphasis should be laid on the necessity of recognizing our own weakness and need of the Lord, and on what constitutes worthy approach to the Holy Supper, what we should be thinking of as we partake of it, and what the Lord does for us through it. The whole chapter may be taught with these emphases in mind.

In the Gospel of Luke (22:19) we are told that when, at the institution of the Holy Supper, the Lord gave thanks and broke the bread and gave it to the disciples, telling them that it was His body, He added, "This do in remembrance of me." The disciples did not realize—although they had been told—that this would be the last meal they would share with the Lord while He was in the flesh, but the Lord Himself knew it. Read verse 8 of our chapter. He was about to lay down His life for the salvation of mankind. The man who was to betray Him had already made his agreement with the priests, although he was present at the supper with the rest and the Lord shared the bread and wine with him also.

The Passover was celebrated in remembrance of the deliverance of the ancient Hebrews from bondage in Egypt. The Holy Supper is to be celebrated in remembrance of our deliverance from bondage to the hells by means of the Lord's victories over them when He was on earth. We should always have this in mind when we come to the Holy Supper. Judas is in each one of us as the temptation to love self and the world more than the Lord and the neighbor. When the Lord said that one of those present at the table would betray Him, each of the apostles began to ask, "Is it I?" The proper preparation for receiving the Lord's Supper worthily is honest self-examination. No one can do this for us. Each must do it for himself.

Eating together is the symbol of conjunction. We invite our friends to share a meal with us as a token of our friendship. We also know that when there is one person present at the table who is out of harmony with the rest, the enjoyment of all is lessened. The Lord is present in the Holy Supper whenever it is celebrated just as really as He was present with His disciples at its institution. The bread is His body and the wine His blood, goodness and truth from Him. If we recognize and put away our selfish and worldly feelings and thoughts and come to the Lord's table in the sincere desire to receive goodness and truth from Him, we shall draw close to Him and our souls will be fed, each according to his need.

In the Gospel of Matthew as well as in that of Mark the account of the institution of the Holy Supper is immediately preceded by the anointing of the Lord while He sat at supper in Bethany. John tells us that it was Mary, the sister of Martha and Lazarus, who anointed Him and that it was Judas who raised the objection that the precious ointment should rather have been sold and the money given to the poor. This is a picture of the contrast between genuine love to the Lord and the attitude of those who place virtue in externals. The Lord taught the true relation of these things in His words to the scribes and Pharisees in Matthew 23:23. We should not neglect the outward good works, but they are not the thing of first importance. The attitude of the heart and mind is the thing which determines whether external good works are genuine or hypocritical.

Study the prayer of the Lord in the Garden of Gethsemane. We should not think that the cup from which He asked to be delivered was the physical suffering on the cross. The Lord never spared His physical body or was concerned about it. The Lord could have saved Himself from the cross. We shall take up this question in our lesson on the crucifixion. The point to note here is that the spirit of this prayer of the Lord is our example when we are facing possible hardship or sorrow, and that it is in keeping with the petitions of the Lord's Prayer: "Lead us not into temptation," and, "Thy will be done." We should recognize our weakness and pray to be kept out of temptation, but when temptation comes, we should know that it is permitted by the Lord and that He sees that we are strong enough to resist it with His help if we choose, and that we shall profit by the experience.

You may sometimes hear people say that the Lord never claimed to be the Messiah. This is not true. There are several places in the Gospels where He makes the claim clearly. One of them is in verse 62 of our chapter and in verses 63 and 64 we are told that it was this very claim which the high priest made the basis for condemning Him. We need to read the Gospels often and with attention so that we may be sure for ourselves of the recorded facts. People are sometimes very blind to things they do not want to see.

Finally in our chapter there is the story of Peter's denial of the Lord. Read first verses 27 to 31 and then 66 to 72. This incident, too, teaches our own weakness and constant need of guidance and strength from the Lord. Peter was one of the three closest followers of the Lord, one of the four first called to follow Him. Like Reuben, the oldest son of Jacob, he represents faith. How strong is our faith? If, like Peter, we are inclined to boast of our devotion to the Lord— even to ourselves—we shall soon be tested, and we may need to be shown how weak we really are. When we see someone else yield to temptation, we are very apt to feel that we should have been stronger if the same temptation had come to us. But we should remember that each person's temptations are different from those of any other. We never know just when or in what form our own temptations will come, but we should know that we can never meet them in our own strength. We need the Lord's help from day to day. We get this help by keeping close to Him through regular reading of the Word, through prayer, through regular worship, and especially through the Lord's Supper when we go to it in the right spirit.

## Adult

A topic for this lesson with the Adults might well be: "How we as members of the church may be betraying the Lord." Some of the younger and newer members of the class will also need a discussion of the meaning and value of the Holy Supper and of what constitutes proper preparation for approach to it.

We read in AC 5915 that sustenance in the spiritual sense is "nothing else than the influx of good and truth through heaven from the Lord. From this are the angels sustained, and from this is the soul of man (that is, his internal man) sustained. To this sustenance corresponds the sustenance of the external man by food and drink; and therefore, by 'food' is signified good, and by 'drink' truth. Such also is the correspondence, that when a man is partaking of food, the angels with him are in the idea of good and truth, and wonderful to say with a difference according to the species of the food. Thus when a man in the Holy Supper receives the bread and the wine, the angels with him are in the idea of the good of love and the good of faith . . . for the reason that bread corresponds to the good of love, and wine to the good of faith; and because they correspond, they also signify the same in the Word."

The New Church recognizes only two sacraments, baptism and the Holy Supper, considering these two to have been specifically instituted and commanded by the Lord Himself. In Luke (22:19) we are told that when the Lord gave the bread to His disciples, He said, "This do in remembrance of me." As we have seen before, the disciples in spite of all the Lord had told them did not realize that the Lord would actually be put to death. Even Judas, as his later acts indicate, obviously expected the Lord to save Himself as He had so often done before. But the Lord knew what was about to happen. On the previous day in Bethany, as our chapter tells us, when the woman anointed Him with the precious ointment, He told them: "She hath done what she could: she is come aforehand to anoint my body to the burying." We are told in John 12:4-6 that it was Judas who voiced the objection to Mary's act on the ground that the precious ointment should have been sold to benefit the poor, "not that he cared for the poor; but because he was a thief, and had the bag, and bare what was put therein." And in both Matthew and Mark it is immediately after the Lord's commendation of Mary that Judas goes to the chief priests with his offer to betray the Lord. Judas, we have seen, represents his nation, which put the all of religion in the externals of worship. Yet Judas was one of the twelve chosen by the Lord Himself, and in TCR 791, in connection with the historical Second Coming, we are told: "After this work was finished the Lord called together His twelve disciples who followed Him in the world; and the next day He sent them all forth throughout the whole spiritual world to preach the Gospel that THE LORD GOD JESUS CHRIST reigns." Judas, we may infer, was still one of the twelve. In TCR 4 in the same connection it is said, "his twelve disciples, now angels." Apparently Judas the man had in him the basis of salvation. As a representative character he belongs with the apostles; the externals of worship are an essential part of the complete Christian life. But we must always keep in mind that it is through them, when the emphasis is put on them rather than on the celestial and spiritual things which they represent, that the Lord is betrayed. The first Christian Church betrayed the Lord in this way by adding interpretations and regulations of its own to the simple and beautiful teaching and example of the Lord as given us by Him in the Word of the New Testament. When we compare the elaborate rituals of some churches today with the simple ceremony of the Holy Supper as the Lord first gave it, we realize the danger into which the love of the externals of worship can lead.

We should note in our chapter that a state of humility preceded the institution of the Holy Supper. The Lord told the twelve that one of them would betray Him, and instead of looking at each other with suspicion "they began to be sorrowful, and to say unto Him one by one, 'Is it I?' " This is the pattern for our own approach to the Holy Supper. "What weaknesses are in me which may be leading me to betray the Lord?" The thirteenth chapter of TCR (nn. 698-752) is devoted to the subject of the Holy Supper. Section VI of this chapter is headed: "Those come to the holy supper worthily who have faith in the Lord and charity toward the neighbor." See the excerpt from n. 726 below.

We recall that even James and John had in their minds thoughts of their own power and glory, and this universal tendency in man to wish to place himself first is further impressed upon us by the story of Peter's denial of the Lord. Peter, we know, represents faith, and Peter was sure that though all others failed, he would remain true. He needed to see and acknowledge his own weakness, and each of us needs the same lesson. Another example of the same weakness is found in verses 51 and 52. This little incident is recorded only in the Gospel of Mark, and commentators with some reason have suggested that the young man may have been Mark himself. We remember that Mark lived in Jerusalem and that his mother was among the most prominent of the early Christians. Tidings of the exodus of the multitude with swords and staves in the direction of the garden where the Lord had gone might well have reached her home and prompted young Mark to leave his bed hastily and follow. The important thought for us, however, is rather that in the correspondence the linen garment represents the possession of truth from the divine—"the fine linen is the righteousness of saints"—and nakedness represents lack of truth. When the enemy laid hold on the young man's garment, he left the linen cloth and fled from them naked. Although he had received and accepted the Lord's teaching, his belief was not strong enough to stand in the face of personal danger.

There are other things in this chapter which we need to note especially. One is the prayer of the Lord in Gethsemane. We may be sure that the Lord was not praying to be spared physical suffering. What the suffering on the cross was we shall consider in our next lesson. The form of the prayer, however, is a divine recognition of the weakness of human nature; "For he knoweth our frame; he remembereth that we are dust." What the Lord is saying to us here is that it is not wrong for us to pray to be delivered from some impending trial or bereavement provided that at the same time we are at heart willing to go through it if the Lord sees that it is for our good.

We all recognize the betrayal of the Lord by Judas with a kiss as picturing the betrayal of the Lord which is involved in professing to be a Christian while inwardly serving self instead of the Lord. One of the strongest arguments men offer against uniting with a church is that so many of its members are obviously sinners.

Finally we should note verses 61-64, because sometimes people say that the Lord never claimed to be the Messiah, when in fact this very claim was made the basis for His condemnation by the high priest. Note that there is nothing in this chapter which has to do with Gentiles—people outside of the church. Its lessons concern those who profess religion, and it shows us our constant need of humility and of the consciousness of our own weakness and selfishness, of not pointing at others but at every point asking sincerely, "Is it I?"

## From the Writings of Swedenborg

*True Christian Religion*, n. 726: "Eternal life and salvation are impossible without conjunction with the Lord. . . . Only those come to the holy supper worthily who are interiorly conjoined with the Lord, and those are interiorly conjoined with Him who are regenerated. . . . There are many who confess the Lord, and who do good to the neighbor; but unless this is done from love to the neighbor and from faith in the Lord, they are not regenerated, for such do good to the neighbor solely for reasons that look to the world and themselves, and not to the neighbor as the neighbor. The works of such are merely natural, and do not have concealed within them anything spiritual; for they confess the Lord with the mouth and lips only, from which their heart is far away. True love to the neighbor, and true faith, are from the Lord alone, and both are given to man when he from his freedom of choice does good to the neighbor naturally, and believes truths rationally, and looks to the Lord, doing these three things because they are commanded in the Word. The Lord then implants charity and faith in the midst of him, and makes both of these spiritual. Thus the Lord conjoins Himself to man, and man conjoins himself to the Lord, for no conjunction is possible unless it is effected reciprocally."

## Suggested Questions on the Lesson

J. What did the Lord say about little children? *of such is kingdom of heaven*

J. What did the rich young man ask?  *what must I do to inherit eternal life?*

J. What did the Lord tell him to do as the first thing necessary?  *obey commandments*

P. What was the young man not willing to do?  *give up his riches*

J. What did the Lord say about [trust in] riches?  *makes it hard to enter heaven*

P. What did James and John want?  *seats of honor*

J. What did the Lord say true greatness is?  *being servant to all*

J. When the Lord was at supper in Bethany, what did a woman do for Him?  *anointed Him*

J. What did some of the disciples say?  *this was wasteful*

J. What did the Lord tell them?  *she has done a beautiful thing*

P. How did the Lord tell the two disciples to find the house where they should prepare the Passover feast?  *follow man with water jar*

P. Where was the room in the house?  *upstairs*

J. What did the Passover commemorate?  *release from Egyptian slavery*

P. When the Lord told the disciples that one of them would betray Him, · what did each one ask?  *"Is it I?"*

P. What did the Lord do with the bread and wine as they were eating?  *blessed, gave to disciples*

P. Of what Christian sacrament was this the beginning?  *Holy Supper*

I. What do the bread and wine represent?  *divine goodness and truth*

J. Where did the Lord go after supper?  *Gethsemane*

J. What was His prayer there?  *to "remove cup"*

J. Who betrayed the Lord?  *Judas Iscariot*

J. How did he betray Him?  *with a kiss*

J. Where was the Lord taken to be tried?  *before the high priest*

S. What accusation did the high priest make against Him? Why?  *blasphemy, claimed to be the Christ*

J. What did Peter do which he had been sure he would not do?  *denied the Lord three times*

S. What do we commemorate in the Holy Supper?  *our redemption from power of evil*

# THE CRUCIFIXION
## *Mark 15*

Review the institution of the Holy Supper and make your connection through the betrayal of the Lord by Judas. In all the classes make clear that it was the high priests who actually condemned the Lord, but that Pilate had to give his consent.

---

## Doctrinal Points
*The passion of the cross was only the last in a whole lifetime of temptations the Lord faced in order to redeem mankind.*
*Evil can have no power over us unless we allow it, by failing to call on the Lord to help us overcome it.*

---

## Notes for Parents
When we think about the crucifixion of the Lord, it is likely to seem to us a terrible crime which was committed long ago, in which we are glad that we had no part. We live in a nominally Christian nation after centuries of recognition of the Lord. And we live in an age which has learned—as a result of Christianity—to think of physical torture as barbarous. But the people in the Lord's time took cruel punishments for granted, and to the chief priests the Lord was just a Nazarene who was stirring up the people and threatening their own authority. They did commit a cruel crime, but our thought should be about the motives which prompted them and about how far we may have those same motives in our own hearts.

Do we ever refuse to recognize the truth because it would interfere with what we want to do? Do we ever try to discredit and silence someone who presumes to criticize us? Do we ever try to ridicule other people into agreeing with us?

The Lord had power to save Himself from His enemies. He had proved it many times. He could have performed a great miracle which would have forced everyone to believe in Him. But this would not have changed their hearts. Nothing really brings people happiness but love freely given, and the Lord wants us to be happy. So He leaves us free. He came into the world to show us the whole way of life, and that had to include the way through death. He had said to His disciples, "Be not afraid of them that kill the body, and after that have no more that they can do." If we will learn this lesson from Him and try always to follow His example, evil will have no power over us, and we shall be what He wants us all to be, inheritors of the kingdom of heaven.

## Primary

Stress the reason why the Lord did not save Himself from death on the cross. Tell the children very simply what crucifixion was, as they will be sure to see pictures of it, but do not let them think that the physical suffering was too important. The older children will also be interested in the other details of the story.

You remember that the Lord ate the Passover feast with His disciples, and after the feast He blessed the bread and wine and shared them among the disciples and told them to observe the new feast afterward in memory of Him. That is why we have the Holy Supper in the Christian Church instead of the Passover.

What did He tell them one of them would do?
What did they all say?
It was Judas Iscariot who betrayed the Lord.
He took money from the high priests for leading their servants to the Lord.
He told them that the one he would kiss would be the one for them to take.
Judas was the apostle who had charge of the money from which all their expenses were paid.
He had become more interested in adding money to the bag than in serving the Lord.
But he probably thought that the Lord would save Himself, as He had at other times.

After the Passover supper Judas led a company of people from the high priest out to the Garden of Gethsemane where the Lord had gone to pray. In order to show them the right person to capture, He went up to the Lord, as he had agreed to do, and kissed

Him. Then they took the Lord prisoner, and the chief priests con-demned Him and sent Him to Pilate, the Roman governor, to be put to death.

Pilate, the governor, could find no fault in the Lord.
Read verses 6 and 7 of our chapter.
Pilate wanted to release the Lord.
What did the Jews say?
How was the Lord put to death?
Who carried His cross to Golgotha? [Cf., however, John 19:17.]
What was written over the cross?
Who were crucified with Him?
What do we call the day on which this happened? ["Good" in this context means "holy."]
What happened the next Sunday?
What do we call that day?

## Junior

Bring out the position of the Roman governor and his relation to the high priests. The children may like to discuss how far each was to blame for the Lord's death. They are also old enough to understand why the Lord did not save Himself. They should learn the details of the whole story.

For what feast did the Lord come to Jerusalem on Palm Sunday?
On what day did He celebrate it?
What new feast did He institute at that time?
Which of the apostles betrayed the Lord?
How did he show the high priest's servants which person to seize?
Before whom was the Lord first tried?
Of what did the high priest find Him guilty?
Why?
What did Peter do that he was sure he could not do?

At this time the Hebrew nation was under the rule of the Roman empire. The Romans had conquered most of the world. They kept each nation subject by sending out to it a Roman governor with trained troops to take control. The Hebrew priests could not con-demn anyone to death. So the high priest sent the Lord to the Roman governor, whose name was Pontius Pilate, and asked him to have the Lord put to death.

What did Pilate ask the Lord?
What did the Lord say?

As we learn from verse 6, it was the custom for the Roman governor at the time of the Passover to free one prisoner—anyone the people chose.

What other prisoner did Pilate have at this time?
What crimes had he committed?
What did Pilate ask the people?
Which prisoner did they ask to have released?
What did they ask Pilate to do with the Lord?
Where was the Lord crucified?
What was written above the cross?
Who were crucified with the Lord?
What did His enemies who were watching tell the Lord to do?

The Lord could have saved Himself from the cross as He had saved Himself at other times. Read Luke 4:28-30, John 8:59, John 10:17-18, 39, and John 19:10-11. No doubt Judas expected Him to save Himself, for when he saw that the Lord was actually taken prisoner, he went to the high priest and tried to save Him by giving back the thirty pieces of silver which had been paid him, and when the high priest refused, Judas threw the money on the floor and went out and hanged himself (Matthew 27:3-5). But the Lord had come into the world to show us the whole way of life, and the life of every one of us in this world reaches its end in what we call death. The Lord had to die and rise again to show us that death is only one of the necessary steps in our life and that we need not be at all afraid of it. And He wanted to show us that if we are good, nothing that anyone can do to us will really hurt our souls. So He let His enemies do the very worst they possibly could to His body.

What happened in the temple when the Lord died?
What did the centurion (the soldier in charge of the Roman guard) say?
Who asked permission of Pilate to bury the Lord's body?
Where did he place it?
Who watched to see where it was laid?

You remember from the Easter account that it was these two

Marys who came to the sepulcher early on Sunday morning with spices, hoping to be able to anoint the body of the Lord, as was the custom, and so were the first to know that the Lord had risen.

The story of the crucifixion seems to all of us a very terrible story, but it is one we need to read and think about because it teaches us especially two things. One is that human beings—all men and women—are selfish by nature, and that if this selfishness in each of us is not recognized and checked, it can lead us to do very cruel and wicked things. The crimes that we read about in the newspapers today can for the most part be traced back to unchecked selfishness. Most of them no doubt began in little acts of dishonesty and cruelty in childhood. We must begin while we are young to hate such things in ourselves as well as in others, and to be honest and kind every day with everyone.

The other lesson is one of gratitude to the Lord for being willing to come into the world and live in a body like ours and suffer not only the physical pain which all material bodies are subject to but the hatred and scorn of the very people whom He was trying to save. Remember always that He could have saved Himself but that if He had, He would not have been able to save us. He won a great victory over all the power of evil by choosing as He did.

———

## Intermediate

The correspondence of the chief priests and of Pilate and how this story applies to our everyday lives is important for his class. Emphasize what it means to condemn the Lord and free Barabbas. Be sure the young people understand what the temptation on the cross really was and how the Lord, by His victories over temptation, made salvation possible for us.

In the time of the Lord the chief priests did not have the power to pronounce a death sentence on anyone. That had to be done by the Roman governor. So the chief priests sent the Lord to Pilate, asking him to sentence the Lord to death. Pilate could find no fault in the Lord, but he soon gave in to the urging of the priests and agreed to sentence Him to be crucified. Let us see if we can understand what this means in our lives. We all know something of the

Lord's truth in the Word. If we are selfish, we want to put that truth away where it will not bother us. The high priests represent this selfishness in our hearts. But we are made in such a way that our thinking does not have to agree with our will. Our minds can tell us that we ought to do right even when we want to do wrong. Our minds, like Pilate, can see that the Lord is right. So we often, like the priests, try hard to make our thinking agree to what we want to do. And very often our minds give in just as Pilate did. Remember this when you find yourself trying to make up excuses for doing what you want instead of what you really know is right. Pilate could have released the Lord, but instead he was persuaded to release Barabbas, a rebel and murderer. When our reasoning ability gives in to our selfishness, evil things instead of good ones are given their freedom in our minds and hearts.

Crucifixion was considered the worst form in which death could be inflicted on anyone. The physical suffering was severe and prolonged, and the exposure to the ridicule of the crowd was an added torment. We can understand this latter suffering if we read verses 29 to 32 of our chapter. People have always talked a great deal about these aspects of the Lord's death on the cross, but they were actually the least of His suffering. The Lord, we know, could have saved Himself from the cross. Read Luke 4:28-30, John 8:59, John 10:17-18, 39, and John 19:10-11. He was afraid neither of the physical suffering nor of the ridicule of the people. But because He loved all men—even His enemies—He was tempted to use His divine power to keep them from committing so great a crime. If He had come down from the cross as His enemies dared Him to, they would have had to acknowledge Him as God, but it would not have changed their hearts. The Lord wants us to love Him, not fear Him. Love has to be given freely.

Now read verse 38. To know what the veil of the temple was, read Exodus 26:31-33. It hid the Holy of Holies, where the ark was kept, in an earlier day, from the sight even of the priests who ministered in the Holy Place. In the Word a veil always pictures the covering over the Divine itself which the Lord provides in order

that men can bear to look toward Him, just as we put on dark
glasses when we need to look toward the sun. While the Lord was in
the world, the human nature which He had taken on from Mary was
such a "veil." On the cross, when He overcame the last human temptation, He finally put off this veil. That was why, because of its correspondence, the veil of the temple was rent (torn) at that time,
and you notice that immediately the centurion who was on guard
at the cross–although he could not have known of the rending of
the veil in the temple–was given to see that this was indeed God.

The last part of our chapter tells us how Joseph of Arimathea,
"an honourable counsellor," asked Pilate for the body of the Lord
and placed it in a tomb hewn out of a rock, and rolled a stone in
front of the door. The ruling body of Judaism was the Sanhedrin,
a council of about seventy of the leading men, including the high
priests. Joseph of Arimathea and Nicodemus (John 3:1-13) were,
so far as we know, the only members of the Sanhedrin who believed
in the Lord. We learn from John 19:39 that Nicodemus assisted
Joseph with the burial. As prominent men they could get the ear
of Pilate as the other disciples could not. Joseph had bought fine
linen in which to wrap the body and Nicodemus brought the spices
used in burials. The linen and the spices correspond to different
kinds of truth. Both of these leaders had recognized that the Lord's
teachings were the truth, and they wished to honor Him and to
preserve the truth which they had found in Him even after the life
had left His earthly body. Linen pictures truth from the divine and
spices truth from love. These two men and the three women (verse
40) were the only ones of all His followers who did not desert the
Lord when He seemed dead. They represent true faith and true
love which serve the Lord for the sake of the truth and goodness
which they have found in Him and not from any thought of their
own future honor or gain.

### Basic Correspondences

linen  =  truth from the divine
in the natural plane of the mind
the veil  =  the Lord's finite humanity

Senior

The difference between the New Church doctrine of salvation and that of other churches should be stressed. The nature of the Lord's temptation on the cross is important, and the reason why He did not save Himself. Show how every detail of the story has an application to our own temptations.

The symbol of the Christian Church is the cross, and the cross reminds all Christians that the Lord laid down His life to save mankind. But there is a wide difference of belief among Christians as to just why the Lord allowed Himself to be crucified and as to the nature of the salvation thus accomplished. Some churches believe that by His physical suffering on the cross the Lord paid the penalty for all the sins of man and so purchased from His Father forgiveness for all who would claim forgiveness in His name. The New Church does not believe this.

The Lord did voluntarily die on the cross to save mankind. That He could have saved Himself we know from several other incidents recorded in the Gospels. (See Luke 4:28-30, John 8:59, John 10:17-18, 39, and John 19:10-11.) But if He had, the work for which He came into the world would not have been completed. We believe that although the Lord, as He appeared during His life on earth, was called the Son of God, He was in Himself no other than our heavenly Father. He took on for a time a body and mind like ours on purpose to meet and conquer the power of the hells which were becoming too strong for any finite human being to resist, and with which He Himself could come in contact in no other way. In the body and mind which He assumed He felt all the weakness and temptation we feel, and from the power of the divine love within He was able to overcome them. The temptation on the cross was merely the last and deepest of the whole series of temptations He had been meeting and conquering throughout His life.

It was not the temptation to save Himself from physical suffering—this is a comparatively light temptation which brave men are constantly overcoming. The Lord on the cross was tempted to perform a miracle so great that all men would be forced to acknowledge

Him to be God, not for the sake of His own glory, but in the hope that through fear of Him they might be led to amend their lives and be saved. The thought of this possibility was the last remnant of His assumed human nature, for it was contrary to His divine wisdom which knew that salvation must be the result of the free choice of good. Love to the Lord is salvation, and love cannot be forced. So the Lord conquered this last temptation. He let His enemies do their worst and died on the cross. Then on the third day He rose again and in this way showed His followers—those who wanted to believe—that He had told them the truth when He said, "Be not afraid of them that kill the body, and after that have no more that they can do." (Luke 12:4) The Lord saved us by making the hells subject to Him and by showing us that with His help it is possible to overcome every temptation we may meet from the cradle to the grave. This is the salvation of which the cross is the final symbol.

In addition to these general thoughts about the crucifixion, there are many interesting points in our chapter. One is in the correspondence of the chief priests and Pilate. At this time Rome ruled the world, sending out governors with Roman troops to keep the conquered nations in subjection. So, although Roman policy did not interfere with the religion of any nation, the chief priests had only religious power. They could not condemn the Lord to death but could only urge Pilate to pronounc that sentence. The chief priests represent evil in the heart and Pilate falsity in the understanding. Pilate could find no fault in the Lord, but he allowed himself to be persuaded. When we are selfishly bent on having our own way, we always manage to justify ourselves for going ahead with it, even when our arguments are contrary to reason. Then we are apt to bolster up our position by ridiculing the standards of right which we are transgressing, as the soldiers of Pilate mocked the Lord. The freeing of Barabbas instead of the Lord pictures the fact that when we reject the truth which the Lord shows us, we let loose in our minds and hearts the falsity and evil which we should be trying to destroy.

The parting of the Lord's garments among the soldiers pictures the way in which people treat the letter of the Word, taking what they like of it and leaving the rest. This action prefigured the origin of the many Christian sects today, each based on a particular interpretation of a few chosen statements in the Word.

The fact that the Lord was crucified between two thieves represents that His teachings were rated by the leaders as falsities, for thieves correspond to falsities. We shall take up this incident in more detail when we study the Gospel of Luke.

The rending of the veil of the temple—the curtain which hid the Holy of Holies—at the time of the Lord's death is a symbol of the removal of the final separation, thus the final complete union of the Lord's divine human with the Divine itself when the last of the finite humanity was put off. When this takes place in our thought about the Lord, the rational principle in our minds—represented by the centurion—immediately recognizes that Jesus is God.

In the Word burial corresponds to resurrection. We should note that it was not the apostles who buried the Lord's body. Although they had been His closest followers, they all deserted Him when He was taken prisoner. Their hopes were bound up in the person of Jesus. When He died, they felt that the end had come. But there were two men of a different position from the apostles, Joseph of Arimathea and Nicodemus (John 19:39). They were both "counsellors," members of the Sanhedrin, the high court of Judaism, and they had reached their conclusions about the Lord on the basis of rational consideration of what He said and did rather than through the influence of personal association with Him. They gave the Lord's body the burial necessary for the fulfillment of the spiritual requirements of the Word. And the women, who picture simple unselfish affection, remained with the Lord to the last and watched where He was laid. These women were the first to learn of the resurrection on Sunday morning.

## Adult

Take up first the New Church doctrine of salvation and the nature of the

Lord's temptation on the cross. Then be guided by the interest of the class as to which details of the story you discuss. They may have questions as to one or another incident in the chapter.

In the New Church we are familiar with the thought that the passion of the cross was not a matter of physical suffering voluntarily endured by the Lord as a vicarious atonement for the sins of the world. But even today this idea is still frequently expressed, especially by revivalists, and converts are actually solicited through pity for the Lord's physical suffering. Crucifixion was indeed a painful form of death, a true expression of the cruelty in men's hearts at the end of that dispensation. But many others besides the Lord underwent crucifixion, some of them—probably including the apostle Peter—voluntarily. And we know that when the soul is under stress of emotion, men can suffer severe injuries without being conscious of the physical pain. The Lord on the cross was not thinking of His physical body.

The passion of the cross was the last and most severe of the Lord's temptations. See the passage from AC 1690 below. The Lord, from His earliest childhood up to the last hour of His life in the world, was assaulted by all the hells, against which He continually fought, and subjugated and overcame them, and this solely from love toward the whole human race. AC 1787 says: "Every temptation is attended with some kind of despair (otherwise it is not a temptation) . . . He who is tempted is brought into anxieties, which induce a state of despair as to what the end is to be . . . The Lord also, as He endured the most dire and cruel temptations of all, could not but be driven into states of despair." Since the Lord's love was the love of the whole human race, His deepest temptation was despair because they would not be saved. He might have performed a miracle and come down from the cross and so convinced their minds. That this was at least a part of His last temptation we know from verses 29 to 32 of our chapter, for the cry of His enemies was certainly inspired from hell. But such a miracle would not have changed their hearts. He could not interfere with their free choice without destroying them. Read Matthew 23:37.

We recently thought of what betrayal of the Lord means in our own lives. The first part of our chapter today shows us just how that betrayal leads us to crucify Him. The chief priests, we recall, condemned the Lord as a blasphemer because He said He was the Christ. The chief priests represent self-love in the heart. Self-love refuses to acknowledge that the Lord is divine and that the Word is divine truth, because it wishes to determine all things in the interests of self. But our will has to have the cooperation of our understanding. Pilate represents falsity ruling in the mind, and the mind has to consent before truth can be utterly rejected. Pilate could find no actual fault in the Lord—the reason has to admit that His teaching is harmless—but Pilate was "willing to content the people." The people in this case represent all the considerations of self-interest which are stirred up by self-love. So Pilate condemned the Lord and released Barabbas, a rebel and murderer. Is not this a clear picture of the course we take when we are determined to have our own selfish way? We force our minds to justify what we wish to do and so we reject truth altogether and let loose in our souls the willful and evil things which we should be destroying. And we thus mock at the truth, as the Roman soldiers mocked the Lord, pretending to reverence it, but actually falsifying it at its very fountainhead. This falsification of divine truth is pictured by the crown of thorns.

We recognize that the parting of the Lord's garments pictures the way in which the Christian Church was to treat the letter of the Word, each sect taking certain passages as the basis for its separate existence and discarding the rest.

In AE 519[2] Swedenborg gives us an interesting interpretation—based on Matthew 27:34, 48 rather than on Mark—of the two drinks offered to the Lord at the crucifixion: "Their giving the Lord 'vinegar mingled with gall,' which was also called 'wine mingled with myrrh,' signified the quality of the divine truth from the Word with the Jewish nation, namely, that it was mingled with the falsity from evil, and thus altogether falsified and adulterated, therefore He would not drink it. But that afterwards 'they gave the Lord vinegar in a sponge and placed it upon hyssop' signified the kind of falsity there was among the upright Gentiles, which was falsity from ignorance of the truth, in which there was something good and useful; because this falsity is accepted by the Lord He drank this vinegar. The 'hyssop' upon which they placed it signifies the purification of the falsity." The hyssop is mentioned in this incident as given in John 19:29-30.

When the Lord "gave up the ghost," He finally wholly separated Himself from the finite humanity. AE 220[5] says: "That 'the veil of the temple was rent in two parts from the top to the bottom' . . . signified the union of the Lord's Divine Human with the Divine itself." The veil was the curtain which hid the Holy of Holies from the view even of the priests who ministered in the Holy Place. The Holy of Holies represented the Divine itself, which after the crucifixion was one with the divine human.

That the Scripture (Isaiah 53:9) might be fulfilled and the scene laid for the resurrection story, another person is active in our chapter. It was not the custom to bury the bodies of those who were crucified. In Europe and in England even up to a century or so ago criminals were hanged on gibbets set up to public view at crossroads, and their bodies were left hanging indefinitely as a warning to other would-be malefactors. So it was with the crucified in the Lord's day. Presumably the two thieves who were crucified with the Lord were left in this way. But the Lord had two disciples who were members of the Sanhedrin, the high court of Judaism, and one of them obtained permission from Pilate to bury Jesus' body. Only Joseph of Arimathea is mentioned in Mark, but John (19:39) tells us that Nicodemus came to assist him with the burial. Nicodemus was the one who came to the Lord by night (John 3:1-21), and John tells us (19:38) that Joseph also was the Lord's disciple "secretly for fear of the Jews." But both of them were brave enough to show their reverence for Him openly when their associates had put Him to a shameful death.

The women who watched with the Lord after the disciples had left Him, and who waited to see where His body was laid represent the simple affection for the Lord which cannot be alienated by adversity. It was to these women that the resurrection was first made known. The sepulcher or tomb in the rock with the great stone rolled in front of the entrance represents the Word as it appears to those who know only the letter, and especially to those who believe that letter to be the product of the minds of men only, and not divine wisdom.

## From the Writings of Swedenborg

*Arcana Coelestia*, n. 1690: "All temptation is an assault upon the love in which the man is, and the temptation is in the same degree as is the love. If the love is not assaulted, there is no temptation. To destroy anyone's love is to destroy his very life; for the love is the life. The Lord's life was love toward the whole human race, and was indeed so great, and of such a quality, as to be nothing but pure love. Against this His life, continual temptations were admitted, as before said, from His earliest childhood to His last hour in the world. . . . He fought against the love of the world, or all things that are of the love of the world . . . He fought against the love of self, and all things that are of the love of self . . . And because this love was not human but Divine, and because such as is the greatness of the love, such is that of the temptation, it may be seen how grievous the combats were."

## Suggested Questions on the Lesson

P. What feast did the Lord celebrate during His last week on earth? *Passover*
J. What did this feast commemorate? *release from Egyptian slavery*
J. What new feast did He institute at that time? *Holy Supper*
J. What does this Christian feast commemorate? *redemption from slavery to evil*
P. Who betrayed the Lord? *Judas Iscariot*
J. Before whom was Jesus first tried? *the high priests*
J. Of what did the high priests declare Him guilty? *blasphemy*
P. To whom was He sent to be condemned? *Pontius Pilate*
J. What did Pilate think of Him? *found no fault in Him*
J. Why did he not release Him? *wanted to satisfy the crowd*
J. Whom did he release instead? *Barabbas*
P. What did Pilate's soldiers do to the Lord? *mocked Him*
J. Where was the Lord crucified? *Golgotha*

J. Who carried His cross to Golgotha? *Simon of Cyrene (but see John 19:17)*

P. What did the soldiers do with the Lord's garments? *divided them among themselves*

P. Who were crucified with the Lord? *two thieves*

J. What did the Lord's enemies tempt Him to do? *come down from the cross*

J. What happened in the temple at the time of His death? *curtain tore in two*

J. What did the centurion say? *truly this man was son of God*

J. Who asked Pilate for the Lord's body? *Joseph of Arimathea*

J. What did he do with it? *laid it in new rock-hewn tomb*

J. What women stayed near the Lord until His body was placed in the tomb? *the two Marys*

I. Why did the Lord allow Himself to be put to death? *to show that evil is really powerless against good*

S. What is pictured by the parting of the Lord's garments? *picking and choosing from the Word what we want to believe*

# THE EASTER LESSON
*Mark 16*

The teacher may start with the fact that it is Easter and draw from the class their knowledge of what Easter means before taking up the lesson himself. The older classes are so familiar with the story that a very brief review of it will be enough to begin with.

---

## Doctrinal Points
*Love for the Lord's character enables us to overcome our natural inclination to believe only in what we can see and touch.*
*Life in this world is only the beginning of our life.*
*The promise of the Lord is always fulfilled spiritually with those who have true faith.*

---

## Notes for Parents
We all know that Easter is the anniversary of the day on which the Lord rose from the dead. Our chapter shows us how hard the disciples were to convince that He was really alive, even though He had told them beforehand just what would happen. Verse 14 tells us that He "upbraided them with their unbelief and hardness of heart, because they believed not them which had seen him after he was risen." Many people today are like the disciples. They know the record in all the four Gospels, but they will not believe it. They go on thinking of the material world as the only real world and of death as the end of everything. And they spend their whole thought and energy in getting all the material things they can for themselves and trying to keep their bodies alive, while their souls—which are going on forever—are being starved and warped and shriveled.

We ought to know better even from what this earth teaches us. Every fall the flowers in our gardens die, the fields become bare, and the earth freezes into apparent death, but in the spring new life pushes up out of the earth, the twigs become green and the

162

buds begin to swell, and presently the earth is overflowing with life and beauty again. The Lord said to His disciples early in the last week of His earthly life, "The hour is come, that the Son of man should be glorified. Verily, verily, I say unto you, Except a corn of wheat fall into the ground and die, it abideth alone: but if it die, it bringeth forth much fruit. He that loveth his life shall lose it; and he that hateth his life in this world shall keep it unto life eternal." Spring is a picture of the resurrection. Life goes on forever. The soul never dies.

It is a curious but not meaningless fact that even the name which we have given to the day on which we celebrate the Lord's resurrection from the dead is a name associated with our earthly spring. *Easter* is a respelling of *Eastre*, the name of the Teutonic goddess of spring. And we have adopted the custom of giving our children Easter eggs and little bunnies and fluffy chicks. There is every reason why they should have these pretty symbols if we show them at the same time how they teach us of the constant renewal of life and tell them how the Lord showed us that our life goes right on after the body dies.

No Christian should fear death for himself or for his loved ones. For a good person, death is the crown of life, when his eyes close on the struggles and disappointments and limitations of this world and open to the beauty and freedom and endless progress of the life beyond the grave. It was to show us this that the Lord let Himself be put to death and rose again on the first Easter.

The children may like to have you read them the Easter story from another Gospel also. A good chapter to read is Luke 24. Chapters 20 and 21 of John give a still longer account which you should read for yourself and with your older children especially.

---

## Primary

See what the children have in their minds about Easter. Refer to the Palm Sunday lesson, mention what happened to the Lord afterward, and tell them how discouraged and unhappy the disciples were and how they forgot all that the Lord had told them about what would happen. Then read the lesson from the Word and talk to them about the spiritual world and about death as the gateway to that world. The important thing is to emphasize the religious character of the Easter celebration.

You know that every year in the spring we celebrate Easter. Christmas and Easter are the two great days in the Christian Church.

What did we celebrate on Christmas? The Lord lived in the world about thirty-three years. Last Sunday we learned how, at the beginning of the last week of His earthly life, He rode into Jerusalem as a king, welcomed by crowds of people. But you remember the people turned against Him very soon when they found He was not going to do the things they wanted, and the very next Friday they let His enemies put Him to death.

They put His body in a sepulcher or tomb hollowed out of a rock, and rolled a great stone in front of the entrance, and they sealed the stone and set a guard of Roman soldiers to make sure that no one should open it. They thought they had got rid of Him.

What happened on the first Easter morning?
Who came first to the sepulcher?
Why did they come?
What did they find?
What did the angel tell them?
To whom did the Lord show Himself first?
The Lord had to show Himself to all the disciples before they would believe that He had risen.
He had told them just what was to happen, but they would not believe Him.
When He was crucified, they thought that all their hopes were ended.
But after they saw Him alive again, they understood what He had told them.
The Lord's resurrection showed us that our life does not end at death.
It goes on forever.
This world is only the beginning of our life.

You know, of course, that each one of us will die someday, but we do not have to worry about it or be afraid, because the Lord showed us that death is nothing but going to sleep and waking up again just as we do every day. Only when we die, we wake up in the beautiful world which the Lord has prepared for us to live in forever, where there is no pain or sickness or trouble. There, if we have learned to be the loving, honest, useful people the Lord wants us to be, we shall be happy always. It was to teach us this that the Lord let Himself be put to death and then showed Himself to His disciples that first Easter day.

———————

## Junior

It is important to give this class a sense of the weight of evidence concerning the resurrection. Children need to feel sure and also to be able to say why they are sure. So give them as wide a factual background as possible for their Christian faith.

What special Sunday is today?
What was last Sunday?
Why was it called Palm Sunday?
What animal did the Lord ride into Jerusalem?
Why did the people welcome Him?
Why did they so soon turn against Him?
What happened on Thursday night?
What new feast did the Lord institute?
What happened on Friday?

The body of the Lord had been placed in a tomb belonging to Joseph of Arimathea. A great stone had been rolled against the door of the sepulcher, and at the request of the religious leaders Pilate had had this sealed and had placed a guard of soldiers to prevent anyone's stealing the body.

The accounts of the events of the first Easter Sunday differ slightly in the four Gospels, but they really merely supplement each other. Matthew and Mark are quite brief and simple, Luke is more detailed, and John gives much more of the Lord's teaching as well as several facts which are not in any of the other Gospels. It is clear that the women who loved the Lord were the first to discover that He had risen, that Mary Magdalene was the first to see Him, and that the eleven closest disciples—Judas, who had betrayed the Lord, had hanged himself—would not believe that He had risen until they saw Him with their own eyes.

In our chapter we learn (verse 14) that when He did appear to them, He "upbraided them with their unbelief and hardness of heart, because they believed not them which had seen him after he was risen." In the account in John (John 20:29) the Lord says to Thomas, who had been the most doubtful of all, "Thomas, because thou hast seen me, thou hast believed: blessed are they that have not seen, and yet have believed." We wish sometimes that we might have lived in the time when the Lord was on earth and might have known Him personally, but you see how little the men who had that privilege really understood of what He taught them. For He had told His disciples just what must happen to Him and that He would rise again on the third day, and yet when He was taken captive, they all deserted Him, and when they saw Him die, they thought everything was over.

Sometime you may hear someone say, "How do I know there is a life after death? No one ever came back to tell us about it." This is simply not so. It has been said that the testimony of the four Gospels would stand up in any court of law. We may believe their testimony. The Lord did "come back" to show us that death is only a step in life. We go to sleep in this world and wake in the other. It is as simple as that. We leave our physical body behind because we have no further use for it, but we have a spiritual body formed of the substance of the spiritual world. It is a much more perfect body than the one we have here, for it exactly expresses what we really are. We need to remember that when we get into the other world we cannot put on a pleasant look to hide our hateful feelings, and we cannot change our real character after we die; so it is very important for us to get rid of our hateful, selfish feelings while we are here. When the Lord appeared to His disciples after the resurrection, they were frightened and thought they were seeing a ghost, and He said (Luke 24:39), "Behold my hands and my feet, that it is I myself: handle me and see; for a spirit hath not flesh and bones as ye see me have"; and yet, as we are told in John 20:19, He appeared in their midst although the doors were shut. John tells us in the very last verse of his Gospel that the Lord did many more things than could possibly have been recorded. We have evidence of the fact that He must have told His followers something of the difference between the natural and the spiritual body in the statement of the apostle Paul in his first letter to the Corinthians (15:42-44).

From the Gospel of Mark we might think that the Lord's ascension into heaven took place very soon after the resurrection, but we learn from Acts 1:3 that the Lord was seen for forty days after He rose from the dead.

What commission did He give His disciples?
What signs did He say would be given to those who believed in Him?

In the early days of the Christian Church such miraculous signs were necessary, because people had for so long been in the habit of thinking of this world as the only real world. But the Lord does not want us to have to be convinced by miracles. He wants us to use our minds and see and believe in Him from reason and from love of His ways.

So we should think of the change which the Lord's resurrection made in the whole history of the world and the difference it makes in our lives to believe in the reality and nearness of the spiritual world. The Gospel testimony and history both teach us why Easter Sunday should find us each year more grateful and faithful followers of our Lord and Savior, Jesus Christ.

--- --- ---

## Intermediate

The correspondence of the sepulcher and the stone and of the coming of the women with their spices are the lesson for this class especially. Be sure they understand why it was the women who first saw the risen Lord.

When the Lord was crucified, His body was placed in a rock tomb and a great stone was rolled in front of the entrance. You remember that stone is one of the symbols of truth. It pictures the hard foundation truths on which one builds the house of character and with which he walls it in for protection against spiritual enemies. In a lower sense it pictures the hard facts which we must accept and recognize. There are many other things which truth does for us which are not like the uses of stone. So in the Bible there are many other symbols of truth. Water, for example, pictures truth as it comes down to us from heaven, as it is stored in our memor- ies—the seas—or as it cleanses our lives, as symbolized in baptism. Silver is truth as a shining ornament to the mind and as a medium of exchange of thought with other people. It was a fact that the Lord was rejected and put to death. It was a fact that His body was placed in a rock tomb. The letter of the Word, in which these facts are recorded, is pictured by the sepulcher itself. It was a fact that the people wanted no king who did not promise them material prosperity and that they wanted to know nothing of spiritual life. This hard materialism was the stone with which they closed the entrance.

But these things do not apply only to the ancient Jewish nation. The material body in which the Lord comes to us is the letter of the Word. When we refuse to believe that this is divinely inspired, we are really rejecting the Lord, and when we argue away the necessity of obedience to the truths of the Word, we are crucifying Him and putting His body in a tomb. The stone which we roll in front of the entrance to prevent access to the Lord is our refusal to raise our minds above the level of natural truth, the things which our senses perceive.

The women who came to the sepulcher on the first Easter morn- ing had loved the Lord. They had known He was wonderful and had believed Him to be the Messiah, but it probably had never occurred to them that the Messiah, after He once came, could die. So when they saw Him die, they too lost hope. But even with their hopes blasted they loved Him just the same and, while the men merely mourned their disappointment, the women thought about what they could still do for Him. So they came to the sepulcher with the spices they had bought to anoint His body, hoping they could find someone to roll away the stone.

"And when they looked, they saw that the stone was rolled away." It is love for the Lord's character which enables us to over- come our natural inclination to believe only in what we can see and touch and to realize that those are not the real and living things. So the women were the first ones to be told that the Lord had risen, and they believed what the Lord's messenger told them. And Mary Magdalene, whom the Lord had healed of a terrible obsession, was the first to see Him after He rose. Spices are another symbol of truth—this time the interior or higher truth which is perceived by those who are good.

The disciples were very hard to convince. They did not believe the report of the women. And when the Lord finally appeared among them, He "upbraided them with their unbelief and hardness of heart." The Lord had told them several times how He must die and that He would rise again on the third day but, as we say, it had gone in one ear and out the other. Our parents try hard sometimes to prepare us for things they know will happen to us, but we are too much interested in something else to pay attention. This is one reason why the Lord has to let troubles come to us—because sometimes we will learn in no other way.

That the Lord really did rise from the dead and appear to the disciples not only because the Gospels tell us so but because His appearance so changed the disciples that from being discouraged and fearful they became bold and brave and went out and told all the world about it. Most of them—tradition says all but John—were put to death for their preaching, but they were not afraid of death because the Lord had proved to them that death is only a step in life. Because they had seen Him alive again they knew that everything He had told them was true, and they wanted nothing better than the opportunity to tell everybody else the good news—the Gospel.

Doesn't it seem strange that after nearly twenty centuries, in which this good news has made wonderful changes in men and in the world, there are still people who refuse to believe it? In verse 16 of our chapter the Lord says, "He that believeth and is baptized shall be saved; but he that believeth not shall be damned." This sounds to us very hard, but it is the truth. You remember that baptism pictures the determination to make our lives clean according to the truths that the Lord gives us in His Word. Those who do not have this desire nor make this effort must necessarily be led by their own judgment, which is essentially worldly and selfish. And to be selfish is to be in hell or damned. Selfishness is the very spirit of hell both in this world and in the life after death.

The Lord also told the disciples certain signs which should "follow" those who believed. In the early days of the Christian Church these signs did at times literally follow them. If you would like to read some of the things which happened, look up Acts 2:1-4, 5:12-16, 10:44-46, 28:1-6. These things happened because the simple people of that time needed to have their faith confirmed and strengthened in this way. But men have developed intellectually since then and should not need such physical evidences. For us the signs are pictures of the spiritual results of belief. Those who truly believe in the Lord can cast out their evil desires; they can understand different kinds of people and say the right thing to help each one; they enjoy the pleasures of the world without being hurt by them; they can hear and read things that are false without believing them; and they can help other people to overcome their weaknesses also. Think of these things as you read verses 17 and 18.

The resurrection not only means to us that the spiritual world is real and near and that death is nothing more than going to sleep in this world and waking in the other, but it means that everything the Lord said about Himself and everything He teaches us in the Word is true, because He is life itself, our heavenly Father, who created us and cares for us always.

*Basic Correspondences*

spices  =  interior truths from good

---

### Senior

For this class the emphasis should be placed on the nature of materialism and how it closes the mind to spiritual enlightenment. The subtle influence of materialism in the world which they are about to enter should be pointed out to them so that they may be armed against it. Their answers to questions on the Easter story will suggest other points which need to be brought out for them.

We are told that when the Lord was crucified, all the disciples, those who had been with Him almost constantly for three years, forsook Him and fled. He had prophesied that they would do this, and there was a reason for it. Before they could go out and preach the Gospel, they had to be made to recognize fully their own weakness. We do nothing in our own strength. Self-confidence and pride in our own intelligence have no part in true missionary work.

There was one group of the Lord's followers, however, who did not desert Him, although they had no power to prevent His crucifixion. This was the women. The last verse of the fifteenth chapter of Mark shows them still at hand when His body was taken from the cross and placed in the sepulcher, and they were first to return to the sepulcher when the sabbath was over. Their love for the' Lord had been based not so much on what He taught as on what He was, and there was no personal ambition in it as there was in that of the apostles. They still wanted to minister to Him. This was why they were the first to learn of the resurrection, and why Mary Magdalene, who loved Him most, was the first to see Him afterward. Even before they saw Him, they did not question the word of the "young man" who told them that He was risen. But the disciples would not believe until they themselves had seen Him.

This teaches us a lesson which we all need. The twelve apostles, like the twelve sons of Jacob, represent all the faculties we have which enable us to serve the Lord. They are all in us, Peter as the capacity to believe, Andrew as the capacity to obey what truth teaches, and so on. It is these capacities which enable us to be instructed by the Word and to bring our lives into order and finally to serve as the Lord's agents in the world. But we tend to be proud of these faculties, to expect praise and reward when we develop and use them, and to be easily discouraged when unexpected failure comes. Fortunately the women are in us, too, states of simple trust and affection remaining from our infancy and childhood, developed before we begin to reason and act for ourselves, and added to from time to time in our best moments. These are what carry us through periods of failure and discouragement and enable us to recognize the Lord in all that happens to us.

In our Palm Sunday lesson we saw that, while our natural reason is a necessary and useful faculty, it must be kept subject to the direction of truth from the Word. It was the natural reason—which sees only the earth side of things—that caused the complete discouragement of the disciples when the Lord was crucified. Although He had told them that He would rise on the third day, that assurance had meant nothing to them. For them death was still death, the end of everything. They had counted on Him and He had left them. As the two disciples on the way to Emmaus (Luke 24:13-35) said to the Lord before they recognized Him, "We trusted that it had been he which should have redeemed Israel." Even after three years of personal association with Him they still thought of His kingdom in terms of this world.

We all begin our active careers in this same natural state of mind. What happens to us in this world seems so important! We want to be good men and women and we know—theoretically—that virtue is more important than worldly success, that we are here to build for eternity, and that the Lord has told us that His kingdom is not of this world. But we are still very much of this world and our spiritual eyes are closed. Physical health, worldly learning, professional advancement seem to us the immediate and important things. It takes us a long time to realize that the "women" in us are wiser than the "men," that the Lord can make Himself known to us only as we cultivate states of humility, trust, and love for the divine qualities which are Himself.

The story of the resurrection teaches us this lesson. It teaches us, of course, many other things too, especially that life in this world is only the beginning of our life, the seed-time which leads to an endless harvest of good or evil fruit depending on how we form the seed. It teaches us that the spiritual world is real and near, not in some far-off star; that we wake in that world immediately, not on some far-off judgment day; that everyone wakes there the same person who went to sleep here, in a body in which he may be recognized even though it is not the physical body. It teaches us, as it finally taught the disciples, that everything the

Lord said of Himself is true, that His character was the divine character and His voice the divine voice.

It was not a mere man, however good, whose life is recorded in the Gospels. It was not a second person in the Godhead, sent by another and mightier God to pay the price of man's sins. It was our heavenly Father Himself, showing us for a time by means of an earthly body as much as we can see and understand of His divine nature. And the record of His earthly life, which we know as the Gospels, was not any mere putting down by four men of what they remembered or had been told of His life. These facts were indeed in their memories, but they were drawn forth, arranged, and inspired by the Lord Himself just as the Word of the Old Testament was given by inspiration to the prophets and others. Unless we believe this we cannot see the Lord in it. The belief that the letter of the Word is the product of men's minds is the "stone which seals the sepulcher" for many today. The Gospel of Matthew (28:2) tells us that there was a great earthquake and that the angel of the Lord came and rolled back the stone from the door and sat upon it. Sometimes it takes a great earthquake in a person's life to loosen the grip of materialism so that the heavenly messenger can roll back the stone and show him the empty tomb. On the first Easter morning the Lord rose in fact. He rises in us when we become willing to recognize that all real life is spiritual and not material, cease to think in terms of this world only, and begin to look to Him as our ever-living and ever-present Lord.

---

## Adult

This is such a familiar story to the Adults that the teacher needs to give special thought to his preparation and to try to bring the material to them in a new way which will illustrate the depth and variety still untapped in even the best-known parts of Scripture.

The resurrection of the Lord changed history. After the crucifixion the disciples were completely discouraged. The Lord had told them that He would be put to death, but they had not really believed Him. He had told them that He would rise again, but they had not been able to imagine such a possibility. All the Gospels tell us that they would not believe until they actually saw Him. Thomas would not believe until he could touch the nail prints. Yet after the resurrection and ascension they went out into the world and preached the good news—the Gospel—without fear. Tradition says that all except John suffered martyrdom. Our natural reason alone should tell us that the Christian Church was not founded on a myth.

But the story of the resurrection shows us that it was not the disciples who rolled back the stone and revealed the empty tomb. It was a divine work. It is a divine work with us. The stone represents in this case the materialism of the people of that day which made them unwilling to acknowledge anything spiritual, and it represents similar materialism in all times. The sepulcher in which the Lord was laid pictures the letter of the Word, which must be opened if we are to see the Lord as a living and present being.

Three types of disciples appear in the Bible story of the resurrection. There were the apostles, who had been close to the Lord for three years and had been instructed by Him, and yet deserted Him when their earthly hopes seemed to be over. There were the two "rulers" of the Jews, Joseph of Arimathea and Nicodemus, who had believed in Him without daring to acknowledge Him openly while He was alive, yet when He was dead came forth publicly and cared for His body. And there were the women, who loved Him for what He was, remained near Him throughout the hours on Calvary, watched to see where His body was laid, and returned to the sepulcher at the first opportunity to do what small services they could still perform for Him.

The disciples, like the twelve sons of Jacob, represent the faculties we have which enable us to serve the Lord. These faculties "mean well," but are very much under the influence of the materialistic thinking of the world. In the face of disappointment and apparent failure it is hard for them to take a firm stand. They are dismayed and doubtful. The two counsellors represent the principles which rule in our minds. These, if they are good principles, come out of hiding in times of discouragement and keep us in at least outward order. And then there are the women, the simple affections for divine qualities, which cling to the Lord in spite of appearances and, in the final analysis, are the ground of our reception of a true understanding of the Lord. This is taught in many places in the Word: "Blessed are the pure in heart, for they shall see God," "I thank thee, O Father . . . because thou hast hid these things from the wise and prudent, and hast revealed them unto babes." And Swedenborg tells us: "The Lord flows with power into those who are humble; but not into those who are puffed up, because the former receive influx, but the latter reject it" (AC 9039), "Those cannot possibly be in any enlightenment who have not as their end a life according to Divine truths from the Word; but who have as their end honor, gain, and reputation; and who thus regard the Divine truths of the Word as means" (AC 10551), and "There is no other way than for a man to go to the Lord God the Saviour, and under His auspices read the Word; for He is the God of the Word; and man will then be enlightened and will see truths which reason also will acknowledge . . . A man who reads the Word not under the Lord's auspices but under the auspices of his own intelligence, thinks himself a lynx and better sighted than Argus; and yet he inwardly sees not a shred of truth, but only what is false; and under self-persuasion this falsity seems to him like a polar star towards which he directs all the sails of his thought; and then he no more sees truths than a mole does, or if he sees them he bends them to favor his phantasies, and so perverts and falsifies the holy things of the Word" (TCR 165).

We are told in Acts 1:3 that the Lord's post-resurrection appearances extended over a period of forty days. Mary Magdalene was the first to see Him. Then Mark refers to His appearance to the two disciples as they "went into the country," the incident more fully told in Luke 24:13-35. Then He appeared to the disciples in Jerusalem—Mark says "to the eleven," but John tells us that Thomas was not with them at that time but that he was present

with the others eight days later (John 20:24-29). He had told
them (Matthew 26:32 and Mark 14:28) that after He had risen, He
would go before them into Galilee, and the angel messenger at the
sepulcher tells the women to repeat this message to the disciples.
Matthew tells of one of His appearances in Galilee (Matthew 28:16-
17) and John of another (John 21:1-23). The ascension took place
at Bethany (Luke 24:50-51). The account in Mark is very much
condensed and yet he adds to the others the Lord's teaching concerning the power to be given to "them that believe."

This last teaching is found in verses 17 and 18 of our chapter.
The Lord had given similar powers to the seventy when He sent
them out (Luke 10:19), but now He says that all who believe shall
have them. We know that in the early church such signs were literally given. See Acts 5:15-16, 8:7, 9:18, 16:18, 19:12, 28:5-8.
Some people think that one who has sufficient "faith" should be
able to do the same now. But we read in the writings: "No one is
reformed by miracles and signs, because they compel. It has been
shown above that man has an internal and an external of thought,
and that the Lord flows into man through the internal of thought
into its external, and thus teaches and leads him; also that it is of
the Lord's Divine providence that man should act from freedom in
accordance with reason. Both of these would perish in man if
miracles were wrought and man was thereby driven to believe"
(DP 130). The people in the Holy Land at the time of the Lord's
Advent were so external that they were not compelled even by
miracles, as is evidenced by the fact that those who had witnessed
the miracles nevertheless rejected the Lord, but the Lord through
His life and teaching on earth reopened the spiritual plane of
thought, and when interior thought is possible, miracles compel
and are disorderly.

Yet the promise of the Lord is always fulfilled spiritually with
those who have true faith—the faith which leads to obedience. The
devils who infest the will are cast out, a new understanding and
speech are given, sense pleasures no longer injure, falsities heard
or read do not poison the mind, and a new power is given to help

others in times of weakness and disorderly living.

Easter should mean more to us than merely the assurance that we shall continue to live after the death of the physical body. It should impress upon us the fact that even while we are in the body the real and living part of us is the soul and the important thing from day to day is not what is happening to our body but what is happening to our soul. The body, whatever its physical condition, is only a tool for temporary use. We should keep it in reasonably good condition as we would any tool, but if we are doing our real work in the world well, we may trust the Lord to enable us to go on here as long as He sees best, and we may be sure that He is preparing within us the spiritual body which will serve us to eternity.

## From the Writings of Swedenborg

*Apocalypse Explained*, n. 400[14]: "'The angel rolled away the stone from the mouth and sat upon it' signifies that the Lord removed all the falsity that had shut off access to Him, and that He opened Divine truth, 'stone' signifying Divine truth which the Jews had falsified by their tradition."

## Suggested Questions on the Lesson

P. What do we call this Sunday? *Easter*

P. What do we celebrate on Easter? *Jesus' rising from death*

P. What was last Sunday? *Palm Sunday*

P. Why was it called Palm Sunday? *people spread palm branches before the Lord*

I. Why did the Lord ride into Jerusalem on an ass? *sign of kingship*

J. Why did the people welcome Him? *thought He would be worldly ruler*

I. Why did they turn against Him so soon? *found out his kingdom was not of this world*

J. What happened on Thursday evening of that week? *last supper*

J. What happened on Friday? *crucifixion*

P. Who came to the sepulcher on Sunday morning? *two Marys, Salome*

P. Why did they come? *to anoint body*

J. What question was in their minds? *who would roll away the stone for them*

P. What did they find? *stone rolled away, the Lord gone, young man in white*

P. What did the angel tell them? *He is risen*

J. To whom did the Lord appear first? *Mary Magdalene*

J. Did the disciples believe when they were told that He had been seen? *no*

J. What did He say when He finally appeared to them all? *upbraided them for unbelief*

J. What did He tell them to do? *go and preach Gospel, baptize*

J. What did He say about those who believe? *will be saved*

J. How did He leave them? *taken up into heaven*

I. What is pictured by the stone which sealed the tomb? *materialistic thinking*

S. Why did the women see the Lord first after He rose? *they represent our affections for divine qualities*

# THE BIRTH OF JOHN THE BAPTIST
## Luke 1

The lessons we are taking from the Gospel of Luke do not in themselves depend at any point upon geographical background, and yet the pupils should be aware of the final divisions of the Holy Land as a completion of their map study for the year. It is suggested, therefore, that in connection with this lesson the Sunday school be shown a map of the Holy Land in the Lord's time, pointing out the three divisions and the location of Jerusalem, Bethlehem, Nazareth, the Sea of Galilee, Capernaum, the cross-Jordan country, and Jericho.

We have assigned the whole first chapter of Luke, which includes the annunciation to Mary, and with all classes above the Primary this should be taken up and the events of the Lord's birth as told in Luke 2 should be mentioned briefly. The principal lesson, however, is about John the Baptist, and this should be taken up as the fulfillment of the prophecy in Malachi.

---

### Doctrinal Points
*Jesus Christ is God come into the world.*
*The New Testament is bound to the Old by constant references. Neither can be understood apart from the other.*
*True faith cherishes every bit of knowledge of the Lord.*
*It is selfishness in the heart which leads men to reject the Lord.*

---

### Notes for Parents
This is a long chapter but a very important one for all of us. People in the Christian world today sometimes think that the New Testament is the only part of the Bible we really need to read, and that all we have to know of the Old Testament is the ten commandments, and some people even think that those are out of date.

179

But if we read this chapter carefully, we see that it is full of things which we could not understand at all without our knowledge of the Old Testament story, and that is true of all the Gospels. The two cannot be separated.

In the book of Malachi we find prophecies of two messengers: the one Elijah, who was to prepare the way of the Lord; the other "the messenger of the covenant," who was to be the Lord Himself. Today we read about the fulfillment of both these prophecies. For the angel told Zacharias not only that the child his wife Elisabeth was to bear was to prepare the way of the Lord, but that he was to come "in the spirit and power of Elias." *Elias* [KJV] is the Greek form of the name *Elijah*. And the angel told Mary that her child was to be called "the Son of the Highest."

The Lord came into the world almost two thousand years ago. We Christians take that fact so much for granted that we sometimes forget that even today there are millions of people in the world who do not know it. But there is something else we do not consider which comes much closer home to us. The Lord came into the world to stay. He said, "Lo, I am with you always." And He said, "Behold, I stand at the door, and knock: if any man hear my voice, and open the door, I will come in to him, and will sup with him, and he with me." (Revelation 3:20) Has the Lord come to us? Have we listened to His voice and opened the door of our hearts and minds so that He could come in?

John was sent to prepare the way of the Lord. The message he preached was, "Repent ye: for the kingdom of heaven is at hand." (Matthew 3:2) The kingdom of heaven is always at hand. The Lord is always at the door waiting to come in with heavenly blessing and happiness. But He cannot come in while the door is shut against Him by our concern with ourselves and our worldly advancement. We open the door by repentance. Repentance, however, means more than saying we are sorry when something we have done has produced unpleasant consequences. It is examining ourselves in the light of the truth as the Lord gives it to us in His Word, and trying with His help to root out and put away the feelings, thoughts, and conduct which He shows us to be wrong.

═══════════

## Primary

If this lesson is used following lessons from the Prophets, first see if the children can name the two parts of the Bible. Then introduce the New Testament by reminding them of the meaning of Christmas. Then see if they remember the prophecy about Elijah in Malachi and go on from there with today's story. With the older ones, more should be done, if possible, with the message of John and its effect, and possibly with baptism as a sign of repentance.

You have learned that there are two divisions in the Bible, the Old Testament and the New Testament. Our lesson today is our first one in the Gospel of Luke. Christmas marks the birthday of the Lord, and the New Testament is about the life of the Lord when He came into the world.

I wonder if you remember a prophecy from the book of Malachi that someone would be sent to prepare people to receive the Lord when He came into the world. Do you remember who it was to be? It was the prophet Elijah.

Today we read about the fulfillment of that prophecy.
Read verse 17 of our lesson.
The Old Testament was written in Hebrew, but the New Testament was written in Greek.
*Elias* is the form which *Elijah* takes in the Greek.
So you see the angel told Zacharias that his son was to be the promised Elijah.
What was Zacharias doing when the angel appeared to him?
Read what is said about Zacharias and his wife Elisabeth in verse 6.
You see they were among the good people we spoke about last Sunday.
The angel also gave Zacharias a sign so that he would be sure the promise was true.
Zacharias was made dumb and could not speak again until after John was born.
The first words he spoke were the *Benedictus,* which is sometimes sung in church.

When John grew up, he lived in the wilderness, and the people came out to hear him preach. He dressed just like Elijah and everyone recognized that he was a prophet of the Lord, and once the Lord Himself told the people that John was the messenger promised by Malachi. John showed the people the bad things they were doing and told them: "Repent ye; for the kingdom of heaven is at hand." So they knew that the Lord was about to come, and all those who wanted to be good and welcomed the Lord's coming did repent, and John baptized them in the River Jordan.

That is why he is usually called John the Baptist.

======

## Junior

Both stories in this chapter should be given to the Juniors with the emphasis on their factual content and on the connection with the Old Testament. Be sure they look up all the references. At the end they should be taught what repentance is and why it is necessary.

What is the last book in the Old Testament?
What does the name *Malachi* mean?
What great event was foretold through Malachi?
Who did Malachi say would be sent to prepare the way of the Lord?
What is the general theme of all the Gospels?

Now we are studying the Gospel of Luke. We shall not take up the story of the Lord's birth because we have that story on Christmas Sunday.

Our chapter for today contains two stories, one concerning John the Baptist and one concerning the Lord. You remember that in the first verse of the third chapter of Malachi, which was part of our lesson for last Sunday, two messengers were promised. One was the messenger to prepare the way, and the other was "the messenger of the covenant" or the Lord Himself. So our chapter today tells about the fulfillment of both these promises. The prophecy said that there would be wicked people to whom the coming of the Lord would be like a destroying fire, and good people to whom it would be like the rising sun. Two of these good people were Zacharias and his wife Elisabeth.

What was Zacharias's profession?
Who is named as the ancestor of Elisabeth?

You remember that Aaron, the brother of Moses, was the first high priest, that the tribe of Levi and especially the descendants of

Aaron were set aside from the other tribes to be the priests, and that instead of a single lot in the land they were given cities throughout the territories of all the tribes to live in. After the people established their worship in the Holy Land, the priests were divided into groups called "courses" (divisions or groups), and each course served in the tabernacle and later in the temple at Jerusalem for one month out of each year. You remember that the altar of incense stood in the Holy Place in front of the entrance to the Holy of Holies, and that incense was burnt upon it regularly as part of the worship.

What was Zacharias doing when the angel appeared to him?
What was the angel's message to him?
What sign did he give him?

The last part of our chapter tells about the fulfillment of the angel's promise, which was also the fulfillment of the last prophecy of Malachi. After John was born and Zacharias was able to speak again, he spoke words which are probably familiar to us all because we sometimes sing them as part of our morning service. They are called the *Benedictus* from the first word in the Latin version. *Benedictus* means "blessed."

Who else in our chapter saw an angel?
What did the angel tell Mary?
Where was Mary's home?

In the time of the Lord the Holy Land had come to be marked off in three divisions: Galilee on the north, Judea on the south, and Samaria between them. The Samaritans were descendants of the foreigners who had been brought in from Assyria when the people of Israel were carried away. Most of the Jews lived in Judea where Jerusalem was, although there were some in the other divisions of the land. Galilee was called "Galilee of the Gentiles" because there were so many foreigners there—people from many other nations.

Mary was another of the good people who believed the prophecies of the Old Testament and hoped for the coming of the Lord. There was one particular prophecy which must have come to her when the angel spoke to her. Read it in Isaiah 7:14. It must have been hard for her to believe that she was really the one chosen after all those years to be the mother of the Lord.

What was the child to be named?
What name is commanded in Isaiah 7:14?

Look up Matthew 1:21-23. Both names expressed the character of the Lord. *Immanuel* means "God with us" and *Jesus* means "Jehovah is salvation." By these two names it was made clear that the child to be born was Jehovah Himself come into the world to save mankind.

The angel Gabriel is mentioned four times in the Word: Luke 1:19 and 26 and in Daniel 8:16 and 9:21. Swedenborg tells us that there is no one angel who is called Gabriel but that this is the name of a whole society of angels, those who particularly love the teaching of the Word that Jehovah Himself came into the world as the savior.

The angel spoke to Mary of her cousin Elisabeth and so Mary went to see Elisabeth, and as soon as Elisabeth saw Mary the Lord showed her that Mary was to be the mother of the promised Messiah. *Messiah* from the Hebrew language and *Christ* from the Greek both mean "the anointed one." The words which Mary spoke (verses 46-55) after Elisabeth confirmed the angel's message are called the *Magnificat*, from the word with which the Latin version of them begins. They are also set to music to be sung in church, especially at Christmas time.

The angel had told Zacharias that the son who was to be born to him would go before the Lord "in the spirit and power of Elias." *Elias* [KJV] is the Greek form of *Elijah*. Elijah had gone about the country telling people of their sins and warning them to change their ways or disaster would fall on them. The message of John was the same: "Repent ye: for the kingdom of heaven is at hand." John dressed just as the old prophets had dressed (Mark 1:6), and there was a power in his words which made all the people recognize him as a prophet. Those who were looking for someone to tell them the right way to live welcomed him and believed him and were baptized by Him in the Jordan. That is why he is called John the Baptist.

No one can really receive the Lord into his heart and mind as long as he is satisfied with himself and bent on having his own way. He has to recognize his faults and overcome them. This is repentance. But the Lord is always "at hand" to help us and to fill our hearts with His unselfish love as fast as we make room for Him there.

---

## Intermediate

The meaning of the mission of John the Baptist for our own lives is the important lesson for this class, but the fulfillment of prophecies in this chapter should also be studied and explained. Be sure the pupils know the meaning of baptism.

We turn now to the account of the life of the Lord as it is recorded in the Gospel of Luke. Some four hundred years had passed since the Lord last sent a prophet, and in that time the Scriptures, which had been given for their instruction, had been so overlaid by the priests and scribes with man-made laws and traditions that the people no longer knew what the law of the Lord was. Most of the people were satisfied to perform the various ceremonies required of them and then to feel free to be as worldly and selfish as they pleased. But a few cherished in their hearts the longing for a really good life. We see this pictured in the last chapter of the Old Testament. The prophecies contained in that chapter were fulfilled in the birth of John the Baptist, followed by the birth of the Lord. In verse 17 of our chapter for today the angel gives us the reason why it was prophesied that Elijah would come. *Elias* [KJV] is the Greek form of *Elijah*. Look up also Matthew 11:13-14 and 17:10-13.

The story of the appearance of the angel Gabriel to Zacharias is a striking one. The same angel had appeared to Daniel to prophesy the coming of the Messiah (Daniel 8:16 and 9:21). *Gabriel* means "God is mighty." Swedenborg tells us that by Gabriel are meant all in the heavens who especially love to know and to teach the great truth that the Lord Jesus Christ is God Himself. It was really a whole angelic society which appeared to Daniel and to Zacharias, although in the form of one man. The dumbness of Zacharias pictures his inability, in the state in which he then was, to understand the great promise well enough to believe and talk about it. You see, even in slang we sometimes speak in correspondences, for we call a person "dumb" when we mean that he is too ignorant to understand what we are trying to tell him and discuss it with us. When John was born, Zacharias could speak again, because then he could believe. Notice that the first words he spoke were the *Benedictus*, which is sung from time to time in church.

Mary, as well as Zacharias and Elisabeth, was of those who remained devout and faithful. It was the angel Gabriel who was sent to her also with the wonderful announcement that she was to be the mother of the Lord. The Old Testament is full of prophecies of the Lord's birth. The most direct, perhaps, is that in Isaiah 7:14, which is cited in Matthew 1:22-23. The good Jews of that day were acutely conscious of the condition of their people, and clung to these prophecies as their only hope and comfort. See what is said of the prophetess Anna in Luke 2:36-38. It is evident in the letter of our lesson that Mary had no doubt of the meaning of the angel's words, and that Elisabeth also received divine confirmation of the function Mary was to serve.

John had to be sent to prepare the way of the Lord because only the humble mind, conscious of its evils and need of the Lord, is open to receive Him. John's message was "Repent ye: for the kingdom of heaven is at hand." The kingdom of heaven is always at hand, but repentance must come before salvation. We must recognize and put away our evil thoughts and feelings before the Lord's spirit can enter our hearts. This is something we need to think about. We take it for granted sometimes that we are Christians because we have been baptized and brought up in the Christian Church. And indeed baptism is the sign of Christianity. But it is only a sign that we have the great privilege of knowing that Jesus Christ came into the world to be our savior, and of knowing that we ought to live according to the example He gave us. We are not really Christians unless we do follow His example. We receive

Him when we get rid of our selfish ways and allow His unselfish love to enter our hearts and work through us in the world. He says in John 13:35, "By this shall all men know that ye are my disciples, if ye have love one to another."

So John's work was to show the people their selfishness and lead them to struggle against it, and it was the people who had listened to John and obeyed his injunction to repentance who were ready to listen to the Lord and follow Him. In Malachi the Lord's coming was likened to the rising of the sun. When we turn away from the sun, the thing we see nearest to us is our own shadow. When we turn away from the Lord, the shadow of our own self is between us and everyone else.

Those who did repent were baptized by John in the Jordan. That is why, of course, he is called John the Baptist. Baptism with water is a symbol of the intention to cleanse our lives by means of obedience to the truths of the Word.

### Basic Correspondences

dumbness = inability to "confess" or
acknowledge the Lord openly

baptism = cleansing the life by means of
truths from the Word

## Senior

The immediate connection between the Old and the New Testaments through the fulfillment of prophecy should be stressed, as well as the early connection between John the Baptist and the Lord. Then discuss the mission of John the Baptist—what it did for the good in the Lord's day and what it means in our lives.

Not only Malachi but many other books of the Old Testament contain wonderful prophecies of the Lord's Advent. In the four hundred years which elapsed between Malachi and the Advent these prophecies were the subject of much study, as we know by the prompt reply given by the chief priests and scribes when Herod asked them where Christ should be born. Some of this study was prompted by fear of a judgment, and some by unhappiness under existing evil conditions. The Jews of that day—like people in all places and at all times—were divided into two groups, those who longed for the coming of a time of righteousness and those who preferred not to change their lives.

The first chapter of Luke gives us more clearly than either Matthew or John the relationship between the Lord and John the Baptist. We can know from the prophecies in the Old Testament that a part of the divine plan was that when the appointed time came, the way of the Lord should be prepared by a forerunner. Malachi calls him Elijah the prophet. That such a forerunner was expected we know from Matthew 11:10-14. Yet, in spite of his own denials, many of his followers wished to believe him the Christ.

The angel Gabriel—Swedenborg tells us that this is the name of a whole angelic society—was sent to announce the birth of John and also that of the Lord. His words to Zacharias concerning John's mission should be carefully compared with those to Mary concerning the Lord. John's mission was "to make ready a people prepared for the Lord," whereas the Lord's was "to reign over the house of Jacob forever."

Even those good people who looked and longed for the coming of the Messiah were in gross darkness and in deep evils. The teachings of the Law and the Prophets had been so confused with the traditions of the elders and so buried under selfishness and worldliness that without preparation no one could have received the Lord. The Lord's truth comes as a destroyer if we have nothing but evil and falsity in our hearts and minds. Humility and repentance are the only ground of salvation.

The angel Gabriel told Zacharias that the child to be born to his wife Elisabeth and to be called John would go before the Lord "in the spirit and power of Elias," *Elias* [KJV] being the Greek form of *Elijah*. John himself later (Luke 3:4) claimed to be the promised forerunner of the Lord, and the Lord Himself revealed the same truth to Peter, James, and John after the transfiguration (Matthew 17:10-13). John also dressed like Elijah and, like him, lived in the wilderness.

John's message was "Repent ye: for the kingdom of heaven is at hand." The burden of Elijah's message was likewise the need for repentance. The wilderness pictures the barren nature of all of the merely external life, the rough clothing the harshness with which the thought of repentance comes to us, the locusts and wild honey which John ate the scanty satisfaction we derive from the act of repentance.

Although we are told that Zacharias and his wife Elisabeth "were both righteous before God, walking in all the commandments and ordinances of the Lord blameless," yet even Zacharias was slow to believe the promise of the angel, because from a worldly point of view it seemed impossible of fulfillment. This unwillingness to believe resulted in his dumbness. Swedenborg says that in the internal sense of the Word "dumb" means "those who are not able to confess the Lord, thus neither to preach faith in Him, from ignorance; in which state are the Gentiles outside the Church, and also the simple within the church." It took the actual birth of John to open the mouth of Zacharias, and his first words were the beautiful confession of the Lord which we call the *Benedictus*.

John preceded the Lord even as to his natural birth, and even before his birth his mother Elisabeth was enabled to recognize that the promise of the Messiah was to be fulfilled in the child of her cousin Mary.

The Lord can come to us only after the work of John is performed in us—only after we open the way for Him by recognizing and fighting our evils. We see people sometimes claiming to be instruments of the Lord, but actually inflated by self-love and proclaiming falsity. This is the effect which religious zeal has in the mind of one who has not first seen and fought his own evils. We need always to pass judgment on ourselves rather than on others. It is a popular fallacy to imagine that man of himself is good; this is contrary to the teaching of the Word and of the church. By nature we incline to evil, and this must be acknowledged before our hearts and minds are open to receive the Lord. Repentance is absolutely necessary to any degree of regeneration and salvation.

Unless we are willing to face honestly our own specific weaknesses and shortcomings, we must remain filled up with self-satisfaction and with the pride of our own intelligence. The Lord's loving, unselfish spirit cannot enter the proud heart.

―――――――

### Adult

In many of the other Christian churches there is a strong tendency to relegate the Old Testament to the past and to feel that the New Testament is the only part of the Word we really need to study. This lesson is a good one in which to bring out the inseparable nature of the two and the fact that no one can understand the New Testament without knowing the Old. The meaning of John's message in our own lives is also important for Adults.

Concerning the state of the church at the time of the Advent Swedenborg says: "The church was then altogether vastated, so that there was no longer any good, or any truth" (AC 2708). The Roman Empire, whose doctrine was "might is right," controlled the world. The Jews had the Word but had made it "of none effect" through their traditions. The Scriptures were read, and worship was carried on in the temple with all the traditional ceremonies; but the aim of the church was temporal power, and the temple was in reality no longer a house of prayer, but a den of thieves. Yet even in this bleak situation there were a few simple pious people who cherished the prophecies of salvation and longed for their fulfillment. Examples of such people were Zacharias and Elisabeth, who "were both righteous before God, walking in all the commandments and ordinances of the Lord blameless"; Joseph and Mary; Simeon (Luke 2:25-35) and Anna (Luke 2:36-38); the shepherds and the apostles. And outside the church among the Gentile nations were multitudes who knew that they walked in darkness and longed for light. The song of Zacharias (Luke 1:68-79) is a glorification of the Lord for His mercy in fulfilling the prophecies and visiting His people, "To give light to them that sit in darkness and in the shadow of death." Swedenborg tells us that visitation is predicated of the exploration of both the good and the evil as to their real quality, preceding a judgment, and that darkness may be the darkness either of falsity from evil or of falsity from ignorance. The death in whose shadow they were was spiritual death, which must have overtaken the whole world if the Lord had not come to restore the light of truth; for those who had the truth had perverted it so that those who came seeking it found only falsity. The Lord said of the scribes and Pharisees, "Ye compass sea and land to make one proselyte, and when he is made, ye make him twofold more the child of hell than yourselves. (Matthew 23:15) The whole of the twenty-third chapter of Matthew, as also most of Luke 11, is a vivid description of the conditions existing in the church.

Zacharias and Elisabeth were both descendants of Aaron. Zacharias was of the "course" or division of Abia, or Abijah. The house of Aaron was divided into twenty-four "courses" or groups of priests, who took turns in administering the worship of the temple (I Chronicles 24:1-19). When a course finished its period of ministry, its members returned to their homes until their turn came again (Luke 1:23). The duty of Zacharias on this particular day was to burn incense on the altar of incense. AE 298 explains that the angel appeared to Zacharias standing on the right side of the altar because the "right hand" in reference to angels and men means "the wisdom and intelligence that they have from the Divine good through the Divine truth preceeding from the Lord." Swedenborg also tells us that Gabriel, Michael, and Raphael in the Word are not the names of individual angels but of angelic societies, named from particular functions, and that by Gabriel is meant "the ministry of those who teach from the Word, that Jehovah came into the world, and that the Human He there assumed is the Son of God, and Divine" (AR 548). Study also the messages which the angel Gabriel brought to Daniel (Daniel 8:16 and 9:21 ff.).

The Gospel of Luke gives the most complete, although not the most detailed, account of the life of the Lord. It begins with the annunciation concerning John the Baptist, and it is the only Gospel which describes the ascension. Miracles attending John's birth link the New Testament directly with the Old, bridging a period of four hundred years, for the last verses of the last chapter of Malachi are a prophecy of the coming of Elijah to prepare the way of the Lord.

Swedenborg tells us what is meant by these last words of Malachi: "John the Baptist was sent before to prepare the people for the reception of the Lord by baptism, because baptism represented and signified purification from evils and falsities, and also regeneration by the Lord by means of the Word. Unless this representation had preceded, the Lord could not have manifested Himself and have taught and lived in Judea and in Jerusalem, since the Lord was the God of heaven and earth under a human form, and He could not have been present with a nation that was in mere falsities in respect to doctrine and in mere evils in respect to life; consequently, unless that nation had been prepared for the reception of the Lord by a representation of purification from falsities and evils by baptism, it would have been destroyed by diseases of every kind by the presence of the Divine Itself; therefore, this is what is signified by 'lest I come and smite the earth with a curse' " (AE 724). The Lord says of John, "And if ye will receive it, this is Elias, which was for to come." (Matthew 11:14) The angel says that John will come "in the spirit and power of Elias." John himself says that he is the fulfillment of the prophecies in Isaiah 40:3 and Malachi 3:1. And after the transfiguration the Lord revealed to Peter, James, and John that John the Baptist had been the promised Elijah (Matthew 17:10-13). *Elias* [KJV] is the Greek form of *Elijah*. We are thus made to realize how close is the relation between the two testaments, the whole of the Old Testament being in reality a prophecy of the life of the Lord. The Lord said that He came to fulfill the Law and the Prophets, and He later expounded to the disciples in all the Scriptures the things concerning Himself "beginning at Moses and all the Prophets."

The dumbness of Zacharias offers an interesting correspondence, for the slang expression "dumb" may be thought of as one of the natural outgrowths of correspondence. "Dumb" of course means unable to speak; yet we use it to mean "ignorant" or "stupid."

Ignorance or lack of intelligence with regard to any subject makes it impossible for us to speak effectively on that subject. Dumbness is thus the direct result of lack of knowledge, understanding, and consequent convictions. The angel said to Zacharias, "And, behold, thou shalt be dumb, and not able to speak, until the day that these things shall be performed, *because thou believest not my words, which shall be fulfilled in their season.*" Swedenborg says that in the internal sense by the dumb are signified "they who cannot confess the Lord, thus cannot profess faith in Him, by reason of ignorance, in which state are the nations outside the church, and also the simple within the church" (AC 6988). In the same number he says that the miracles wrought by the Lord all signify the state of the church and of the human race saved by His coming into the world. The healing of the dumb man by the Lord thus pictured the deliverance of men from falsities which prevented their acknowledging Him. Of the idols that men make it is said, "They have mouths, but they speak not" (Psalm 135:16). Of the coming of the Lord's kingdom Isaiah prophesies: "Then shall the lame man leap as an hart, and the tongue of the dumb sing; for in the wilderness shall waters break out, and streams in the desert." (Isaiah 35:6) The wilderness and the desert picture the state of the church at the time of the Advent—for this reason, of course, John was in the desert—and the waters and streams breaking out picture the truth which the Lord came to restore. When John was born according to the angel's prophecy, and Zacharias had signified that his name was to be *John*—the name means "the Lord is gracious"— it is reported, "And his mouth was opened immediately, and his tongue loosed, and he spake, and praised God." Ignorance in regard to the Lord, lack of understanding of Him and of His purposes make it impossible for one to confess Him in such a way as to convey any impression to anyone else. If we do not wish to be spiritually "dumb," we must learn all we can about the Lord as He reveals Himself in His Word, and by living according to what we learn acquire that spiritual wisdom which will also enable us to show forth the Lord's praise "not only with our lips, but in our lives."

The good people of that time recognized in John a power which cut through all the superficialities with which the scribes and Pharisees had obscured the Scriptures, and revealed to them anew the fundamental principles of right and wrong which the Scriptures laid down for their own daily lives. Once they were able to recognize their evils and falsities and to make the effort to overcome them, they were prepared to recognize the Lord, to welcome Him, and to listen to the deeper truths He preached. This is equally true for us. The Lord's spirit cannot enter except where the way is prepared by humility and obedience to truth from the Word. We recall that in the Old Testament the period of the wilderness wanderings represented a similar period of reformation, a setting in order of the external life by obedience to the commandments, and that this had to precede entrance into the Holy Land, which pictures a state of inner achievement and happiness. John's whole appeal was to reformation of the external life. He wore a garment of camel's hair, which represents the truths of the literal sense of the Word as to good (AC 5620[12]).

John's message, "Repent ye: for the kingdom of heaven is at hand," is eternally valid. The kingdom of heaven is always at hand. The Lord stands at the door, always ready to enter. Our part is to open the door, to clear the way for the Lord's spirit by rejecting the things in us which stand in His way.

Our chapter weaves together the fulfillment of two prophecies in Malachi. The angel Gabriel appeared first to Zacharias and then to Mary. Mary was told that her cousin Elisabeth was to have a child, and was moved to visit her. And even before he was born John bore witness—the child leaped in the womb—and Elisabeth and Mary were given divine confirmation of the promises which had been made to them. So we have given us in this same chapter both the *Benedictus* spoken by Zacharias and the *Magnificat* spoken by Mary. John was born first; he entered upon his public mission first; and at the time of his baptism of the Lord he made the first public proclamation of the Lord's identity, which was immediately confirmed by the voice and sign from heaven. Then, as the Lord's ministry became established, John's came to its end, as he himself prophesied: "He must increase, but I must decrease." (John 3:30) He was imprisoned during the second year of the Lord's ministry and put to death early in the third year. So the Lord takes fuller and fuller possession of the prepared heart and mind, and the ordering of the external life becomes a matter of course as the expression of the spirit within.

## From the Writings of Swedenborg

*Arcana Coelestia*, n. 6988: "That this signifies no utterance, is evident from the signification of 'dumb,' as being no utterance. . . . By 'utterance' is not here meant that of the voice, or speech, for this utterance is natural; but by 'utterance' is meant confession of the Lord, and the profession of faith in Him; for this utterance is spiritual. Hence it is evident [*inde patet*] what is signified in the internal sense by the 'dumb,' namely, they who cannot confess the Lord, thus cannot profess faith in Him, by reason of ignorance, in which state are the nations outside the church, and also the simple within the church."

## Suggested Questions on the Lesson

J. What is the last book in the Old Testament?  *Malachi*

J. What event did Malachi foretell?  *coming of the Lord*

J. Of what two messengers did he speak?  *(1) to prepare the way, (2) of the covenant*

J. What two kinds of people would the Lord find in the Holy Land when He came?  *(1) self-satisfied, (2) those who wanted to be good*

P. How would his coming affect the wicked?  *burn like an oven*

P. What would His coming be like to the good?  *healing*

J. Who was the first messenger to be?  *Elijah (John)*

P. What angel is named in our lesson for today?  *Gabriel*

J. To whom did he come first?  *Zacharias*

P. What message did he give to Zacharias?  *he would have a son*

J. What sign did he give him?  *unable to speak until son was born*

J. To what other person did Gabriel appear?  *Mary*

J. What was his message to Mary?  *she would have a son*

I. How do we know that John was the promised Elijah?  *the Lord said so*

J. What was John's message?  *Repent!*

P. Why was he called John the Baptist?  *he baptized*

I. What does dumbness represent?  *spiritual ignorance*

S. Why did John have to "prepare the way of the Lord"?  *only the humble and repentant can receive the Lord*

S. What does baptism represent?  *our intention to cleanse our lives*

# THE BIRTH OF THE LORD
## Luke 2:1-20

Although the Christmas lesson follows in order here, it probably will be studied separately, making it necessary to tell the classes that you are interrupting your regular sequence just for the Christmas lesson and that you will go back to it next Sunday. Be sure that they know what the next lesson will be. Then tell them that the Lord came into the world many hundred years later than the time about which they have been studying.

---

### Doctrinal Points

*The New Testament is the fulfillment of the Old.*

*If the Lord had not come in the fullness of time mankind would have destroyed itself.*

*The Lord must be born in our "Judea" (hearts), grow up in our "Galilee" (outer lives), and frequently pass through our "Samaria" (thoughts).*

---

### Notes for Parents

We all know that the Advent of the Lord made such a change in the world's history that eventually the calendar was changed to date from it. This alone should prove to us that Jesus was not a man like ourselves. No mere man could have accomplished what He accomplished.

Throughout the Old Testament there are prophecies that one day God Himself would come into the world. The Hebrew word *Messiah*, "the anointed one," was the name used by the Jews to refer to this promised savior, and the Greek word which means the same is *Christ*. *Jesus* means "Jehovah saves," and it was also said that the child was to be called *Immanuel*, which means "God with us."

The Lord said that He came into the world not to condemn but to save. He took on a human nature from Mary in order that He might come in direct contact with all the temptations which we feel, and by overcoming them give us the power to overcome them in His strength as we try to follow His example. He came to show us the way to safety, happiness, and peace—the way to heaven. He came because He loves us.

Nothing was accidental about the way in which this great event took place. Every detail of the Christmas stories in Matthew and Luke has a deep meaning which the older children are studying. They are beautiful stories which we all love, and they should mean more and more to us as the years go by. We should never forget that on the first Christmas day God gave us the greatest gift of all: Himself.

————

### Primary

Be sure that this class knows all the basic details of the lesson. A good plan is to ask them first what they know of the story of the shepherds, then ask them to pay close attention while you read the story from the Word, and then ask for the additional details which they did not mention at first.

Do you know whose birthday we celebrate on Christmas day? The Lord Himself was born on that day many, many years ago.

We know, of course, that this was not the beginning of the Lord. The Lord has lived always. He made the world and everything in it. But men needed to see Him. He had always told them about Himself and about how they must live if they wanted to be truly happy. But they had not really believed Him.

Men thought they knew enough to live without the Lord's help. They wanted to have their own way instead of to learn from Him. So they became very selfish and very unhappy. The people who could read the Word, the scribes and Pharisees, told the others what they wanted them to do instead of what the Lord had said. So those who wanted to do right could no longer find out what really was right.

Then the Lord finally had to come into the world Himself to show people how to live.

Where was the Lord born?

What is Bethlehem called in verse 11?

This is because David was born there.

Mary and Joseph were descendants of David.

Their own home was not in Bethlehem, but at this time they had traveled to Bethlehem on business.

The Holy Land had become part of the Roman Empire.

The Emperor of Rome had issued an order that everyone should be taxed, and everyone had to go to his ancestral home to be enrolled for taxation.

When Mary and Joseph arrived, the city was crowded with people, and there was no room for them in the inn.

Where did they find lodging?

About how many years ago was the Lord born?

How can you remember?

The Lord came into the world to save men from evil by showing them the right way to live, making it possible for them to see and to overcome their temptations.

That is why He is called the savior.

When He was born, only a few people could be told.

This was because most people were evil and did not want to know the truth.

What did the shepherds see?

What did the angel of the Lord tell them?

What message did the heavenly host give?

Where did the shepherds find the Lord?

What did they do after they found Him?

Most of the people soon forgot what they had been told by the shepherds.

Who did not forget?

Sometimes at Christmas we think so much about the presents people give us that we forget the most wonderful present of all, our present from the Lord, the knowledge of our heavenly Father, which He gave us by coming into the world Himself on the first Christmas day.

The prophet Isaiah had foretold His coming long before. This is what he wrote: "For unto us a child is born, unto us a son is given: and the government shall be upon his shoulder: and his name shall be called Wonderful, Counsellor, The mighty God, The everlasting Father, The Prince of Peace."

## Junior

The class will be interested to know that the Advent took place at least eleven centuries after the time of the Judges. Call attention to the fact that in the Lord's time the Holy Land had come to be divided into three parts, and on a map point out Nazareth and Bethlehem. The Juniors should remember the story of the Wise Men and also something about John the Baptist, so that a more general picture of the Advent can be discussed. They are old enough to get some idea of why the Lord came.

What great event was often prophesied in the Old Testament?
Who was born to prepare the way of the Lord?
How did he prepare it?

We celebrate Christmas because it is the birthday of the Lord Himself into the world. In Matthew 1:23 we are told that the baby was to be called *Immanuel*, which means "God with us." He came as a little baby and grew up as we do, so that He could feel all the weaknesses and temptations that come to us in our everyday life and show us how to recognize and overcome them. This is what makes Him our savior. We can be saved from the power of the evils that are within us if we will learn of the Lord and with His help fight against them. The name *Jesus* means "Jehovah saves"; *Christ* means "the anointed one." Anointing with olive oil pictures conse-cration by love. Think how much Jehovah must love mankind to have been willing to come down and live among us just to show us the way to happiness. What this has meant to the world is shown by the fact that long afterward the calendar was changed so that its years are counted backward and forward from the Lord's birth.

Where was the Lord born?
Where was Mary's home?
Why did Mary and Joseph come to Bethlehem?
Why was the Lord born in a stable?

There are two stories about the Lord's birth which we all know well. In the second chapter of Matthew is the story of the Wise Men, who lived a long way from the Holy Land. Do you remember how they learned of the Lord's birth? They knew what the star meant because they had cherished the prophecies of the Ancient Word. They picture all people who really love to know the truth and are willing to live according to it when they find it. Some people say they love the truth, but they close their ears to any truth they do not like. The Pharisees were such people. People are really wise only when they do what truth teaches.

In our chapter for today we have the story of the shepherds. In the Word we read a great deal about shepherds, and the Lord Himself is called our shepherd. The shepherds of the Holy Land lived with their flocks, leading them from place to place to find pasture, keeping them safely in folds at night, and defending them from fierce animals even at the risk of their own lives. They knew their sheep by name and the sheep knew the voice of their own shepherd and came when he called. Sheep are gentle, harmless animals. They picture trustfulness and innocence; the word *innocent* comes from a Latin word meaning "not harming." People who love and cherish innocence and trust are shepherds, spiritually speaking. They may not have much knowledge of the truth, but they are close to the Lord in heart. To the shepherds in the fields of Bethlehem tending their flock on the night when the Lord was born the light which broke upon the world at His birth was not a distant star but an opening of the very heavens above them. They saw the angels and heard the glad tidings, and they did not have to go a long way to find the Lord. But we must notice that both the Wise Men and the shepherds believed at once and did go to find the Lord. This is one of the requirements of all who would be Christians: willingness to believe and readiness to act on our belief.

What message did the heavenly host have for the world?

This message expresses what is in the heart of everyone in heaven and what must be in the heart of every truly good person on earth: worship of the Lord and the desire to help and serve all those around him. This is later expressed by the Lord in the two great commandments: "Thou shalt love the Lord thy God with all thy heart, and with all thy soul, and with all thy mind . . . And . . . Thou shalt love thy neighbor as thyself." (Matthew 22:35-40) So the angels were expressing the sphere of heaven, which the Lord had come to make possible for men on earth.

What did the shepherds do after the angel message?
Where did they find the Lord?
Whom did they tell about Him?
Who remembered all they told?

─────────

## Intermediate

The correspondence of many of the details of the story can be given, and the class should be encouraged to begin to think more deeply about the meaning of Christmas to us and to the world.

The whole of the Old Testament looks forward to the coming of the Lord into the world. The child that is promised in the prophecy in Isaiah 9:6 is to be called, among other things, "The everlasting Father." It was Jehovah Himself who was to come in the form of a child. The Jews of that day believed that this promised child, whom they called *Messiah*, "the anointed one," would be a mighty king who would overthrow their earthly enemies, and set up their nation as the greatest on earth.

So when He came as a lowly babe in a manger in Bethlehem, most of the people could not possibly have been made to believe that He was really their promised Messiah. Only the few simple, good people who were looking for guidance for their personal lives and the few really wise people who saw more than external meaning in the prophecies could be told of the Advent. The shepherds represent those who cherish innocence and the Wise Men those who cherish truth for the sake of life.

It was nighttime when the Lord was born. You remember that light is one of the representatives of truth and that darkness pictures ignorance. The Lord came at a time when people were about to lose all true knowledge of Him because the religious leaders, who were the custodians of the Word, had overlaid it with their traditions. The only way in which the Lord could save men was by coming down to them in a form which they could see and touch. Moreover, the power of evil in the world had become so great that good people could no longer stand against it. Only the Lord could overcome it, and to do this He had to take on a human nature in which evil could reach and attack Him. It was because He loves us that He gave Himself to us on the first Christmas day, the most wonderful gift ever given. We should never forget, when we are thanking people for our Christmas presents, to thank the Lord for this greatest gift of all.

The fact that the Lord was born in a stable and laid in a manger pictures His coming to feed our good affections, for you remember that cattle* represent our affections for useful labor. The Lord did not come, as some of the people expected, to set them up above others, but to teach them how to serve others. Only the humble recognized Him, and only the humble really recognize Him today. With the others, whose minds are full of self, there is no room for Him, just as there was no room in the inn.

The shepherds, keeping watch over their flock by night in the field near Bethlehem, represent all those simple good people who cling to kindness and goodness even when they cannot find anyone to tell them about the Lord and His truth. To such people knowledge of the savior comes as a great burst of light. They welcome it and hurry to learn more and to tell everyone else about it, just as the shepherds did. And the message of the heavenly host, "Glory to God in the highest, and on earth peace, good will toward men," expresses the very heart of heaven, love to the Lord and love to the neighbor. The Lord came into the world to teach us both by His words and by His example, that it is these two loves which make heaven both in the other world and here in this world in the heart of everyone who is willing to overcome his selfishness, learn of the Lord, and try to obey Him.

## Basic Correspondences

manger = doctrine of truth from the Word

shepherds = those who cherish innocence

---

*Although it is usual—and certainly not harmful—to associate cattle with the scene of the Lord's birth, in AE 706[12] we read (in relation to Luke 2:12) that "a manger, as a feeding place for horses, signifies the doctrine of truth from the Word." —Ed.

Wise Men  =  those who cherish truth
for the sake of life

the star  =  guiding truth

―――――

## Senior

The important lesson for this class is in the states of mind in us which are receptive of the Lord's entrance into our lives, as contrasted with the states which bar His entrance. The message of the heavenly host and the two kinds of people who were told of the Lord's birth gives us the picture we need.

When we realize that the Advent of the Lord, obscure as it seemed at the time, had such an effect on history that the calendar was changed to make it the central point, we wonder how anyone can imagine that He was a mere man. Yet many do so imagine.

The familiar stories of the Lord's birth picture clearly the conditions necessary to recognition of the Lord. First we must either, like the Wise Men, love and cherish truth, or we must, like the shepherds, cherish innocence and trust. In either case, we must be willing to believe and willing to act on our belief, no matter what personal sacrifices are involved.

You have perhaps heard people say, "Your belief is beautiful; I wish I could believe as you do." You might answer, "Do you really wish that? Do you wish it enough to study the grounds for our belief and, if you find them to be sound, to change your life accordingly?" This is the real test. Belief is primarily a matter of the will.

John the Baptist was sent before the Lord to prepare His way. John the Baptist and his message picture the necessity of genuine self-searching and repentance as a preliminary to reception of the Lord. If we study the individuals to whom the announcement of the Lord's birth was made—Mary and Joseph, Zacharias and Elisabeth, the shepherds and the Wise Men, Simeon and Anna—we see that they were all looking for the Lord, open-minded to the Gospel, and ready to manifest their belief. We have to choose to believe, to be open to the reception of new truth. If instead we choose to close our minds to anything which upsets our accepted way of life, the Lord knocks at our door in vain.

Swedenborg tells us that the angels are very careful not to inter-fere with this freedom of ours. The message "Glory to God in the highest, and on earth peace, good will toward men" was spoken by permission and is a beautiful expression of the sphere of heaven. It makes us think of the petition in the Lord's Prayer, "Thy kingdom come, thy will be done as in heaven so upon the earth." If the Lord is truly glorified in the heart, there will be innocence and good will in the outward life. Peace is the outcome of innocence—harmlessness—and good will. The Lord is called a lamb and also the prince of peace. His spirit, received in the heart, is what leads to peace, whether in the individual life or in the life of the world. Apart from it, no external measures will bring peace.

Notice that, while the Lord was born in Bethlehem of Judea, He was brought up in Nazareth of Galilee. Here again is the same sequence, for Judea represents the plane of the will and Galilee the plane of the outer life. Between the two lay Samaria, which represents the plane of the understanding, the thought which con-nects will and act. We remember that during His ministry on earth most of the Lord's work was done in Galilee, but that He went up to Jerusalem periodically for the feasts, and that both going to Jerusalem and coming from it "he must needs pass through Samaria." This is a picture of what our lives should be. We begin with a desire to serve the Lord, but our good intention is not enough. We must work this intention out in active service in our outward life, and we do so by means of study and thought. What we meet in our experience in the world should lead us to go back often to a state of worship for renewal of our will to do good; and our worship, to be effective, must be the climax of a period of meditation.

The Lord came into the world on the first Christmas day in order to meet and overcome the evils which were growing so strong that even those who longed for goodness could not fight against them. He came to restore to men a true knowledge of Himself and to be our example in all things. He came as the savior of the world, but He can save each one of us only as we learn of Him and seek to follow His example, recognizing and fighting our evils in His strength. He endowed mankind with rationality and freedom of choice, which alone make us human beings instead of animals, and He cannot save any one of us against his will.

―――――

## Adult

Discuss the necessity of the constant growth of our concept of the Lord and of our understanding and appreciation of the meaning of the details of the familiar Christmas stories. Use Isaiah 9:6 to point this up and Isaiah 9:7 to suggest the effect which this growing concept should have on our lives.

Looking back after nearly two thousand years we can see that the Lord's Advent changed the whole course of history. We all know that our calendar dates from the birth of Christ and that the Christian nations, in spite of their obvious shortcomings, are the progressive and dominant nations. The life of the Lord gave the world a new standard, a new ideal, without which spiritual life would have perished; for men, looking to themselves or to other men for wisdom, were becoming more and more confused, uncertain, and fearful. The only genuine truth in the world was in the Hebrew Scriptures, and the church of that day had so perverted these that they were no longer read with an open mind. The object of the lifelong search of Socrates was for the wise man. No man could be found who could point out the way of life.

This spiritual darkness was the night upon which the great light broke. The star which the Wise Men saw afar off and the "glory of the Lord" which shone round about the shepherds were the same light, the Lord coming into the world as the truth, "the way," "the light of the world," "a light to lighten the Gentiles," the only wise man, to whom men in all time to come could look for light and guidance. When we are little children, we love and cherish the picture of the holy babe in the manger with Mary and Joseph and the shepherds in adoration, but as we grow older every detail of this picture must be filled with deeper and deeper meaning. We begin to glimpse the tremendous significance of this seemingly obscure event which is celebrated all over the world on Christmas day, and to see that nothing less than the coming into the world of the Lord God Himself could so profoundly have affected the history of the world and the course of individual lives.

Then comes the question, "Why did so few recognize the Lord?" This is answered for us many times in the Word. "For this people's heart is waxed gross, and their ears are dull of hearing, and their eyes they have closed" (Matthew 13:15); "And men loved darkness rather than light, because their deeds were evil" (John 3:19). Owls, which depend upon the darkness to help them surprise their prey, see in the dark and are blinded in the daytime. We can all refuse to see truths which we have not prepared ourselves to use, just as a child who has not studied his lesson or the lessons which went before it is not prepared to understand what the teacher is talking about. "God sent not his son into the world to condemn the world, but that the world through him might be saved." His light would have destroyed eyes not prepared to receive it if He had not permitted the eyes to be closed. So His Advent was accomplished in a way which represented His accommodation of Himself to men, and only those who were prepared knew of it. But the light which was at first seen by so few grew and spread and continues to grow and spread throughout the whole world.

The Lord was born in Bethlehem, the birthplace of Benjamin as well as of David. Of Himself He said, "I am the bread of life." *Bethlehem* means "house of bread." To each of us, when we are children or in childhood states, the Lord comes in simple instruction as to how we may be good and useful, and the beautiful story in the letter of the Word of His coming as a humble babe in the manger at Bethlehem moves our hearts. But as we pass out of our childhood states, our knowledge of the Lord and our concept of Him must grow. We are all familiar with the general correspondence of the Christmas stories: the Wise Men, those who cherish and love the truths of spiritual living; and the shepherds, the simple in heart who love what is good and innocent. These are the two classes of people who are able to recognize the Lord: those who love and cherish the knowledge of Him which they have received through

the Word from their parents and teachers, as the Wise Men cherished
the prophecies which they had from the Ancient Word; and those
who, in the absence of knowledge of the Lord, still are humble
and loving, preserving their own good innocent affections in spite
of the worldliness which surrounds them, as the shepherds watched
their flocks by night.

There was no room for the Lord at the inn. An inn represents
a "place of instruction." The church was the only place of instruction to which men could go who wanted to learn of the Lord, but
it had so perverted the precious knowledge entrusted to it that the
divine truth was altogether crowded out. So the Lord was laid in
a humble manger, the feeding place of horses and cattle, the few
humble minds and hearts which still found some instruction for
life, and He was wrapped in swaddling clothes, which represent the
first simple truths which clothe our early perceptions of the Lord
(AE 706[11]).

To many it seems strange that so few people acknowledged the
Lord's birth when it was accompanied by signs and wonders and
when the Hebrew nation had looked forward through all its history to this very event. But we must not think that the signs and
wonders were visible to everyone, though many stories based on
this assumption have been written. Verses 17 and 18 of our lesson
gives us a suggestion here. They make it rather evident that others
knew of the shepherds' vision only as the shepherds told of it and
that, while they wondered at it, only Mary really thought much
about it. Belief is a matter of the will. We do not believe unless
we want to. Even the Lord never forces us to believe in Him, and
when He came into the world, He came in such a way that only
those recognized Him who really longed for His coming and so
would worship and protect the child Jesus. These few were told,
each in a way that would be most assuring to him: the Wise Men,
who understood something of correspondences, saw a star; the
simple shepherds had in common a beautiful and awe-inspiring
vision and heard the actual announcement; Mary and Joseph,
Zacharias and Elisabeth were told by an angel (and the doubting

Zacharias was still further impressed by being struck dumb); and Simeon and Anna were taught by a perception within their own hearts when they saw the child. Most of the people who wanted no truth which might condemn them, neither saw nor heard.

It is much the same with people today. Swedenborg tells us that the angels never try to instruct men on earth. They know that the Lord has given men the Word and leaves them in freedom to receive or reject its teaching, and that this freedom must be preserved at all costs. Only evil spirits seek to speak to men.* But at the time of the Advent the angelic host was permitted to express in one great beautiful message the very sphere of heaven: "Glory to God in the highest, and on earth, peace, good will toward men." The more accurate translation is "to men of good will." Love to God and love to the neighbor, afterward pointed out by the Lord Himself as the two great commandments, are the way to peace both for the individual and for the world. This is a message which we should ponder most deeply at Christmas time. The angel told the shepherds where to find the Lord. That is all the angels can do for us. If we are wise, we shall do as the shepherds did: go quickly to find the Lord in the manger of the letter of the Word: and we shall worship Him and tell others what we have found; and then we shall go back to our daily tasks "glorifying and praising God."

---

## From the Writings of Swedenborg

*Apocalypse Explained*, n. 706[12]: "It is said in the seventh verse of the same chapter that this was done 'because there was no place in the inn,' an 'inn' signifying a place of instruction. Because this was the state with the Jews, who were then in mere falsities, through the adulteration of the Word, this was signified by 'there was no place in the inn'; for if it had pleased the Lord He might have been born in a most splendid palace, and have been laid in a bed adorned with precious stones; but He would thus have been with such as were in no doctrine of truth, and there would have been no heavenly representation.

---

*See, e.g., HH 249. —Ed.

He is also said to have been 'wrapped in swaddling clothes,' because 'swaddling clothes' signify first truths, which are truths of innocence, and which are also truths of the Divine love."

*True Christian Religion*, n. 92: "The Lord frequently says that the Father sent Him, and that He was sent by the Father . . . and this He says, because 'being sent into the world' means to descend and come among men; and this was done by means of a human which He took on through the virgin Mary. Moreover, the Human is actually the Son of God, because it was conceived from Jehovah God as its Father . . . He is called 'the Son of God,' 'the Son of man,' and 'the son of Mary'; 'the Son of God' meaning Jehovah God in His Human; 'the Son of man' the Lord in respect to the Word; while 'the son of Mary' means strictly the human He took on. . . . In regard to the Lord, the Divine that He had was from Jehovah the Father, and the human from the mother. These two united are the Son of God. . . . That the Divine Trinity— God the Father, Son, and Holy Spirit—is in the Lord, and that the Father in Him is the Divine from which, the Son the Divine Human, and the Holy Spirit the Divine going forth, will be seen in the third chapter of this work where the Divine Trinity is treated of."

---

## Suggested Questions on the Lesson

P. What do we celebrate on Christmas day?  *the birth of Jesus Christ*

J. About how many years ago was the Lord born on earth?  *two thousand (more or less)*

P. Where was He born?  *Bethlehem*

P. Who was His mother?  *Mary*

P. Who was her husband?  *Joseph*

J. Who in a far-off country were told of His birth?  *Wise Men*

J. How were they told?  *"We have seen his star . . ."*

P. Who were told near Bethlehem?  *some shepherds*

P. Where were these shepherds and what were they doing?  *in the field watching their sheep*

P. How were they told?  *by an angel*

P. What did the angel tell them to do?  *"You will find the babe wrapped in swaddling clothes lying in a manger"*

P. What was the message of the heavenly host?  *peace on earth to men of good will*

J. Where did the shepherds find the Lord?  *in a stable*

J. Whom did they tell about Him?  *everyone they saw*

J. Who remembered all they said?  *Mary*

J. Who was Jesus? *God with us*

I. Why did He come into the world? *to save us from our sins*

S. What did He accomplish for us? *redemption, making salvation possible for all*

# THE WIDOW OF NAIN
## Luke 7:1-30

As noted in the first lesson from Luke, our effort after covering the basic story of the Lord's life in Matthew is to center the lessons as far as possible in stories in the particular Gospel under consideration which do not appear in the other Gospels. This means that the facts of the Lord's life must be brought in by the way. In this lesson, for example, the teacher should tell briefly the story of the Lord's early years and of His baptism before taking up the chapter for the day. The latter part of the lesson ties in with the review and with the Old Testament.

---

### Doctrinal Points
*The Lord is life itself.*
*All the prophets represent the Word.*
*Faith involves confidence.*
*True charity inevitably expresses itself in works.*

---

### Notes for Parents
There are two very wonderful stories in our lesson for today. One is about a Roman soldier who heard of the Lord's miracles and, believing what he heard, knew that such power could come only from God and so it was not limited by any earthly conditions. We see evidences all about us of the Lord's power in the lives of other people. Are we as willing as the centurion was to acknowledge it and turn to the Lord ourselves, sure that He can help us?

And the other story is of a poor widow whose only son had died, and the Lord "had compassion on her" and with the one word, "Arise," brought her son back to life. Nothing that is recorded in the Bible is there by accident. It is the Lord who gives us this story. He gives it to us to show us that He has power over life and death, and that we never really die. When He sees that it is best for us and for others to pass out of this world, our bodies die. But to each one of us He then says, "Arise," and, like the widow's son, we sit up and begin to speak. In the sight of the angels the thing which we call death is resurrection, for they then see us rising to active consciousness in their world. We should never fear death. It is always a blessing to the one who goes. We should look forward to it. And we will, if we believe and trust the Lord and try to live the kind of life which is taught in His Word. Shall we be like the people in our chapter whom John had baptized, or like the Pharisees and lawyers who rejected his counsel?

———————

## Primary

Follow the outline suggested, drawing as much as possible of the story of the Lord's early life from the children's own memory. Some of the older ones in the class should know most of it. With this class something can be done with the importance of the miracle itself, and with the latter part of the chapter.

Our lesson today is about a miracle. A miracle is a wonderful thing done by the Lord.

After the Lord was born in Bethlehem, He was taken down into Egypt for a while because Herod, the wicked king, wanted to kill Him. Then after Herod died, the Lord was brought back and grew up in Nazareth, where Mary and her husband Joseph lived. When He was twelve years old, He was brought to Jerusalem for His first Passover feast. After that He grew up in Nazareth, and no one knew anything more about Him until He was about thirty years old.

Who was sent to prepare the way of the Lord?
Who were John's father and mother?
Who told his father what he was to be?
What sign did Gabriel give Zacharias?

John grew up and began to preach in the wilderness, and many of the good people went out to hear him and believed what he told them about the bad things they had been doing. So they knew that they must change their lives, and John baptized them in the Jordan as a sign that they were going to try to do better. This was the way he prepared them to welcome the Lord.

Then one day the Lord came to the Jordan and asked John to baptize Him, because He came into the world to show us the things we ought to do and being baptized is one of those things. And after the Lord was baptized, the people saw a dove fly down and light upon Him, and they heard a voice from heaven which told them that He was the promised Lord.

He did not need to be baptized, but He was showing us what we ought to do. Then He began to go about preaching and teaching and working miracles of healing.

The miracles recorded in the Bible are wonderful things done by the Lord.

What miracles does our lesson today describe?

You see, the Lord is life itself.

He is the one who gives us our life from day to day.

He raised the widow's son to show us that no one ever really dies.

By this time John had been put in prison by a second Herod.

What did John's messengers ask the Lord?

What did He tell them?

What did He tell the people about John?

―――――――

## Junior

The review and introductory material are covered in the questions in the Junior notes. The teacher should see that the pupils know the answers to all these questions. Both miracles in the chapter should be taken up in this class, but the first one with the emphasis on the question of faith. In the discussion of the raising of the widow's son have the children look up and read the three other stories suggested and stress the Lord's control of life. Point out that it was from the Lord that power came to Elijah and Elisha. Use the last part of the reading for today to reinforce the review of John the Baptist.

Who was sent to fulfill the prophecy of Malachi about Elijah?

Who were John's parents?

By whom was Zacharias told what was to happen?

What sign was given him?

What do we call the first words he spoke after John's birth?

To whom else was the angel Gabriel sent?

What did he promise her?

What other familiar song of praise do we find in this chapter?

Now let us see how much you remember about the early life of the Lord.

Where was He born?
Where was He taken to save Him from Herod?
Where was He brought up?
Where did He appear in public when He was twelve years old?
How old was He when He began His public ministry?
Where did He find John?
What did He ask John to do for Him?
What sign was given from heaven at that time?
Where did the Lord spend forty days after He was baptized?
What happened to Him there?

After His temptations in the wilderness the Lord entered immediately upon His public ministry. He went about the country preaching, teaching, and healing. Today our lesson tells of two miracles. The word *miracle* means "a wonderful thing." The miracles in the Bible are wonders done by the Lord Himself. If we study them, we find that there are two conditions necessary to the healing of any person: he must recognize that he needs help, and he must believe that the Lord can help him.

A centurion was a Roman soldier who commanded a hundred men. The people hated their Roman conquerors as a rule, but they liked the particular centurion mentioned in our lesson for today.

Why?
What did the centurion ask the Lord to do for him?
How did he show his faith in the Lord?
What did the Lord do for him?
How did He say he was better than the people of Israel?

The other miracle in our lesson is even more wonderful. The widow, grieving for the loss of her only son, longed for help. The Lord has power over life because He is life itself. All our life comes from Him. When we are sick, it is really only the Lord who knows whether or not we shall recover. Many people have recovered after the doctors have given them up, and many people have died whom the doctors expected to recover. We know that what seems to us to be death is only the laying off of the body which we have used in this world, and that we always go right on living. We just go to sleep in this world and wake up in the spiritual world, where our souls have been all the time even though we were not conscious of it. In this miracle the Lord merely waked the widow's son again in ths world. There are two similar miracles in the Old Testament and another in the New. Look up I Kings 17:8-24, II Kings 4:8-37, and Luke 8:41-42; 49-56. Both Elijah and Elisha, because they were faithful prophets, could use the Lord's power.

As we learn from Luke 3:19-20, John the Baptist had been cast into prison by Herod. While he was in prison, it must have seemed to John that he had failed, and he began to doubt his mission, and even whether it was really the Messiah whom he had seen and baptized. So he sent two of his disciples to the Lord.

What did they ask Him?

What did He answer?

What other miracles did He perform so they could give John a sure report?

Even the best of the people in those days, like John, judged everything according to the way it looked outwardly. So they needed to see miracles in order to confirm and strengthen their faith. But we can see with our reason that the Lord was the Messiah, God Himself come into the world. We do not need miracles to convince us, and this is a higher type of belief. For many people who saw the miracles did not believe in the Lord, as we see from the last two verses of our lesson.

What did the Lord tell the people about John?

---

### Intermediate

In this class more should be done with the reason why the Lord performed miracles and with the correspondence of the miracles in our lesson, as well as with the meaning of the last part of the assignment.

To the messengers sent by John the Baptist the Lord cited His miracles as proof that He was the Messiah. The people of that day were a wholly materialistic and external people. Even those who longed for the coming of the Messiah had to have their faith confirmed by visible miracles. The Lord does not want us to require this external proof. We have a higher sight than that of the body. We know that the body is of secondary importance—only a tool for the soul. We need to keep it in as good condition as possible because of its usefulness, but it should never be of first concern to us. People who are always worrying about their health are not only unhappy but are seldom very useful.

The Lord had the power to perform physical miracles. He still has it and still performs them. It is the Lord's power which heals the body today, whenever He sees that continued life and health in this world will be good for us and for others. Both our life here and our continued life in the spiritual world after the death of the body are from the Lord alone. There is only one who is life.

But the miracles which the Lord performed when He was on earth had a twofold purpose. They did confirm the faith of those Jews and Gentiles who wished to believe in Him, and they also could be recorded in the Word to teach us the deeper lessons which we draw from their correspondence. So the centurion's servant is a picture of some useful faculty of ours which has suddenly failed us. If we have the real faith which the centurion had, we shall turn to the Lord for help, knowing that He has the power to restore us. All that is needed is the humble recognition of our own weakness and the conviction that "with God all things are possible."

The other miracle in our lesson was performed for a widow. We remember that in general men picture the understanding and women the affections. So a widow—and there are many widows mentioned in the Word—pictures some good desire which has lost the knowledge of truth which properly belongs with it. When this knowledge is lost, the ideas which spring from our desire have no life in them. People often say, "I wish I could believe in God and the Bible as I did when I was a little child." This merely means that they have allowed worldly thinking and living to kill the truths which were in their minds. In this state, only a realization of the Lord's presence and power in our lives can make the truths live again. The Lord restored to life the son of the widow of Nain to teach us just this lesson. If we realize our own weakness and ignorance and look to Him for help, He will restore our spiritual powers also.

It is not by accident that the verses about John the Baptist follow the story of this miracle. Nothing in the Word is accidental. Naturally, no miracles of the Lord aroused greater wonder and comment than those in which He brought back to life people who had already died. The people knew from the books of Kings (I Kings 17:8-24 and II Kings 4:8-37) that Elijah and Elisha had each raised someone from the dead. But the time had come when they must be shown that the Lord was not a mere prophet but the Messiah Himself whom John had promised them. So the messengers came from John and received the assurance he asked for.

And then the Lord told the people that all John had said to them was true. The truth which the Lord gives us is not a reed shaken by the wind. Reeds, a simple growth on the water's edge, are pictures of the letter of the Word as it comes into our natural memory. They are shaken with the wind when we make the letter of the Word teach whatever we happen to want to believe instead of what the Lord means it to teach. And the Lord's truth is not always easy and pleasing to us in this world. Kings' courts, where soft clothing is worn, are found in heaven after we have overcome our evils. The letter of the Word is a prophet, speaking for the Lord. At first it comes to us like John the Baptist pointing out our evils, telling us to repent, and leading us to try to make our lives clean according to its truth. But when we have done this—this is what verse 28 means—and begin really to feel the Lord's spirit in our hearts, John the Baptist passes away, and we begin to grow in joy and peace from the Lord Himself.

### Basic Correspondences

| | | |
|---|---|---|
| a widow | = | a good desire which has lost the truth which belongs with it |
| a reed | = | the outmost letter of the Word when we see no deeper into it |

kings' courts  =  heaven

———

## Senior

The lesson for the Seniors may well be centered on the meaning of the miracle of the widow's son and the power which trust in the Lord instead of in self brings into the life in small things and in great. Whatever the young people are going to do in the world, obedience to the Lord's truth as He has given it to us and trust in His power to accomplish should be their constant support.

The New Church teaches that the miracles recorded in the Word are fact. It does not try to explain them away, or imagine that they were made up later by the apostles in order to convince people. Believing that Jesus was actually Immanuel, God with us, who created and maintains every living thing, we have no difficulty in accepting His power to control natural as well as spiritual forces.

But the Lord never performed miracles in order to convince doubters, and His miracles did not convince the doubters who saw them any more than they convince doubters today. The doubters then attributed His power to the devil. He performed miracles to confirm and strengthen the faith of those who, in a wholly worldly and materialistic nation and age, still felt their need of Him and wished to accept Him, and also in order to teach in the Word, through the knowledge of correspondence later to be revealed, lessons of the healing and reviving power of His spirit in the soul.

Since the Incarnation the Lord's spirit working in the world has increased man's power of rational and spiritual sight, and in this latter age through the Second Coming the necessary knowledge has been given to implement the new power. So we should not ask for external miracles. The Lord said to Thomas, "Thomas, because thou hast seen me, thou hast believed: blessed are they that have not seen, and yet have believed." (John 20:29) Spiritual reason creates a higher type of faith than physical sight. So, although we believe the miracles, and recognize them as evidence of the power exerted by the Lord when He was on earth, their chief interest for us is in their correspondence.

For example, the miracle of the healing of the centurion's servant pictures the Lord's power to revitalize even the activities of our everyday life in the world provided we wish, as did the centurion, to make that life serve our own spiritual development and that of the world. The good centurion is a picture of the well-ordered external life, ministering to the spiritual and looking to the Lord for correction and renewal. The complete submission of this external plane to the will of the Lord is the final test of faith.

The story of the raising of the son of the widow of Nain pictures the Lord's power to revitalize all our powers in times of doubt and discouragement, when we seem to have lost even the power to see what we ought to do. The widow of Nain stands for our good desire, bereft of its proper knowledge of truth, and so inevitably of its ability to produce an effective decision. In such a case we must put aside all thought of our own worldly wisdom and lift our problem into the clear light of the Lord's teaching of love to God and the neighbor.

Every one of us over and over again in our lives is in the position of the widow of Nain. We want, perhaps, to help someone with advice and comfort, but we do not know just how—the right words will not come. Or we want to decide some important question in the right way, but we don't know just what is right. Or we want to show a child or a friend just how some weakness is leading him astray, but we are not sure how to go about it. Or perhaps we want to give some friend an understanding of what our church teaches and stands for, but we find we are too ignorant. When we are in this state, we seem to ourselves to be good for nothing. We seem unable to produce anything that will live. This is pictured by the death of the widow's only son. When we are dwelling on our discouragement, we are like the mourning widow and her friends following the bier out of the city toward the tombs.

But the Lord is always standing at the gate. If we will "stand still" when He touches the bier and look to Him instead of thinking of ourselves, we shall always hear Him say, "Arise!" Do you remember how Joshua, after the first defeat at Ai, "rent his clothes, and fell to his face upon the earth," and how the Lord said to him, "Get thee up; wherefore liest thou thus upon thy face?" and set him to work to find out and correct the sin in Israel? Think what Joshua accomplished after that!

The coming of the messengers from John the Baptist, who was now in prison, expresses the same sort of doubt and discouragement. The Lord answered by pointing to His works. If we study history and look about us in the world, we shall find ample evidence of the Lord's power to save in spite of human weakness. The troubles of the world are man-made. But the Lord also shows us in our lesson that His truth is not something that can be twisted according to our desires—a reed shaken with the wind—nor yet always easy and pleasant this side of heaven. Like John the Baptist it tells us exactly what we must do if the Lord's power is to make itself felt in our lives and through us in the world. Verse 28 tells us, however, that after we have received that life-giving power, all the hard part of the struggle is behind us.

## Adult

Two parts of this lesson will lead to helpful discussion: the meaning for us of the raising of the widow's son, and the Lord's words concerning John the Baptist. Verses 29 and 30 help to point up His meaning.

We are all familiar with the Gospel story of the Lord's life. Therefore, after following its basic outline in Matthew, we have tried in the other Gospels to pick out, for most of the lessons, stories which are told in only the one Gospel we are studying. It is interesting to look at the lists of the Lord's miracles and parables as given in the reference section of a teacher's Bible. The Gospel of Luke is preeminently noteworthy for its parables, giving us seventeen which are not found in any other Gospel, as well as ten of the more common ones. It is not known whether or not Luke came in direct contact with the Lord, as he is not mentioned in any Gospel narrative. He was one of the early Christians and a companion of Paul on some of his travels, and is generally believed to have been for seven years at least in charge of the group at Philippi in Macedonia, the first Christian Church established in Europe. Paul calls Luke "the beloved physician" (Colossians 4:14). His name indicates that he was not of Jewish descent. He is accepted as the writer of the book of Acts as well as of the third Gospel. His brief introduction to the first chapter of his Gospel (Luke 1:1-4) indicates that his memory-knowledge of the Lord's life and teaching was the result of eager application to all possible sources of information, but we know, of course, that his Gospel as recorded was set down under inspiration like the other three.

The first of the two miracles recorded in our chapter is also recorded in Matthew. From the point of view of healing, it is noteworthy as being a case in which the Lord healed at a distance with no physical contact with the person healed. This miracle is usually remembered, however, because of the Lord's comparison of the faith of the centurion with that of the Jews. The second miracle, the raising of the dead son of the widow of Nain, is one of the seven miracles recorded only in Luke. Both were performed in Galilee. The centurions's message was delivered to the Lord at Capernaum. Nain was a village not far from Nazareth. We remember that Galilee was called "Galilee of the Gentiles" and that it represents the outward life. The Roman conquerors also represent the life of the world, usually in its character of usurper of time and effort which should be devoted to higher things, but in the person of the centurion in its less common character of the friend and benefactor of the spiritual life. So the healing of the centurion's servant represents the restoration of some useful external ability through inspiration from the Lord.

The story of the widow of Nain teaches a similar lesson. Throughout the Scriptures a widow pictures a good desire which is bereft of the truth needed to support and make it productive. A son pictures a derivative truth. People who want to be good but have no true knowledge of the Lord and His purposes are easily deprived of such simple truths as they may have. They are easy to deceive and mislead and become a prey to evils. All of us are in this state so far as we are in ignorance of truth which we need in order to do good.

Swedenborg speaks of two kinds of resurrection: the natural, when a man's body is laid aside and he rises to life in the spiritual world, and the spiritual in which the life of the natural selfhood is put away and a new will is given from the Lord. "He that loseth his life for my sake shall find it." See the passage from AE 899[11] below.

In the spiritual sense the sequence in the Word is always interesting. We have in the story about John the Baptist which immediately follows an illustration of the sort of distress pictured by the condition of the widow of Nain. John at this time has been cast into prison by Herod. His active preaching was ended, although his disciples still resorted to him in the prison. John is pictured as discouraged at the seeming frustration of his life work, even to the point of allowing himself to wonder if he could have been mistaken. How often when our own efforts for the church and for others seem to come to nought, we allow ourselves to wonder if our work and sacrifice have been worthwhile! John in prison could not see the Lord at work. When we are shut up within the narrow circle of our own accomplishment, we cannot see the Lord at work. The Lord allowed John's messengers to see the miracles His presence was accomplishing, as He will always let us see them if we are willing to face the fact that it is He and not we from whom the good is to come. This is the lesson taught in verse 28.

John the Baptist, like all the prophets, represented the letter of the Word. The letter of the Word is not a reed shaken with the wind, something which may be twisted to suit our passing desires and imaginings. It is not a man clothed in soft raiment; as long as we are in this world it will present to us truths which go harshly against our preferences. It is a prophet: it speaks for the Lord. And when we see it so, it becomes more than a prophet: it becomes the medium through which the Lord enters our minds and hearts.

Of the statement made in verse 28 Swedenborg says in AC 9372[6]: "That in the internal sense, or such as it is in heaven, the Word is in a degree above the Word in the external sense, or such as it is in the world, and such as John the Baptist taught, is signified by, 'he that is less in the kingdom of the heavens is greater than he'; for as perceived in heaven the Word is of wisdom so great that it transcends all human apprehension."

## From the Writings of Swedenborg

*Apocalypse Explained*, n. 899[11]: " 'Death' signifies resurrection, and thus 'the dead' signify those who rise again into eternal life, because 'death' signifies hell, and thus evils and falsities; and these must die that man may receive spiritual life; for until these are dead and extinct man has no spiritual life, which is the life that is meant in the Word by 'life," 'eternal life,' and 'resurrection'; therefore 'to die' means here and elsewhere in the Word the extinction of the life that is man's own, which regarded in itself consists solely of evils and falsities from them . . . Resurrection from the dead, both in the natural and in the spiritual sense, was represented and thus was signified by the dead whom the Lord raised."

## Suggested Questions on the Lesson

J. What prophecy did John the Baptist fulfill? *Malachi's regarding Elijah*

J. Who were his father and mother? *Zacharias and Elisabeth*

P. Who announced his coming? *the angel Gabriel*

P. What sign did the angel give Zacharias? *that he be dumb till John's birth*

P. What other announcement did the same angel make? *that the Lord would be born*

P. To whom was it made? *Mary*

J. What two familiar selections do we find in the first chapter of Luke? *Benedictus, Magnificat*

I. What was the message of John the Baptist? *Repent!*

J. What did he do for the people who believed him? *baptized them*

P. Why was the Lord baptized? *to show us what we ought to do*

J. What is the first miracle described in our lesson for today? *healing centurion's slave*

P. What is the second? *raising the widow's son*

S. Why could the Lord bring the dead man back to life? *He has power over life*

J. What did John want to ask the Lord? *"Are you he who is to come?"*

J. What did the Lord tell John's messengers?   *tell him what you have seen and heard*

I. What did He tell the people John was?   *a prophet*

S. Who did He say was greater than John?   *he who is least in the kingdom of God*

# THE APOSTLES ARE SENT OUT
*Luke 9:1-36*

There are really four parts to this lesson. We have chosen the sending out of the apostles as the center of our study because we have had a lesson on the feeding of the multitude and one on the transfiguration in our studies of the other Gospels. Both these stories, as well as the Lord's question and Peter's answer can easily be taken up in direct relation to the assigned topic, as examples and types of the Lord's preparation of the apostles for their life work.

———

### Doctrinal Points

*Jesus Christ, risen and glorified, is the only God.*
*Moses and the Prophets teach of Him.*
*Faith gives the power to help others.*
*The more we do for others the more we are able to do.*

———

### Notes for Parents

Did you ever think of the fact that we are all capable of being apostles of the Lord?

We sometimes hear a person say, "I didn't ask to be born; I can't help being what I am." This is his excuse for not trying to overcome his evils. The first part of his statement is true of every one of us. Under divine providence and without any choice of our own each one of us was born in a particular family, in a particular community, with a particular heredity, and with particular abilities and particular weaknesses.

But the second part of his statement is false. No one remains just what he was at birth, and what he becomes—his final character—depends on his own choice and not on anyone or anything else. Others may put stumbling blocks in his way, but we develop

226

strength only by overcoming obstacles. Other people may tempt him to do wrong but he, like every person in the world, has an all-powerful friend always at hand to help him do right if he really wants to. We should look at the circumstances of our birth as our own special place and opportunity in the world—the place which no one else can fill. Our few short years of life here are given us just for the purpose of choosing what kind of people we want to be. And the choice is a very important one, for the character we choose for ourselves here is the character we shall keep to eternity.

Out of all His followers the Lord chose twelve men to be His apostles. They were very simple men. At least four of them were fishermen—three of them His closest disciples—and one was a tax collector, despised by his fellow men because of his occupation. But the Lord saw in each of them qualities which were needed for the establishment of His kingdom among men, and because they followed Him wherever He went and did what He told them to do, He could teach them and give them power to teach others and to help others to overcome their evils and weaknesses and mistaken ideas. Our lesson today tells us about some of this teaching and what the apostles were enabled to do. And because the Lord has recorded it for us in His Word, it is for us too, and we can learn to be His apostles in our world of today—if we choose.

———

### Primary

Try to teach the children the number of the apostles, what the words *disciple* and *apostle* mean, and the names of the Lord's three closest followers. The teacher should do as much as possible with the details of the lesson as abridged. This class should also learn the word *transfiguration* and what it means.

As the Lord went about the country and the villages preaching and teaching and working miracles, more and more people believed in Him and followed Him. Many came to Him only to be healed of their diseases. But others came to learn from Him how they ought to live. These were called His disciples, because the word *disciple* means "a learner."

The Lord knew just what was in the heart and mind of each one of these disciples, just as He always knows what is in the heart and mind of each one of us. From all His disciples He chose twelve men in whom He found certain special qualities which would make them able to go and tell other people the things He came to show them. These were the men who were to go out into the world, after the Lord's life on earth was over, and begin the Christian Church. These twelve were called apostles, because the word *apostle* means "one sent out." See if you can remember the words *disciple* and *apostle* and what they mean.

The Lord gave these men special instructions and also gave them practice in the work they were to do.

When the Lord sent them out, what powers did He give them?
What were they to preach?
What were they to take with them?
How were they to be taken care of?
Three of the apostles were often taken with the Lord when the others were left behind.
Which three were they?
Where did He take them to show them a vision?
What was the appearance of the Lord in the vision?
This vision is called the *transfiguration*, a word which means "change of appearance."
Whom did the apostles see talking with the Lord?
Moses and Elijah represent the Law and the Prophets.
What did Peter want to do?
What overshadowed them which made them afraid?
What did the voice from heaven say?
When the cloud passed, whom did they see?
The apostles were the ones who, after the Lord's earthly life was ended, went out into the world and began the Christian Church.

---

## Junior

The Junior notes this time will give the teacher a suggestion for developing the lesson. In taking up the voice from heaven recall the story of the Lord's baptism and have the class look it up in Luke 3:21-22. Be sure the children know the names Peter, James, and John, and suggest that they learn the full list of the twelve, which will be found in Luke 6:14-16.

What is a miracle?
What did the Lord do for the centurion?
What did He do for the widow of Nain?
What had happened to John the Baptist?
What did John want to know?
What did the Lord tell John's messengers?
What did He say about John?

Naturally the Lord's miracles attracted many people to Him. The greater part of these people came because they wanted to be healed of their physical or mental diseases. The Lord healed those who were humble and believed in His power. But there were many—especially those who had been prepared by John the Baptist—who wanted to be taught by the Lord how to live rightly. They came to Him to learn. They are called His disciples because the word *disciple* means "a learner." The Lord taught them all they were able to learn. You know that in school some children learn more than others. It is true that some have more mental aptitude than others, but this is only a part of the reason. A very great deal of our ability to learn depends on our desire to learn. A pupil in school whose mind is somewhere else than on the lesson does not learn much, does he? And neither does one who thinks he knows enough already. In the things which the Lord wants to teach us—things about God and heaven, about our souls, and about how to live good and useful lives in this world—the desire to learn is the most important thing in determining how much we learn. The Lord found among His disciples a few men whom He could teach much more than all the rest could be given. So He kept them with Him constantly and let them see and do many things not possible for the others. Look up and read Luke 6:13-16.

How many did the Lord choose?
What did He call them?

The word *apostle* means "one sent out," and our lesson today tells of the first time the Lord sent out the twelve.

What powers did He give them?
What were they to preach?

What were they not to take with them?
How were they to live?

This was a part of the special preparation the Lord gave His apostles. You know that when we are preparing for any particular work, it is not enough just to be told how it should be done: we have to have practice in doing it. For instance, no one ever learns to play the piano by just being told about music and what the notes are.

Our chapter tells about some other lessons the apostles had. One of these lessons is told in a story which is found also in the Gospel of Mark.

What did the Lord say to them when they asked Him to send the multitude away to buy food?
What food did they have with them?
How many people were to be fed?
What happened after the Lord had blessed the food?

This miracle showed them that the Lord could give them power to meet people's needs, if they looked to Him for it.

Now read verses 7 to 9 and then verses 18 to 20. Even Herod could see that the power Jesus exercised came in some way from God, but only those who followed the Lord closely really understood that He was the Messiah or Christ, God Himself come into the world. And only three of the apostles could be given the wonderful vision with which our lesson closes. It makes a great difference what we believe about Christ. *Christ* means "anointed." The Hebrew word is *Messiah*. The Old Testament had said that in the fullness of time Jehovah Himself would come into the world in a human form which was to be called "the anointed one" and "the Son of God." In the Gospel of Mark Peter's answer is, "Thou art the Christ, the Son of the living God." They both mean the same, the fulfillment of the Old Testament prophecies, Jehovah in the flesh. Because Peter and James and John believed this, the Lord could open their spiritual eyes to see Him in His glory, as they would see Him in the spiritual world when they went there.

Where did they go for this vision?
How did the Lord look?

Who were seen with Him?
What did Peter want to do?
What overshadowed them which frightened them?
What did the voice from heaven say?
Whom did they see when the cloud had passed?

This vision is called the *transfiguration*, a word meaning "a change of appearance." In the vision, Moses represented the Law and Elijah the Prophets. In another place (Luke 24:27, 44)) after His resurrection, the Lord told His disciples that Moses and the Prophets and the Psalms all taught of Him. So at the end of this vision in our lesson Moses and Elijah disappeared, and the disciples saw only the Lord. This is what happens in our minds when we truly believe that Jesus is God Himself. We read the Old Testament and find Him in it just the same as in the Gospels.

---

### Intermediate

The correspondence of the twelve apostles as a whole and of Peter, James, and John in particular may be used as the beginning and basis of the lesson with this class. The thought that the Lord knows what is in each one of us and will teach and lead and support us all through our lives if we look to Him instead of to ourselves for guidance is one which young people should be given as early as possible.

The Lord chose twelve of His closest disciples to be His apostles, the men whom He would send out into the world to preach the Gospel, the good news of salvation. There were twelve apostles, as there were twelve tribes of Israel, because the number twelve signifies "all truths and goods in the complex," which means all that we can know and feel if we are trying to serve the Lord and the neighbor. The Lord, who knows the heart and mind of each one of us, saw in each of these twelve men particular characteristics which could serve in the establishment of the Christian Church. So He kept them with Him, and gave them special instruction and special experiences.

One of these experiences was practice in the work they would be doing after He left them. As our chapter tells us, He "gave them power and authority over all devils, and to cure diseases. And he sent them forth to preach the kingdom of God, and to heal the sick." Mark tells us that they were sent out "by two and two." They were to provide nothing for their journey—not even money— but were to go about finding their food and lodging with people who were willing to receive them. This would keep them in the feeling that they were not going out in their own strength but were being led and cared for by the Lord. We all need this knowledge. And we learn from it, too, that even if we are sure we are right, we should not try to force ourselves or our ideas on people who do not want what we have to give.

In our stury of the Gospel of Mark we had a lesson on the feeding of the multitude, the only one of the Lord's miracles which is recorded in all four Gospels. You will remember that this miracle taught the apostles—as it teaches us—that if one makes the effort to share with others the good and truth he has, however little it may be, first seeking the Lord's blessing upon it, the Lord will multiply it so that it will meet the need and more.

Now let us think about the rest of our assignment, which shows us still another kind of preparation given to the apostles. It makes a difference what we believe about God, both in this world and in the next. If we say we believe in God but refuse to accept any definite teaching about Him, we are thrown back on our own judgment and that of our community for our standards of right and wrong. We are not led by the Lord but by ourselves and the world. "God is not in all our thoughts" (Psalm 10:4).

That is why, in all three Gospels in which the incident of the transfiguration is recorded, it is immediately preceded by the account of the Lord's question to His disciples and Peter's answer. It is the recognition of the Lord as God come into the world which opens the mind to a true understanding of the Scriptures.

Look up and read Isaiah 9:6. This prophecy shows just how our thought about the Lord should rise, from dwelling on His life in this world—the child, and the son—by steps until we acknowledge Him as our heavenly Father from whom alone can come happiness and peace. Jesus told the woman of Samaria plainly that He was the promised Messiah (John 4:25-26). If we believe Him, we too see Him transfigured. His words are God's words, not only when He is saying tender, comforting things, but when He is pointing out and rebuking our sins. He speaks to us through the letter of the Word just as really as He spoke to Peter, James, and John.

Peter, James, and John, the three apostles who were the Lord's closest followers, represent faith, charity, and the works of charity. It is these three things in us which are able, if we accept the Lord as God, to follow Him up to the mountain—into a state of spiritual perception—and see Him transfigured. Luke says, "The fashion of his countenance was altered"; Matthew, "His face did shine as the sun." All three Gospels speak of the shining whiteness of His garments. The face is the symbol of the interior quality of a person. When we recognize the Lord as God Himself, we see that the love He manifested in His every word and act is the very nature of God; so His face shone as the sun. And the letter of the Word—His raiment—becomes suddenly clear to us and is freed from the apparent difficulties which marred it before. It shines with the light from within.

Peter's first confused thought was to give equal worship to Moses, Elijah, and Jesus; that is, to hold his old faith, and add the new "Christian" one. But when he made his proposal, the cloud—symbol of the darkness of his mind—overshadowed him, the voice was heard, and when the cloud lifted, the Lord "was found alone." Look up and read verses 16 to 18 of the first chapter of the second epistle of Peter, in which he speaks of this vision. The three apostles also learned from this experience that the Lord's coming was for all men, not just for the Jews of that day, although Peter later had to have another vision to remind him (Acts 11:1-17).

### Basic Correspondences

twelve = all truths and goods in the complex
Peter = faith
James = charity

John = the works of charity
Moses = the law or the historical Word
Elias (Elijah) = the prophetical Word
the face = the interior quality of a person

---

## Senior

Try to present this assignment throughout as instruction to us for our guidance in trying to serve as apostles of the Lord. Most of our young people start out in life with a genuine desire to make their lives count for the betterment of the world. If they will keep the lessons of this chapter in their minds, they will avoid many pitfalls, and will grow in ability and in spiritual effectiveness.

The word *apostle* means "one sent out." Each of us should be an apostle of the Lord. Our lives are given us by the Lord for a spiritual purpose—that we may develop the kingdom of heaven within us and help to develop it in the world about us. So when we read the story of the sending out of the twelve apostles, we may know that all the details of it as it is told in the Word apply to us also as apostles of the Lord. The Lord knows what is in each one of us, just as He knew what was in each one of His followers when He was in the world. He shows us in this chapter the spirit in which we should live our lives, the power He is able to give us, the conviction we should have about Him, and the vision it is possible for us to attain.

First He gave the apostles "power and authority over all devils, and to cure diseases." If we look to Him, we shall be given power to conquer our evil tendencies and to correct our faults and weaknesses.

Then He gave them their mission: "to preach the kingdom of God, and to heal the sick." Our business in life is to promote the kingdom of God in every possible way, and to help others to spiritual health.

Then He told them to take with them no provision of their own for their support while they were doing His work. This is a very important instruction for all of us. We tend naturally to be looking at ourselves in all that we do, thinking of our own abilities and of the impression we are making on others. But our message is not our own, and neither is the power which can make it helpful to others. Self-forgetfulness is essential if we are to be channels for the Lord's spirit.

"And whatsoever house ye enter into, there abide, and thence depart." This means that when we find a willing reception in our efforts to do good, we should "stay with it" until our work is completed. Too often we do some small service or bring some bit of truth to a person who needs and welcomes it, and then do not follow through. Some other interest catches our attention, or some little difference of opinion or manner of life turns us away. On the other hand, we are warned not to try to force entrance where we are not wanted, and also to "shake off the very dust" of such an experience from our feet after it is over. We must not dwell on the thought of those who have been unwilling to hear what we have to say. Such thoughts, remaining in our minds, cloud our zeal and discourage us from other efforts. They are like the dust which adhered to the apostles' feet.

After the apostles returned to the Lord from their "practice teaching," He gave them another experience to drive home the lessons they had learned. We may recall that the feeding of the five thousand with the five loaves and two fishes pictures the power of the Lord to multiply our small supply of knowledge and ability as we try to use it in His name in the service of the neighbor.

Then in our chapter we come to the basic lesson to be learned. As an introduction to our thought suppose we read the following passages in order: Isaiah 9:6, Matthew 1:21-23, Luke 4:17-21, John 4:25-26 and 14:8-9. Many within the Christian Church have allowed themselves to draw unwarranted conclusions from the mere words "son of God," when a little study of the passages in which the term is used would show that even in the letter the "son of God" merely means God in human form, Immanuel, "God with us." This is the obvious meaning in the Old Testament prophecies, and the claim which Jesus clearly made for Himself. This is what those who had the Scriptures expected the Messiah to be. Read John 10:32-33.

When the people refused to accept Jesus as the Messiah it was only because they did not want that kind of God. And that is the real reason today why people refuse to accept Him as God. They prefer to think of Him as a man, a man who said many inspired things perhaps, but with whom they are free to differ when what He says does not suit them.

The thought that Christ is not God Himself closes the door of the mind against light from heaven as it comes to us through the letter of the Word. Because Peter, James, and John believed Jesus to be the Messiah, their spiritual eyes could be opened to see Him transfigured. So our eyes can be opened to see Him in the inner meaning of the Word. Many years later John saw Him again in a still fuller vision. Read Revelation 1:12-18.

Swedenborg tells us that our ability to see the Lord when we come into the spiritual world is measured by the understanding of Him which we have gained in this world. If we have not thought of God as a person, Jesus Christ, we shall never see Him "face to face," but shall be conscious of Him only as a diffused light, even though after death we accept the fact that Jesus is God from our angel instructors as everyone must who enters the heavens; there will be no established basis in our minds for seeing Him as a person.

The lesson of the Lord's question to His disciples concerns us. He asks the same question of us today, and upon our answer depends our ability to see Him transfigured and to find Him in all the Scriptures, to see Moses and Elijah—the Law and the Prophets—as teaching of Him. On our answer also depends our ability to be led by Him and to receive His spirit. Our thought of Him today should be led upward by gradual degrees through the study of the Law, the Prophets, and the Gospels in the light of their inner meaning, until the cloud is lifted and He stands alone as the only object of our worship.

Adult

It is suggested that the outline of the assignment as a whole and its meaning be covered first as briefly as possible by the teacher, and the rest of the time given to any one phase which may appeal to the class. There are many very practical discussion points.

As we take up the story of the Lord's life in this course in each of the different Gospels in turn, we come to the same familiar incidents, as the feeding of the five thousand and the transfiguration. The story in general is the same; yet there are significant variations in context. Isn't this true of the way in which familiar passages from the Word come up in our own minds? The Lord brings them to us in their application to different states and different experiences as we go through life. So today we are thinking of these two familiar stories as a part of the preparation of the apostles for their great life work, and consequently as part of our preparation for true apostleship. The Lord says to all of us: "Ye have not chosen me, but I have chosen you, and ordained you, that ye should go and bear much fruit, and that your fruit should remain." We all want to be true apostles. We want our lives and words to bear testimony to our belief and to lead to lasting good. In this chapter from Luke we are given particular guidance for this task.

This sending out of the apostles was in the nature of a practical experience. They went out as directed and then came back and reported to their teacher. They were given certain powers, which we recognize as the ability the Lord gives each of us to overcome evils in himself and to help others to correct their weaknesses. They were given their mission: "to preach the kingdom of God, and to heal the sick," as we are to "show forth not only with our lips, but in our lives" the power of the Lord to heal and bless. They were to take nothing of their own with them, but to trust to the Lord that they would be received and provided for. We need this instruction especially, because we are all so prone to self-confidence and self-assertion that our ego often looms up between the Lord's message and the people to whom we are trying to bring it. We are to tarry with those who welcome what we have to bring

them; and when our efforts are not well received, we are to withdraw and not to let thoughts of the disappointing experience—the
dust of the city—cling to us. You will find it interesting to go over
the petitions of the Lord's Prayer which we say each morning as
we begin our day, and see how fully they express our desire to
follow these same instructions. Then at night, when we look back
over the experiences of the day, we shall not be ashamed to tell
the Lord, as the returning apostles did, all we have done. And the
Lord will give us the further instruction we need.

In Luke this further instruction first takes the form of the one
miracle which is recorded in all four Gospels, and which we have
studied in the Gospel of Mark. We so often feel inadequate in the
face of an opportunity or obligation to give needed spiritual food
to our neighbors or to our children. How shall I explain New
Church teachings to my friends? How shall I answer my children's
questions? Our impulse is to send them to others for the answers,
as the apostles asked the Lord to send the multitude away into the
villages to buy food. But the Lord says to us as to the apostles:
"Give ye them to eat." However small our store of knowledge and
experience, we have something to give, and we shall always find
that as we try to give it, looking to the Lord for blessing, He will
multiply it so that it will more than meet the need. And as we
study the Word with the help which the Lord has provided for us
in the writings, we shall become better and better able to serve as
the Lord's apostles. Swedenborg tells us that influx is into our
knowledges (AC 4096).

Then in our chapter we come to a different type of instruction.
The story of the transfiguration is given in three Gospels. (The
other accounts are in Matthew 17:1-9 and Mark 9:2-10.) In all
three cases it is directly preceded by the story of the Lord's question and Peter's answer, the prophecy of the crucifixion and resurrection, and the teaching that whosoever will save his life shall lose
it. First comes the necessity of recognizing the Lord as God, then
the understanding of how He laid down His life for our salvation,
then the recognition of the fact that we must lay down our self

life if we are to be conjoined to Him, and finally the ability to see Him in His glorified humanity and to understand in the letter of the Word the teaching concerning Him.

AE 64[2] states the correspondence of the story of the transfiguration more clearly and more briefly than any paraphrase could possibly do: "The Lord took Peter, James, and John, because by them the church in respect to faith, charity, and the works of charity was represented; He took them 'into a high mountain' because 'mountain' signifies heaven; 'His face did shine as the sun' (Matthew 17:2) because 'face' signifies the interiors, and it did shine as the sun because His interiors were Divine, for the 'sun' is Divine love; 'His garments became white as the light' because 'garments' signify Divine truth proceeding from Him; the like is signified by 'light'. 'Moses' and 'Elijah' appeared, because the two signify the Word, 'Moses' the historical Word, and 'Elijah' the prophetical Word; 'a bright cloud overshadowed them' because 'a bright cloud' signifies the Word in the letter within which is the internal sense; 'a voice out of the cloud said, This is my beloved Son, in whom I am well pleased, hear ye Him,' because 'a voice out of a cloud' signifies Divine truth out of the Word, and 'beloved Son' the Lord's Divine Human. And because Divine truth is from Him, and thence all truth of the church, it was said out of the cloud 'in whom I am well pleased, hear ye Him.' " See here the passage from AC 5922[5] below. See also AE 195[18], AC 2576[19], and in AC the preface to Genesis 18.

In the story of the transfiguration, after the cloud passed they saw Jesus only. When we, through belief in the Lord as God with us and faithfulness to His teachings, have been led up into the mountain of spiritual vision where we can see Him in His glory as the internal sense of the Word reveals Him, we come to recognize the Lord alone as God and as the whole of the Word. The three apostles could not share this vision with others "in those days." Such a vision is the crown of faithful service. It cannot be shared with those who have not prepared themselves to see it. The actual Second Coming of the Lord was a revelation of the internal sense of the Word, and the transfiguration is thus a prophecy of the understanding of the Lord made possible by His Second Coming.

## From the Writings of Swedenborg

*Apocalypse Explained*, n. 821[2]: "The twelve apostles, like the twelve tribes of Israel, represented the church in the whole complex, or all things of truth and good, or all things of faith and charity; likewise . . . Peter, James, and John, signified faith, charity, and the works of charity, in their order; from which it follows that when they were together they represented these as one. It is said as one, because without charity there is no faith that is faith; and without works there is no charity that is charity."

*Arcana Coelestia*, n. 5922[5]: "In Luke, when Jesus was transfigured on the mountain . . . the Lord showed Peter, James, and John His Divine Human, such as it was and appeared in Divine light; and the form in which He was then seen presented to view the Word such as it is in the internal sense, thus such as is the Divine truth in heaven, for the Word is Divine truth for the use of the church. For this reason it was also presented to view at the same time that Moses and Elias talked with Him, for by Moses is represented the Law . . . and by Elias . . . the Prophets."

## Suggested Questions on the Lesson

J. What did the centurion ask of the Lord?  *to heal his servant*

J. What did the Lord say about the centurion?  *he had great faith*

P. What did the Lord do for the widow of Nain?  *restored son*

J. What had happened to John the Baptist?  *put in prison*

J. What did the messengers from John ask the Lord?  *are you Christ?*

J. What did the Lord tell them?  *tell John what you've seen*

J. What did He tell the people about John?  *great prophet*

P. How many apostles were there?  *twelve*

P. When the Lord sent them out, what powers did He give them?  *over devils, to heal*

J. What were they to preach?  *kingdom of God*

P. What were they to do?  *preach and heal in all cities*

P. What were they not to take with them?  *no "extras"*

P. Where were they to stay?  *in people's homes*

J. What were they to do if they were not received?  *shake off dust*

J. What miracle is part of our lesson?  *feeding five thousand*

J. What did it teach the apostles? *Lord's power to meet needs*

I. What did Peter believe about the Lord? *the Christ of God*

P. What three apostles were closest to the Lord? *Peter, James, John*

P. What vision were they allowed to see? *Lord dazzling white*

P. Who were seen talking with the Lord in the vision? *Moses, Elijah*

J. What is this vision called? *transfiguration*

I. To what does the number twelve correspond? *all good and truth in complex, all we can know and feel if we are trying to serve God and neighbor*

S. Why could only Peter, James, and John see the transfiguration? *they believed He was the Christ*

S. What do we learn from the Lord's instruction to His apostles about those who would and those who would not receive them? *we should share freely with those who accept, but not try to force belief*

# THE GOOD SAMARITAN
*Luke 10:25-42*

Although there are several chapters in Luke between this one and the entry into Jerusalem, we might note that from verse 51 of chapter 9 we learn that the Lord is already on His way to Jerusalem for the last time. The subject matter of these chapters is largely composed of parables, teaching for the disciples, a few miracles, and the exposing of the states in which the religious leaders were. The first part of chapter 10 contains a condemnation of those whose minds were closed, and the teacher should read it in preparation for the lawyer's question and the Lord's answer, which bring the matter into clear light.

———

### Doctrinal Points
*Worship of the Lord is the first essential of a good life.*
*All the truth we need can be found in the Word.*
*Faith must result in good works.*
*The good in everyone is the neighbor to be loved.*

———

### Notes for Parents
The parable of the Good Samaritan is given us only in the Gospel of Luke, but it has become one of the most familiar stories in the Bible. The lesson of simple, everyday helpfulness which comes to us immediately as we read it is one which every good, kindly person readily sees and accepts. But unfortunately people sometimes misunderstand and misuse this parable, making it teach that if one does the outward good deeds, he is a good man, even though he does not go to church or read the Bible or even believe in God. We have all heard people say, "I do all I can to help my neighbors; that's my religion." Have you ever realized that the person who says this is simply praising himself, and that self-praise is one of

the indications of inherent selfishness? We do many things for the sake of thinking well of ourselves and of being praised by our neighbors.

If you have read the whole lesson for today, you will see that the parable does not teach this at all. In the first place, the Lord made the lawyer admit that the two great commandments of the law are love to the Lord and love to the neighbor. In another Gospel the Lord says of the first of these, "This is the first and great commandment." A lawyer in those days was one who was learned in the laws of the Old Testament, and he had to be outwardly a devout worshiper of the Lord. So the lawyer had no fears for himself on that score. But he was not so sure on the second. The Lord used the Samaritan in the parable because the Jews despised the Samaritans. To them the "neighbor" could only be one of their own people. So you will notice that it was not the man who fell among thieves who is called the neighbor, but rather the Samaritan himself. The Lord was teaching the lawyer that the good in everyone is the neighbor to be loved, regardless of race or color or station.

And the Lord—knowing how prone we are to make things mean what we want them to mean—gives us immediately in the Word another story to prevent our misunderstanding the parable, for He foresaw that the time would come someday when people would be trying to "justify" themselves not for failing in love to the neighbor but for failing in love to the Lord. In the second story Martha was "distracted with much serving"—as many people are today—and the Lord told her that her sister Mary, who sat at His feet and heard His word, had chosen the better part. We do not really do good unless we constantly try to learn from the Lord what is really good, for only in this way can our self-love be driven out and the Lord's unselfish love come in and act through us in the world. Love to the Lord is the first and great commandment.

## Primary

It is suggested that the teacher divide the reading from the Word, first telling the story of the lawyer's question, explaining what a lawyer was in those days, then reading the parable and talking about it, and finally reading the story of Mary and Martha. In this last reading be sure the children understand what "that good part" means. Call their attention to the two great commandments, of which they will often hear. Be sure they understand what the parable means and what it does not mean. They should also know who the Samaritans were and why the Jews despised them.

The Lord came into the world to teach us the right way to live. One day a lawyer—a man who knew well the laws of the Old Testament—came to Him and asked Him, "Master, what shall I do to inherit eternal life?" That is, he wanted to know how to get to heaven. The Lord first showed him that he really knew what was necessary himself, because he knew the Old Testament. He asked the lawyer what the Scriptures taught was the most important thing for us to do. And the lawyer did know. He said, "Thou shalt love the Lord thy God with all thy heart, and with all thy soul, and with all thy strength, and with all thy mind; and thy neighbor as thyself." The Lord told him he was right. But the lawyer had not been living exactly according to this law of love to the Lord and the neighbor, and he tried—just as we sometimes do when we know we have been doing wrong—to find some excuse for himself. He asked the Lord, "And who is my neighbor?"

The Lord's answer was a parable.
A parable is a story made up to teach a lesson.
The priests and the Levites were the ones whom the Jews of that day most respected.
In the parable what did the priest and the Levite do?
What did the Samaritan do?
Do you remember who the Samaritans were?
The Jews despised the Samaritans.
What was this parable meant to teach the lawyer?
But the Lord knew that people might later misunderstand the parable.
So He gave us right afterward in the Word the story of Mary and Martha.
What did Martha do?
What did Mary do?
Which did the Lord say was doing the better thing?
We have to learn from the Lord how best to help our neighbor.

The Lord put this story in the Word right after the story of the Good Samaritan because He did not want us to make the mistake of thinking that just taking care of other people's bodies was what He meant by love and kindness. We have to learn from Him other things we should do for people also—things which will help them even more. We must love the Lord first or we cannot do any good at all.

---

## Junior

There are two simple and needed lessons here for the Juniors: the obvious lesson in the parable, and the lesson pointed out by the last verse of the chapter. The proper relation between the two is brought out by the order of the two great commandments. The children might well learn verse 27.

How many apostles were there?
What does *apostle* mean?
What powers were given the apostles?
What was their message?
Who were the three apostles closest to the Lord?
What vision was given them?
To whom did the Lord speak the parable of our lesson today?
A lawyer in those days was one who knew the laws in the books of Moses.
What did the lawyer ask the Lord?

The Lord made him answer his own question from the law. The laws he quoted are found in Deuteronomy 6:5 and Leviticus 19:18.

What do we call these two laws?

In verse 29, to "justify himself" means to excuse himself for not fully keeping the law. He apparently felt that he had kept the first law, but was not so sure about the second. He hoped the Lord would tell him that his neighbor meant people of his own religion and class. Instead, the Lord told him the parable and then again made him answer his own question.

Jerusalem is built high among the hills, while Jericho is on the low plain near the Dead Sea. The distance between them is about eighteen miles and the road is rough, steep, and lined with jagged rocks among which robbers used to lurk and spring out at travelers.

The priest was one of those most admired and respected by the people, and so was the Levite. The Samaritan, on the other hand, belonged to a group of people who were despised and hated because, you remember, they had been brought in long ago to supplant the Israelites when they were carried away captive by the Assyrians. By the parable the Lord made the lawyer see and acknowledge that it is mercy and kindness which counts, and not race or position or learning.

A *neighbor* means "a near one." It is love which really brings people near together. Selfishness always drives people apart. We are good neighbors when we think kindly of other people and try to help them in right ways. This is one of the lessons of the parable. For you notice that it is not the man who fell among thieves who is called the neighbor, but the good Samaritan himself. We should look for the good in other people and love it and try to help it in every possible way.

Another lesson we may find in this parable is that we often need help ourselves. Do you see how the journey of the man from Jerusalem to Jericho pictures times when we go down from high states—from our ideals and our good resolutions—to the lower plane of our daily work and play? Do we ever "fall among thieves" on the way? Very often temptations take away from us all our good thoughts and intentions and leave us half dead spiritually. Then we need the help of a good Samaritan, someone who will lift us up again and heal us with love and good advice—the oil and wine—and carry us along until we get back our strength. This is one of the things our parents are doing for us constantly because they love us.

Our lesson does not end with the parable of the Good Samaritan. The people then understood the lesson the Lord was trying to teach in it, but the Lord knew that in later times there would be some people who might try to make an excuse of this very parable. You know that there are many people today who do not read the Bible or go to church or take any interest in religion, and some of them point to certain kind things they do for others and say they are like the good Samaritan whom the Lord praised, and that the parable teaches that external good works are all the Lord requires of us. So the Lord, when He wrote the Word, put the story of Mary and Martha immediately after the parable of the Good Samaritan.

When the Lord was in the home of Mary and Martha, what was Martha doing?
What was Mary doing?
What did Martha ask the Lord to do?
What did the Lord tell her?

The Lord did not tell Martha that it was wrong to do the work of the house. All the external services we perform for each other are useful and have their place in our lives. But there is something more important: We should make the most of every opportunity we have to learn of the Lord. If we do not try to learn what the Lord has to say to us, we shall never be able to help our neighbors in the really important things of life. And when we do the outward good works, if we are not doing them from love to the Lord, we are giving ourselves the credit for them, and that takes all the real good out of them.

### Intermediate

The correspondence of the parable should be taken up in some detail. Then discuss the story of Mary and Martha and the relation between the two stories as they illustrate the teaching of the two great commandments.

This is one of the most familiar of the Lord's parables, but it is found only in the Gospel of Luke. The lawyer and his question are found also in Matthew 22:35, and there the Lord Himself answers with the two great commandments. In Matthew the lesson is connected with the question of the Lord's authority, but in Luke it is related to our personal life. The lesson here taught the lawyer was that mercy and kindness are the important thing—not race, or class, or learning. He had to admit that the despised Samaritan might be a better man than the priest or the Levite. We should notice, however, that it is the Samaritan who is called the neighbor, which places the emphasis on his worthiness to be loved.

Every one of the Lord's parables has an obvious lesson of this sort which anyone can see and take to heart. But there is much more to be drawn from the study of their correspondence. Jerusalem, where the temple was, pictures the church, or states of spiritual insight and resolution in which all of us are at times. We cannot stay in these states, however, without being called upon to do something about it. We have to go back to the low plane of every-day living where we are to carry out our good resolutions. The thieves which lurk by the wayside are the evil impulses and wrong thoughts stirred up in us by the hells which are likely to attack us suddenly and rob us of our high ideas and intentions, leaving us half dead spiritually. Doesn't this very thing happen to every one of us over and over again?

The priest and the Levite, representatives of the corrupt church, picture knowledge of what is right and true held in the mind only, with no warm affection for doing good. Such knowledge does not help us when temptation attacks. The Samaritan represents the simple desire to do good which comes to our aid. He binds up our wounds, pouring in oil and wine—love and truth—and mounts us on his own beast, which pictures reasoning from a basis of simple goodness, and brings us to a haven where we can regain our strength. And he promises to do more for us if we have need of it.

So the Lord pointed to goodness as the neighbor to be loved. Swedenborg tells us that it is the good in everyone which we are to regard as our neighbor. It follows from this, for one thing, that to love our enemies is not to condone the evil in them but to try to check it, and to recognize that there is also good in them which we may help to bring out and increase if we try. People are drawn together by similar qualities of good. So in heaven people who are close together in their affections are close together externally— neighbors indeed.

Some people have pointed to this parable as teaching that the only thing really required of us is external good works, but this is not what it means. The very next incident in the Word makes this clear. Notice this particularly. If we will read carefully enough, the

Lord always helps us to avoid misunderstanding His teaching in the Word. Mary and Martha were both good women. But Martha's thought was centered on ministering to the Lord's bodily needs, while Mary sat at His feet and heard His words. When Martha asked the Lord to send Mary to help her in the external good works, the Lord told her that Mary had chosen the better part— the one thing really needful.

If we do not use all our opportunities to learn what the Lord has to say to us, we shall make many mistakes, and often do more harm than good. To help a bad person in external ways may merely be helping him to continue in his evil course. And if we do not care to learn of the Lord, we fall into the thought that the "good works" we do are evidence that we are good. We praise ourselves and condemn people who are not doing just what we do. So our good works are not inwardly good at all.

If we can keep in mind that it is the good in other people which is the neighbor to be helped, and that we can do nothing good except as we look to the Lord for guidance and power, we shall become better and better able to serve both the Lord and the neighbor, and really help to bring about the Lord's kingdom on earth.

### Basic Correspondences

| | | |
|---|---|---|
| Jerusalem | = | a spiritual state |
| Jericho | = | the plane of outward thought and activity |
| thieves | = | wrong thoughts and desires |
| oil | = | love |
| wine | = | spiritual truth |

**Senior**

The lesson for this class should be centered on the lawyer's question and the Lord's way of answering it. The young people need to know Swedenborg's doctrine of the neighbor and what it means in our daily decisions.

The parable of the Good Samaritan is often misused. For the

lawyer who wanted to "justify" himself in his selfish esteem it taught the lesson that mercy and kindness are better than position or learning or birth, and that the neighbor to be loved was everyone who was good. This is one of the true lessons of the parable. But people sometimes assume that this parable teaches that external kindness is the only thing needed to make a man good. They say, "There are better people outside the church than in it," and use this as an excuse for not supporting the church. It is true that some people outside of the church are better than some people in it, but this is only because there are people who are outside the church only because they have not been able to find it, and because the church is not free from hypocrites whose profession of religious belief is lip service only.

The priest and the Levite in the parable do not represent the true church and its doctrines, but the corrupt church, which had forgotten the "weightier matters of the law": justice, mercy, and faith. They picture knowledge of what is right held in the mind merely, with no warm affection for doing good. Such knowledge does not help us in times of temptation, when selfish desires and false reasonings seek to rob us of our good resolutions. Only the simple determination to do good, the Samaritan, can be counted on to help us.

That the parable does not teach the sole importance of external good works is evident from the story of Mary and Martha which follows immediately on purpose to save us from just such a mistake. Martha was "distracted with much serving," and the Lord rebuked her gently, telling her that Mary had chosen the better part in sitting at His feet and hearing His word. Good works must be done under the guidance of the Lord's truth or they are done from self and are not really good.

What the Lord points out to us in the parable is the fact that goodness is the neighbor to be loved—not any individual as such. Swedenborg tells us that it is the good in everyone which we are to regard as our neighbor and to love. This applies to our love for our friends: we are not to let our love close our eyes to their faults, if we can help them to overcome them. True love of the neighbor requires of parents that they recognize and seek to correct their children's faults. And when we are told to love our enemies, it does not mean that we are to excuse and condone evil, but to try to check it and at the same time to look for and foster all that is good in them. In this world people are drawn together by similar states of good, and in heaven such people are neighbors in fact.

This teaching is much needed in the world today. Not only every individual, but every nation and every race has its good qualities and its bad ones. Love to the neighbor demands that, instead of condemning others because they are different from ourselves or of pretending that they are not different—as the inner enemies of race prejudice sometimes do—we must love the good and hate the evil whether it is in others or in ourselves. And we must always keep in mind that love to the neighbor is the second of the two great commandments. The first is love to the Lord. In the Gospel of Matthew, where the Lord Himself speaks these two commandments, He says of love to the Lord, "This is the first and great commandment." So the story of Mary and Martha is tied in with the opening verses of our lesson.

―――――

### Adult

Discussion topics for this class might be: (1) the order of the two great commandments, (2) the meaning of the parable for the lawyer and its meaning for us, (3) the practical applications of the story of Mary and Martha, and (4) the wonderful balance which the Lord always preserves for us if we are careful to study each story in the Word in its context.

With this lesson we enter upon the last period of the Lord's life. The Lord is on His way to Jerusalem for the final scenes of His earthly career (Luke 9:51). The greater part of the teaching in the next few chapters is in the form of parables, most of which are not found in any of the other Gospels.

In our lesson for today the teaching of the Scriptures is reduced at the outset to its simplest terms. The lawyer—we must remember that the law then was primarily the Scriptures—asks his question and is directed to the Scriptures for his answer. In Matthew (22:34-40) the Lord, instead of the lawyer, answers the question and emphasizes love to the Lord by saying of it, "This is the first and great commandment." In Luke He approves the lawyer's answer and says, "This do, and thou shalt live." Love to the Lord and love to the neighbor are a summary of the teaching of the whole Word. Of the two tables on which the ten commandments were originally given, the first contained those relating to our duty to the Lord and the second those relating to our duty to the neighbor. We cannot break the first great commandment and keep the second, nor break the second and keep the first. It is generally recognized today that love to the Lord is not genuine unless it expresses itself in justice and kindness to the neighbor—nothing is more common than criticism of a church because some of its members show a lack of justice and charity in their outward dealings. But it is often asserted that love to the neighbor is possible without love to the Lord. ("So-and-so hasn't any use for religion, but he's always doing things for other people." "There are better people outside of the church than in it." "I always try to treat other people right, and I'll take my chance at salvation with anybody in the church.") The immediate popularity in its day of the poem by Leigh Hunt (1838) *Abou Ben Adhem*, in which love to the Lord is made a sort of involuntary appendage of love to the neighbor, testifies to this feeling. But the fact is that no one can do genuine good to the neighbor without recognition of his dependence upon the Lord for the will and the power to do good, as well as upon the Lord's guidance as to what is good. If a man does not do good from love to the Lord, he does it from love of self, which renders his goodness spurious. People reject this teaching at first, but it is not hard to demonstrate. Those brought up in orderly, respectable homes find it much pleasanter and more profitable to fulfill—even at the cost of some personal inconvenience—the ordinary external requirements of civilized neighborly living which will make them liked and respected in their community than to be openly selfish, miserly, and uncharitable. They like the approval of their neighbors and they like to feel pleased and satisfied with themselves. We remember the story of the rich young man (Matthew 19:16-26). He had kept all the commandments but turned away when the Lord told him to sell all that he had and follow him. To sell all that we have represents giving up the sense of our own goodness and wisdom. And without looking to the Lord for guidance we cannot know what is the neighbor nor how we should express our love for him. The lawyer in our story unconsciously showed this and confessed his own ignorance when he asked, "And who is my neighbor?"

The Lord's answer, the parable of the Good Samaritan, which is recorded only in Luke, is one of the best known and most frequently referred to of the parables, but its lesson is not always carefully analyzed. It is often cited as evidence that we should look outside of the church for true charity and also that the essential of love to the neighbor is caring for the bodily wants of others. We like to imagine ourselves as filling the role of the Good Samaritan. In truth, however, we are all much more likely to play the role of the man who fell among thieves.

A brief study of the correspondence of the story will repay us. "To go down from Jerusalem to Jericho" is to go from "the truth of doctrine to the good of life" (AE 458[10]), that is, to try to put into actual practice something that we have learned of the Lord and His will. On this journey we are all often attacked by our own selfish desires and the false reasonings that come from them, and are robbed of our garments of truth, weakened in our good resolution, and fall by the roadside half dead—with very little of our spiritual vitality left. The priest and the Levite in a good sense represent worship of the Lord and the good of charity; so in a bad sense as here they picture the opposite, namely those who have no love to the Lord and no love to the neighbor (AE 444[14]), who are indifferent to our spiritual condition. The Samaritan pictures those who are in "the affection of truth" (AC 9057[2]), that is, in the love of practicing what truth teaches, or "those who are in the good of charity toward the neighbor" (AE 375[42]). Such people can and do help us, pointing out to us good and true things—the oil and wine—to strengthen our shaken resolution, carrying us along so far as their own understanding permits, and bringing us to those who can give us more instruction and help. An inn signifies a place of instruction. Thus the whole story is a picture of spiritual service. Even in the letter it should be noted that it is the Samaritan and not the injured man who is called the neighbor. Swedenborg tells us (AC 6708) that the Samaritan is called the neighbor because he exercised the good of charity and that everyone is our neighbor in accordance with the quality of his love to the Lord (AC 6711). That is, it is love to the Lord in a man that is the "neighbor" to whom we are to do good, and in all our dealings with others we are to act in such a way as to foster love to the Lord in them. With this end in view we shall not give alms indiscriminately to everyone who asks, for to give alms to an evil man is to make it more possible for him to go on in his evil course. AC 6703 to 6712 states the general principle very clearly, as does TCR 428. When the Lord made the lawyer acknowledge that the despised Samaritan might be more his neighbor than the priest or the Levite, he taught that genuine goodness is to be recognized wherever it is found.

And lest one should feel justified in misinterpreting the parable of the Good Samaritan, the parable is immediately followed in the Word by the story of Mary and Martha. "Martha was cumbered about much serving." How often we are so distracted by our external activities—useful though they be—that we think we have no time to sit at the Lord's feet and hear His word! We see these activities as duties, as services to the Lord, just as Martha was preparing for the Lord's physical entertainment. But we become so "careful and troubled about many things" that we lose our sense of proportion. Churches sometimes become so busy with external service that they almost wholly neglect the study and teaching of the Word. It is a common plea that it is of no use to talk to men of spiritual things until their physical needs are met, but not only is this not true (for many have found peace and joy in spiritual things in spite of physical want): if we take this attitude, we shall never finish the work of supplying physical wants and never find the right time to supply the spiritual. The Lord teaches this elsewhere in connection with this same Mary, when she anointed Him with costly ointment which Judas thought would better have been sold and the money given to the poor (John 12:3). Read also the Lord's words in Mark 14:7. To Martha He said, "But one thing is needful: and Mary hath chosen that good part." Love to the Lord is the first and great commandment. We cannot do good to the neighbor unless we learn of the Lord what is good and perform our services in His name instead of in our own. "What doth the Lord require of thee, but to do justly, and to love mercy, and to walk humbly with thy God?" Further helpful numbers are AE 240, 962; AR 316; TCR 287, 407-411; NJHD 84-90.

## From the Writings of Swedenborg

*The New Jerusalem and Its Heavenly Doctrine*, n. 85: "It is a common opinion at this day that every man is equally the neighbor, and that benefits are to be conferred on every one who needs assistance; but it is in the interest of Christian prudence to examine well the quality of a man's life, and to exercise charity to him accordingly. The man of the internal church exercises his charity with discrimination, consequently with intelligence; but the man of the external church, because he is not able thus to discern things, does it indiscriminately."

*True Christian Religion*, n. 428: "Doing good to an evil-doer is like giving bread to a devil, which he turns into poison; for in the hands of the devil all bread is poison, or if it is not, he turns it into poison by using good deeds as allurements to evil. It is also like handing to an enemy a sword with which he may kill someone; or like giving the shepherd's staff to a wolfish man to guide the sheep to pasture, who, after he has obtained it, drives them away from the pasture to a desert, and there slaughters them; or like giving public authority to a robber, who studies and watches for plunder only, according to the richness and abundance of which he dispenses the laws and executes judgments."

## Suggested Questions on the Lesson

J. What is an apostle? *one sent out*

P. How many apostles were there? *twelve*

J. When the Lord sent out the apostles, what were they to preach? *kingdom of God*

J. How were they to be cared for? *by those they served*

P. How did the Lord help the apostles to feed the multitude? *multiplied loaves and fish*

I. What question did the Lord ask of the apostles? *who do people say I am?*

I. What was Peter's answer? *the Christ of God*

P. Who were the three apostles closest to the Lord? *Peter, James, John*

P. What vision were they allowed to see? *transfiguration*

J. In our lesson for today what does the lawyer ask the Lord? *how may I inherit eternal life?*

P. To what does the Lord refer him for his answer? *Scriptures*

J. What answer does the lawyer find? *love Lord and neighbor*

P. What question does the lawyer ask to "justify" himself? *who is my neighbor?*

P. With what parable does the Lord answer him? *Good Samaritan*

P. Where was the man going when he fell among thieves? *Jerusalem to Jericho*

P. What two men passed him by without helping him? *priest, Levite*

P. Who did help him? *Samaritan*

J. Who were the Samaritans? *people Assyrians had brought in*

J. What did this parable teach the lawyer? *to help anyone in need*

J. What was the difference between Martha and Mary? *first served, latter listened*

P. Which one did the Lord say had chosen the better part? *Mary*

S. Why are we given this story immediately after the parable of the Good Samaritan? *to help us learn how to love the neighbor*

# THE SCRIBES AND PHARISEES
*Luke 11*

With the younger classes we have chosen the latter part of the chapter for emphasis because it is less familiar than the portion on prayer, but with the older classes both parts should be taken up. Verse 33 may be used to bind the two parts together, for it is only as we turn to the Lord as our Father and seek His guidance and help that we can keep the eye of our soul "single" or clear. The scribes and Pharisees are the classic example of what *not* to do with our religion.

---

### Doctrinal Points
*The Lord's deeds showed the divine within Him.*
*The Lord constantly used passages from the Old Testament.*
*Faith comes through knowledge of the Word.*
*It is the heart which most needs cleansing.*

---

### Notes for Parents
We know that the Lord, when He was in the world, gave us a wonderful example of love and self-sacrifice and daily service. We know that He healed people of many diseases and raised the dead. We think of Him as tender and gentle, loving and forgiving. But there were two groups of people whom the Lord condemned in no uncertain terms. They were the scribes and Pharisees, the people who were learned in the law of Moses and made a great show of religion, while at heart they were proud and selfish and hard, expecting everyone to admire and serve them. He called them hypocrites.

Perhaps you have heard of the "unforgivable sin." According to Matthew 12:31 it is blasphemy against the Holy Spirit. People have sometimes worried a good deal about it because they did not know just what it meant and were afraid they might commit the unforgivable sin without knowing it. The Holy Spirit is the spirit of truth proceeding from the Lord to enlighten us and show us what is right and wrong. To blaspheme against the Holy Spirit is to know what the truth is and refuse to try to do it. The scribes and Pharisees really knew they should accept the Lord, but they would not acknowledge it because they did not want to change themselves. They could not deny the Lord's power, for they saw His miracles; so they said His power came from "Beelzebub the chief of the devils." They wanted to appear good, but they did not want to be good.

This sin is unforgivable not because the Lord is unforgiving, but because the person who acts this way will not let the Lord's forgiving spirit enter his heart. This is why we pray, "Forgive us our debts as we forgive our debtors." If we refuse to listen to the truth or to acknowledge it as truth when we do hear it, the truth cannot reach us to purify our hearts and minds and lead us to the Lord. To His disciples, who believed and obeyed Him, the Lord said, "Ask, and it shall be given you; seek, and ye shall find; knock, and it shall be opened unto you." The hypocrite closes the door of his heart and mind against the Lord. It was the scribes and Pharisees who finally crucified the Lord.

If you will read this chapter thoughtfully, you will find that each part of it—and it can be divided into several apparently separate parts—has something to contribute to the general teaching that if we would be good people, we must keep our hearts and minds constantly in a state of willing reception of the Lord's truth. It is not enough to do the outward good deeds which make us popular with our neighbors. Goodness is something within us which can come only from the Lord. The Lord speaks to us today in His Word just as really as He spoke to the people in Palestine nearly two thousand years ago. Are we among those who hear Him gladly, or do we close our minds to His teachings in the Word because it might say something we did not want to hear? The chapter speaks to us all.

## Primary

The children should be told who the scribes and Pharisees were and led to see the meaning of verses 33 and 34. The teacher might read as an illustration the story of the Pharisee and the publican from Luke 18:9-14.

When the Lord was on earth, the good people welcomed Him and listened eagerly to all He had to tell them about the right way to live, because they wanted to do right.

You know that when you are feeling like being good, you ask your parents all kinds of questions and listen to what they tell you and understand it; and if you will think back a little, you will realize that those are the times when you are happiest. Isn't it too bad that we are not always like that?

But you know that there are times when you don't like to hear what your parents say to you and don't want to understand it. These are times when you are feeling like having your own way and doing something you want to do whether it is right or not.

So when the Lord was on earth, there were many people who did not want to listen to Him and who refused to try to understand what He told them, because they were used to having their own way and did not want to change it. These people even said that the Lord's power came from Beelzebub, which is another name for the devil. If they had admitted that it was the power of God, they would have had to believe Him because they had always pretended to be especially religious.

The scribes were men who spent their lives studying and copying the Old Testament and teaching people the law.

And the Pharisees were a sect who pretended to be very strict keepers of the law.

Both these groups knew all the prophecies about the coming of the Messiah. You would think they would have been the first to welcome the Lord when he came.

But they had become used to having everybody look up to them, and they could not bear to have the people turning to anyone else for instruction.

So they tried in every way to prove that Jesus was not the Messiah.

They said His power came from the devil instead of from God.

They knew the Scriptures, but they covered up their real meaning with their own ideas.

They were like a person who covers up a candle so that it can give no light.
What complaint was made by the Pharisee who invited the Lord to dinner?
What did the Lord tell him?
The Pharisees were very careful to pay their tithes or dues to the temple.
What did the Lord say they had overlooked?
Of what did He accuse the lawyers?

We should always listen when our parents are trying to tell us what is right, and be willing to see and understand what is true instead of just seeing what we want to see. Then the eyes of our souls will be "single"—which means pure—instead of evil. The truth which the Lord gives us is like a light by which we see how to live. We should not want to cover it up as the scribes and Pharisees did. This is what verse 33 is saying to us.

Then let us read the verse which follows it in the Bible. [Read Luke 11:34.]
You know that we all say "I see" when we mean "I understand."
The verse means that if we keep our understanding clear and pure, our minds will have light.
But if we let selfishness cloud the eye of our minds, we cannot see what is right.

―――――

## Junior

The Juniors should learn well who the scribes and Pharisees were, why they refused to recognize the Lord, and why the Lord condemned them. They should also learn the word *hypocrite* and what it means. The Bible references in their notes should be looked up.

Our chapter for today begins with the story of how the Lord gave us the Lord's Prayer. The form in Luke is not so familiar to us as that in Matthew, but there are two things about it which we should especially notice. One is that the last sentence in verse 2 gives the order "as in heaven, so in earth," which is actually the order in the original Greek in both Matthew and Luke.* If we are

―――――

*This phrase, however, occurs only in Codex Vaticanus in the Luke version. Later versions omit "Thy will be done . . ." Cf. AC 2009[2], where it is cited as above, although the explanation then renders it "on earth as in the heavens." AE 1217[2] also quotes the Matthew version as "on earth as in the heavens," but then states that "the Lord always rules both heaven and earth." —*Ed.*

to do the Lord's will on earth—in our outward lives—we must first write His will in the heavens within—our minds and hearts. The second is the use of the word *sins* instead of *debts*. As you may know, in many churches the form used is, "Forgive us our trespasses, as we forgive those who trespass against us." This is not the form given in either Gospel, although Matthew introduces it in the Lord's explanation of the prayer. We often do need to pray for forgiveness of our sins or trespasses, but we always need to pray, "Forgive us our debts," for we are in debt to the Lord for everything we have.

Read verses 5 to 10 and then read Matthew 6:7-8, which are the verses just before the Lord's Prayer in that Gospel. These seem to say different things, don't they? Now read Matthew 7:21-23. You see, when the Lord is speaking to His disciples, He is speaking to those who are trying to learn from Him and to obey Him. When we are His true disciples, He is always ready to hear and answer our prayers, even though sometimes for our good the answer has to be, "No," just as it does when we ask our parents for things which they know would do us harm. In the Gospel of Matthew the passage about the Lord's Prayer is part of the sermon on the mount, which was preached to a great crowd of people, who were in various states of life.

Most of our chapter today is about the Lord and the scribes and Pharisees. The scribes or "lawyers" were those who were educated in the law of Moses. They spent their lives reading and copying the books of the Old Testament, and they were the ones who told the people what the law said. Read Matthew 2:3-6. The Pharisees were a sect who claimed to be more religious than any others and who made a great show of their religion and expected to be looked up to by everyone because of it. See what is said of them in Matthew 23:5-7. These two groups had added a great many laws and regulations of their own to the laws of Moses so as to keep people under their own control, and the people—most of whom could not read—had no idea what was really the law of the Lord. The scribes and Pharisees of course knew all the prophecies of the coming of the Messiah, and they should have recognized and welcomed the Lord but, like Herod, they did not really want any ruler in the land instead of themselves.

Where did they say the Lord's power came from?
What did the Lord tell them?
In verse 16 what did His enemies ask for?
What sign did He say they would have?

In Matthew 12:39-40 you will find what He meant by the "sign of Jonas the prophet." He was referring to His own coming crucifixion and His resurrection on the third day. *Jonas* is a Greek form of *Jonah*. The story of Jonah and the people of Nineveh is found in the third chapter of the book of Jonah. The "queen of the south" means the queen of Sheba. If you do not remember that story, read it in I Kings 10:1-10. You see that if we are to understand what the Lord says to us in the Gospels, we need to study the Old Testament.

When in verse 33 the Lord says that a candle should not be lit and then covered up so that the light cannot be seen, He is referring to the way in which the scribes and Pharisees had covered up the truths of the Word so that the people could not see them. In this verse, the translation should be *lamp* and *lampstand* instead of *candle* and *candlestick*. They did not have candles in those days. Their lamps were dishes formed like a very shallow pitcher with a handle. They burned oil in them, which came up to the spout in a wick so that the flame was at the spout. We should also know that the word *single* in verse 34 is an old word for *clear* or *pure*. The Lord's teaching here is that it is selfishness which prevents our seeing the truth. We should remember this when we are refusing to recognize what we ought to do because we want to have our own way instead. We are all sometimes like the scribes and Pharisees.

The Pharisees saw that the people believed in the Lord. So they often pretended to listen to Him, but it was only in the hope that they could find something in His words or actions which they could tell the people was wrong. So in our chapter one of the Pharisees invited the Lord to dinner.

What did the Lord do which he objected to?
What did the Lord tell him?
What did He say about tithes?

The tithe was the tenth of their produce of every kind, which they were supposed to give to the service of the Lord. The Pharisees made a great show of paying their tithes.

What did the Lord call the scribes and Pharisees?

A hypocrite is a person who pretends to be what he really is not, so that people will praise and respect him. We should try to be good all through—in our thoughts and feelings as well as in our acts. The Lord sees our hearts and minds just as He saw those of the scribes and Pharisees.

---

## Intermediate

Center the lesson on the correspondence of verses 33 and 34, using the disciples of the first part of the chapter as an illustration of those whose eye is "single" and the scribes and Pharisees as an illustration of those whose eye is "evil."

From our lesson in Malachi you may remember that the coming of the Lord into the world would be to the wicked like a consuming fire which would burn them up. In our lesson today we find how this prophecy worked out. The scribes and Pharisees in the Gospel story typify that element which at heart hated all the things the Lord came to teach, although outwardly they posed as the most strictly religious of all the people. The scribes—also called lawyers—were the learned men who studied the Old Testament and were regarded as authorities in the law of Moses. The Pharisees were a sect who prided themselves on their strict observance of the law. But both these groups loved the power they had over the people, and they had added many regulations of their own to the law in order to keep the people in subjection to themselves. As long as the people looked to them for instruction, their position was secure, but when first John the Baptist and then the Lord Himself appeared, and the people began to listen to them, the scribes and Pharisees felt their hold on the people weakening, and they "burned" with anger and with hatred of the Lord. They knew the prophecies and should have recognized Him as the Messiah, but, like all of us at times, they believed what they wanted to believe.

This is what is meant by verses 33 and 34 of our chapter. Light is one of the principal symbols of truth. A candle or lamp by whose means light is given forth represents doctrine. "Thy word is a lamp unto my feet, and a light unto my path." Do you remember how the Lord, when He appeared in Revelation to the apostle John, was seen in the midst of seven candlesticks? In Revelation 1:20 we read: "The seven candlesticks which thou sawest are the seven churches." It is the church which is supposed to teach true doctrine so that its people will be able to walk in the light instead of stumbling in the darkness of ignorance. The scribes and Pharisees, who considered themselves to be the church, covered up true doctrine instead of teaching it. Their own self-love had closed their minds to the truth even when it came to them in the person of the Lord Himself.

The eye, you remember, corresponds to the understanding. When the understanding is not clouded with selfish thoughts, the eye is "single," that is, pure or clear. But when selfishness governs the understanding, the light of truth cannot penetrate. You know how this is from your own experience. When you are trying to have your own way about something, your mind is so busy finding reasons why you should be allowed to do what you want that you will not listen to the simple truth. The scribes and Pharisees had to admit the Lord's power to work miracles, but in order that they might not have to admit that He really was the Messiah they claimed that His power came from the devil (verse 15). We should remember this verse, because it shows us how far one can go when he is trying to have his own way, and also it shows us that miracles do not produce faith.

The Lord's description in our chapter of the character of the scribes and Pharisees is summed up in the word *hypocrites* in verse 44. The same charges are made in more detail in the twenty-third chapter of Matthew. In both Gospels there are two charges which most of us remember better than the others. One is that they are careful to pay their tithes but forget to practice the virtues that the tithes stand for—"judgment and the love of God." The other is that they cleanse the outside of the cup and platter, but leave the inside full of wickedness. The cup, which held wine, pictures the knowledges we have in our minds which are capable of containing spiritual truth. The platter, which held food, pictures things in the mind which should contain goodness. So you see how exactly this verse describes the hypocrisy of the scribes and Pharisees. They had all the necessary knowledges from the Scriptures, but they had let their selfish desires and reasonings fill them up so that there was no place for truth or goodness.

There are many other interesting things in this chapter. It gives us, for one thing, our second version of the Lord's Prayer. You will notice that it differs slightly from the version in Matthew. The translation "as in heaven, so in earth" is a more accurate rendering of the Greek than "on earth as it is in heaven" (see footnote to Junior notes). Swedenborg tells us that unless it is the desire of the heart and mind—the heavens of the soul—to do the Lord's will, our outward doing of it—the earth—is not sincere. So this, too, is related to the general subject of our chapter. The parable of the householder and the promise in verses 9 and 10 are addressed to true disciples of the Lord.

The "sign of Jonas the prophet" mentioned in verse 29 means, as we learn from Matthew 12:40, the Lord's resurrection on the third day after the crucifixion. *Jonas* is a Greek form of *Jonah*. We remember that Jonah, after three days in the belly of the great fish, was cast up alive on the shore, and now we see that this was one of the prophecies of the Lord's life on earth. The story of Jonah and the Ninevites is told in chapter 3 of the book of Jonah. In verse 31 the "queen of the south" means the queen of Sheba. The story of her visit to Solomon is told in I Kings 10:1-10.

*Basic Correspondences*
a candle or lamp  =  doctrine

| a lampstand | = | the church |
| a cup | = | a containant for spiritual truth |
| a platter | = | a containant for goodness |
| the eye | = | the understanding |

## Senior

The lessons of sincerity and humility are important for your young people. They are often tempted to pretend to feel and think as the rest of their "crowd" does. Hypocrisy may be an expression of cowardice in that case. If they can be led to see it as a danger signal in themselves, they will be led to do independent thinking and will gain in spiritual strength.

When the Lord was in the world, His severest condemnations were addressed to the scribes and Pharisees, the two religious groups who held the position of highest honor among the laity. Both groups were outwardly devoted to the study and keeping of the law of Moses. The Lord charged them with hypocrisy, and their attitude toward Him proved them to be hypocrites. For they knew all the prophecies concerning the Messiah and pretended to be looking forward to His coming, and yet when one appeared who fulfilled all the prophecies, they were unwilling even to consider whether He might be the Messiah because His presence and teaching were a threat to their own power over the people. They even said His ability to work miracles—which they could not deny—came from the devil.

We all dislike hypocrisy when it is uncovered. But we do not always stop to think what it really is or to ask whether we ourselves may be guilty of it. In *True Christian Religion*, n. 147 Swedenborg says: "It is as yet scarcely known in the church that in all of man's will and thought and his consequent action and speech, there is an internal and an external, and that from infancy man is carefully taught to speak from the external, however the internal may dissent; and that this is the origin of simulation, flattery, and hypocrisy; and thus man becomes double-minded. But he alone is single-minded whose external thinks and speaks and wills and acts from the internal; and such are meant by the 'simple (single)' in the Word (as in Luke 8:15; 11:34; and elsewhere). Nevertheless these are wiser than those who are double-minded." This does not mean that we should always be in the attitude of "calling a spade a spade," as some rather disagreeable people enjoy doing. We remember that our first step toward regeneration is reformation of the outward conduct, even against our natural inclinations, and that the Lord makes use of our natural desire to be liked and praised to help us in the beginning of this reformation. You recall the story of the quails and manna in the wilderness, and that the quails represented natural satisfaction from doing right. But this is only the beginning, and there is nothing genuine about our outward goodness until we reach the point where it comes from the heart. This is why in the original Greek in Matthew as well as in Luke the petition in the Lord's Prayer reads, "Thy will be done as in heaven so in earth" (see footnote to Junior notes), just as it is translated in verse 2 of our chapter [KJV]. This is the true order of doing good and the state of mind and life for which we should pray.

The first part of our chapter emphasized the Lord's unselfish love, His willingness to give all good things to those who look to Him for goodness. This is pointed up by the miracle—told in a single verse—of the dumb man who was able to speak when the Lord had cast out the devil who possessed him. You remember from the story of Zacharias that dumbness represents inability to "confess" the Lord. The scribes and Pharisees saw this miracle. They could not deny the fact. It should have led them to acknowledge the Lord themselves. But their minds were so clouded by thoughts of self-interest that they said the Lord's power came from Beelzebub. Their inner state is described by the Lord in the story of the house that is swept and garnished only that it may become the abode of seven devils instead of one.

All through the chapter the Lord points out to us by one means after another that it is our will—our free choice—which determines whether we acknowledge the truth or not. The men of Nineveh and the queen of Sheba were Gentiles. They did not have the direct knowledge of the Lord in the Scriptures which the scribes and

Pharisees had. Yet they recognized wisdom when they heard it because they were humble-minded before the Lord while the scribes and Pharisees did not recognize the Lord Himself.

In verse 33 the Lord is referring to the treatment His truth had received at the hands of the church. A candlestick—or lampstand, as it should be translated—is a symbol of the church, whose office is to hold the truth high so that men will receive its light. And the next verses sum up the lesson in parable form. Then follow the Lord's specific complaints against the Pharisees and the scribes—or lawyers—which are familiar to us. They are given in more detail in the twenty-third chapter of Matthew.

Young people just starting out in life need to take this lesson very much to heart. Suppose we put it in this way: Whenever I catch myself behaving toward other people in a way which is contrary to the way in which I feel, it is time to take stock of my feelings and try to straighten myself out inside—to give the inside of the cup and platter a thorough cleansing.

## Adult

The whole subject of hypocrisy is an interesting discussion topic. We all condemn hypocrisy, and we should recognize that we are all hypocrites to some extent. The quotations from *True Christian Religion* and *Apocalypse Explained* given in the notes below help us to think this problem through and to meet it in ourselves. The question of the limits we should set upon our judgment of others is also important.

Our chapter begins with the giving of the Lord's Prayer. We are more familiar with the somewhat different form given in Matthew, where it is recorded as part of the sermon on the mount. For the New Churchman such differences of form and context create no problem, because we know that the incidents were recalled to the minds of the different evangelists in each case in a providential order, and that the words were providentially directed each time to serve the needs of the internal sense. We should remember, however, that the Gospel was written in Greek and that, whenever any difficulty arises over differences in form in connection with the

same incident, it becomes important to know what the Greek says.
In the Lord's Prayer, for example, the order "as in heaven, so in
earth" is the order in the Greek both in Matthew and Luke (but
see the footnote at the Junior level). This order has an evident
bearing upon the lesson of the rest of our chapter for today.

In the first thirteen verses of the chapter we are given the picture
of what our true relation to the Lord is. We are children of our
heavenly Father, dependent upon Him for guidance and help in
every phase of our daily life, just as little children depend upon
their earthly parents; and if we acknowledge and accept this relationship, we may look to Him with confidence for the supplying
of our every spiritual need.

Against this background we are given the picture of the scribes
and Pharisees who, while professing to know and keep the law of
Moses above all others, rejected the promised Messiah when He
appeared among them, because at heart they wanted no rule but
their own will. As Isaiah wrote of them, they honored God with
their lips, but their heart was far from Him. Read Isaiah 29:13-19
as an exact description of the conditions presented in our chapter.

We may take verses 33 and 34 as a summary of the teaching
of the chapter. The scribes and Pharisees had done just what is
pictured by putting the candle in a secret place or under a bushel
instead of on a candlestick. They had covered up the light of truth
in the Word of the Old Testament with their own false interpretations and additions, instead of lifting it up where it might give
light to the people around them. They posed as the special spokesmen of the church. We recall words of the Lord to John in Revelation 1:20: "The seven candlesticks which thou sawest are the
seven churches." The primary function of any church is to teach
truth from the Word so that people may walk in the light. When
a church covers over this light with reasonings which spring from
the exaltation of human intelligence above revelation, it is false to
its high calling.

Verse 34 goes to the root of this evil. "The light of the body is the eye." The eye is a symbol of the understanding. The eye has to be "single." Swedenborg renders this word "simple."* The Greek work [and its Latin counterpart], according to the dictionary, means "single, simple, candid, ingenuous, frank, sincere." In our verse this is contrasted with "evil." The Greek word means "wicked, perverse, malignant, evil." So the emphasis is on the state of the heart as influencing the understanding. And in the two words used, the contrast is between an inner state of humility and one of self-will. If we follow this thought through a study of the charges which the Lord makes against the scribes and Pharisees, the picture becomes very clear. We should also read the more detailed record of this condemnation in Matthew 23. The teaching is that we believe what we at heart want to believe, however our outward life may appear.

In TCR 147 we read: "It is as yet scarcely known in the church that in all of man's will and thought and his consequent action and speech, there is an internal and an external, and that from infancy man is carefully taught to speak from the external, however the internal may dissent; and that this is the origin of simulation, flattery, and hypocrisy; and thus man becomes double-minded. But he alone is single-minded whose external thinks and speaks and wills and acts from the internal; and such are meant by the 'simple (single)' in the Word (as in Luke 8:15; 11:34; and elsewhere). Nevertheless these are wiser than those who are double-minded." The rest of this number elaborates and illustrates this thought. Does this mean that we should always say exactly what we think? We have all known individuals who prided themselves on this practice, and they are likely to have been very disagreeable people. Does it mean that we should always do just what we feel like doing? Does it mean that we should not teach our children to observe good manners whether they feel like being polite and considerate or not? The answer to all these questions is, "No." We are

---

*In AE 526[13], e.g., he has *"oculum purum" seu "simplicem"* ("clear or simple [honest] eye").

taught in our doctrines that reformation of our outward conduct must precede regeneration. But the motive in the effort must be the motive of obedience to the Lord, not the motive of being socially acceptable. When we find that our pleasant words and kindly deeds are not sincere expressions of our inner thought and feeling, our duty is not to change our words and deeds but to set to work to change our thoughts and feelings. For we read in AE 394[3]: "When a man does and speaks what is good, true, sincere, and just, for the sake of self and the world he does and speaks them from self, because from the external man without the internal; and such deeds or works are all evil, and if heaven is regarded in them they are meritorious [i.e., self-righteous], and all such are iniquitous." But Swedenborg adds: "In this world no one can determine whether works are from the Lord or from man, since in external form the two kinds appear alike, but they can be distinguished by the Lord alone, and after man's life in the world their origin is disclosed."

The Lord saw the hearts and minds of the scribes and Pharisees. He had the right to utter the condemnation. We have the right to judge the outward acts of other people but not their motives. And as to our own, we can only strive to keep ourselves in a state sensitive to searching and correction by the Lord's truth as it comes to us in the Word. So we pray that the Lord's will may be done in the heavens of our souls and thence in the earth of our outward lives. This is the ideal we set up as our goal.

## From the Writings of Swedenborg

*Apocalypse Explained*, n. 794[3]: "Man has two minds, one spiritual, the other natural. The spiritual mind is what is called the internal and the spiritual man, and the natural mind is what is called the external and the natural man. And as man has an internal spiritual and an external natural, and the internal is conjoined with heaven and the external with the world, it follows that whatever man does from that internal through the external he does from heaven, that is, through heaven from the Lord; but anything that a man does by the external without the internal, this he does from self. This is meant by the Lord's words in Luke . . . (11:39-41). It is said, 'the outside of the cup and of the platter,' and 'the inside' of them, because the 'cup' has a similar meaning as 'wine,' and the 'platter' a similar meaning as 'food'; and 'wine' signifies truth, and 'food' signifies good. It is said also 'give alms,' and this signifies love and charity."

―――――

## Suggested Questions on the Lesson

J. How does the form of the Lord's Prayer in Luke differ from that in Matthew? *[see Junior notes]*

J. Who were the scribes? *men who copied the Scriptures*

J. Who were the Pharisees? *a strict sect who took pride in knowing the law*

J. What law did the scribes study? *Scriptures*

P. Where did they say the Lord's power to work miracles came from? *Beelzebub (devil)*

J. What did the Lord tell them? *a house divided against itself falls*

J. What sign did the Lord say would be given to the Jews? *that of Jonah*

J. To what two stories of the Old Testament did He refer? *Jonah, queen of Sheba*

P. What did the Lord say about a lamp? *put it on a stand*

P. What does this mean? *it is foolish to light lamp and then hide it*

J. What is meant by the eye's being single? *clear or pure*

J. What is meant by the eye's being evil? *blinded by evil*

P. With what great fault did the Lord charge the scribes and Pharisees? *hypocrisy*

J. What is a hypocrite? *one who only pretends to be good*

I. What were some of the ways in which the scribes and Pharisees were hypocrites? *prayed to be seen of men, acted very pious, judged others*

S. Why did the scribes and Pharisees not want to recognize the Lord as the Messiah? *His presence and teachings threatened their power*

## THE GREAT SUPPER

*Luke 14*

The teacher will need to review who the Pharisees were, what their attitude toward the Lord was, and why. Then remind them of the lawyer in the lesson the Good Samaritan since the lawyers were the most learned and honored of the scribes, and the scribes and Pharisees are often mentioned together.

———

### Doctrinal Points

*The Lord invites us all to receive truth and good from Him.*
*Even the Lord's parables present many problems unless we understand the internal meaning.*
*Insincere faith is like insincere friendship.*
*Excuses show the true nature of our affections.*

———

### Notes for Parents

Again we have one of the Lord's parables, this time addressed to the Pharisees, who thought themselves better than anyone else. Did you ever stop to think why so many little stories with a moral to them are written for children? It is because children like stories and remember them, and often they will see the moral for themselves and think about it; whereas if we tried to teach them the same lesson directly, they would close their ears to it. Well, that is why the Lord so often spoke in parables, and indeed why so much of the Bible is in story form. For we are all children to the Lord. We close our ears to His instruction, just as our own children do, when we see immediately that it applies to our faults. But we listen to His stories, which seem at first to be about other people, and afterward we come to see that we are just like the people in the stories, and then the lesson comes home to us.

We all live in a Christian country and most of us think of ourselves as Christians. We consider ourselves friends of the Lord. So

273

if we see that the man in our parable is the Lord, we are all among the friends who were first invited to His table and had accepted His invitation. The Lord gives us our material food, of course, but He also offers us food for our souls which we need still more, for we shall all leave our bodies behind us someday, but our souls are to last forever, and the kind of spiritual food we "eat" determines whether they will be healthy and beautiful or ugly and shrunken and misshapen.

When the invitation to the Lord's table comes to us, the feast which He offers us is in His Word, which is spread before us in His house, the church. Do we ever make excuses? Are we ever so occupied with our own little worldly occupations and ambitions that we can't take time for religion? We know that the poor and maimed and halt and blind—the people who realize their own shortcomings, their sin and weakness and ignorance—go eagerly to the Lord's table to be fed. Do we really think we are better than they? If we do, the Lord tells us in the parable that we shall never taste of His supper.

---

### Primary

Even the little children can get a glimpse of the spiritual meaning in this parable. It is good to emphasize with them the idea of the church as the Lord's house to which they are invited every Sunday.

The Pharisees were the Lord's enemies, but they pretended to be His friends because so many of the people believed in the Lord and followed Him. The Pharisees were a group of people who pretended to be especially religious, and so considered themselves better than anybody else. They would not associate with poor people. But the Lord told them over and over again that their attitude was wrong.

Why did the Lord rebuke them at the feast?
In the parable the Lord told them the man who invited his friends to dinner means the Lord.
The Lord invites all of us to receive instruction and goodness from Him.
Do we ever refuse His invitation?

What three excuses were given in the parable?
Sometimes people today think they are too busy to go to church.
But the church is the Lord's house and it is He who invites us to come there.
Whom did the man in the parable find to sit at his table?
The poor and maimed and halt and blind picture the people who realize how much they need the Lord.

You see, the Lord came into the world to help everybody, but He could not help the people who were so satisfied with themselves that they thought they did not need His help. Such people were like the ones in the parable who were so interested in their own affairs that they could not take time to have dinner with the friend who was kind enough to invite them.

Remember this when you think you would rather stay home and play than go to church and Sunday school. You know that the church is the Lord's house. It is really the Lord who is inviting you to come to church every Sunday and hear the good things He has to tell you in His Word.

## Junior

The Juniors are old enough to understand about spiritual food and drink. Have them try to think for themselves what "bread of life" and "living water" mean. Point out that we could not live without love and truth—we could not grow up if our parents did not love and teach us, and all their goodness and knowledge really comes from the Lord.

In our chapter for today, who invited the Lord to eat at his house?
Who were the Pharisees?
What did the Lord notice about the guests?
What did He advise the Pharisees to do?

Then the Lord told them a parable. The Lord in His teaching spoke many parables. This was because a simple story holds our attention, is easily understood, and stays in our minds afterward. We may not see the point of the story at first, but sometimes it comes to us later. So in our chapter, if the Pharisees had closed their selfish minds to the plain teaching which the Lord gave them first, they might listen to the parable and think it over later.

In the parable whom did the man first invite to his supper?
What excuse did the first man give?
What was the second excuse?
What was the third?
Whom did the man find to eat his supper?

We can see some of the lessons in this parable easily. One is that we should not let our selfish activity about our own affairs interfere with the obligations of friendship. Another is that people we look down upon might make better friends than some we choose. This was taught also in the parable of the Good Samaritan.

But there is a still greater lesson which we may not see so easily. The man in the parable pictures the Lord, who is our greatest friend. The Lord has prepared a great feast for all of us and invited us to come. Of course we know that He gives us our natural food, the food that nourishes or bodies; but the real feast He offers is food for our souls, His love and truth. Again and again in the Word He invites us to come to His house and take freely of the good things He has for us. He calls Himself the "bread of life" (John 6:35) and says He will give us "living water" to drink (John 4:10, 14). You would think that no one would refuse such an invitation, coming from the Lord Himself.

But we do often make excuses, just as the men in the story did. We are too busy with our work and our play and our selfish affairs to study the Bible and to go to the Lord's house. When we hear the invitation, we mean to accept it, but when the time comes, we can't bear to lay aside what we are doing. We are the friends who are invited first, because we call ourselves Christians; that is, we claim to be friends and followers of the Lord, and we know all about the feast and where to find it.

Who do you think are the poor, and the maimed, and the halt, and the blind who do come to the supper? See if you can find the answer in Matthew 5:3-6. There are a great many things in the Gospels about the rich and the poor. It will help us to understand these things if we know that by the rich the Lord does not mean the people that have money, but all those who are rich in their own estimation, who think they have all the goodness and truth they need; and by the poor the Lord always means those who know they are not good or wise enough, but that they need help from the Lord all the time. Read Revelation 3:17, where the Lord is speaking of a Christian Church which had become like the Pharisees. The maimed and the halt and the blind are those who realize that they have done wrong things which have hurt their souls or that they are somehow not quite strong enough to walk in the Lord's way as they should, or that they are ignorant of the Lord's teachings. We are all weak and imperfect in many ways, and we should make the most of every opportunity to receive the help the Lord offers us so freely.

---

## Intermediate

The correspondences in this lesson are simple and very helpful, especially in the three excuses. The Intermediates are reaching the age when many children begin to rebel against going to Sunday school, and the teacher can use this lesson in such a way that it will inspire them to continue. Point out that every new state and experience to which we come in life calls for fresh spiritual food, and that the Word is the Lord's table and we come to it when we come to Sunday school and church.

We wonder sometimes why there is so much in the Bible about eating and drinking. Physically, eating and drinking are essential to our life in this world. Everything we do uses up some of our bodily resources and they have to be continually renewed. The Lord has put into the world a wonderful variety of animal, vegetable, and mineral substances for this purpose. Also we are so made that we enjoy eating and drinking. And we like to eat and drink together. Perhaps the most universal way of showing friendship is the invitation to share a meal.

We are told in our chapter that the Lord went into the house of one of the chief Pharisees "to eat bread on the sabbath day." The Pharisees were the Lord's enemies. Because the people were flocking to hear Him, they pretended first to be His friends and to be willing to hear Him, too, but they were always hoping to catch

Him in some teaching which they could say was contrary to the law. The Lord did not hesitate to accept their invitations although He knew their hearts. He was no one's enemy. But He never hesitated to tell them the truth. So in our chapter He first calls attention to the foolishness of the desire always to be first, and then He tells them a parable, as He often did when His plain teaching was not understood or not well received. The parable would stay in their minds and perhaps make them think afterward.

Our physical bodies, we know, are merely the clothing which our souls wear in this world. They are what they are because they serve and express attributes and powers which our souls possess. So from our physical processes we can know about the unseen things which go on in our souls. Our souls also need constant renewal. Spiritual food—goodness and truth from the Lord—is essential to our spiritual life.

So we may understand that in this parable today the man who "made a great supper and bade many" is the Lord, and we who call ourselves Christians are the invited guests. We know that in the Holy Communion—the Lord's Supper—the bread and wine picture the goodness and truth which the Lord provides for us freely. But the Lord's Supper, like the supper in the parable, is only symbolic of what the Lord offers us all the time. He gives us His truth in His Word, and as we learn and obey it, His goodness flows freely into our hearts.

We all mean to accept the Lord's invitation. But all of us sometimes, when the time comes, make excuses. The three excuses in the parable are typical of the things which come between us and the full acceptance of the happiness which the Lord offers us. "I have bought a piece of ground, and I must needs go and see it." We remember that ground pictures the minds of men. Sometimes we are too interested in our own ideas to read the Word and think about it. "I have bought five yoke of oxen, and I go to prove them." Oxen represent affections for useful work. Sometimes, like Martha, we are so busy with what we consider necessary work that we have no time to sit at the Lord's feet and hear His Word. These two both asked to be excuses. They recognized their obligation although they did not go. But the third man said, "I have married a wife, and therefore I cannot come." He pictures our state when we have become fixed in the intention of going our own way, "wedded" to our selfish ideas and activities.

All the people who make these excuses are apt to consider themselves good—they count themselves among the Lord's friends. But they do not really want to learn from Him and obey Him because they think they have enough knowledge and goodness of their own. But in the parable the man found other people who were glad to accept his invitation. The poor are the "poor in spirit" of the first blessing (Matthew 5:3), those who are humble-minded. The maimed are those who have fallen into sins—like the man in our lesson on the Good Samaritan who had been robbed and wounded—and who feel the need of the Lord's help to become spiritually whole again. The halt, or lame, are those who recognize that they have weaknesses which make it hard for them to "walk in the way of the Lord." The blind are those who realize that they need more understanding of the Lord's teaching. These are the people who are eager to read the Word and to be helped to understand it and to find the strength which can come only from the Lord. Read Revelation 3:17. We are all spiritually halt and maimed and blind in one way or another. If we admit it, we shall accept the invitation to the Lord's table.

### Basic Correspondences

|  |  |  |
|---|---|---|
| oxen | = | affections for useful work |
| marriage | = | the union of heart and mind |
| the poor | = | the humble-minded |
| the maimed | = | those who see that their sins have hurt them |
| the halt | = | those who feel they lack the power to do right |
| the blind | = | those who recognize their lack of knowledge and understanding |

## Senior

The Seniors can profit by the same lesson suggested for the Intermediates, but for them illustrate it from conditions prevailing in the community and the world in order to encourage in them the determination to align themselves with the "poor" rather than with the Pharisees.

In our parable today it is the Lord who prepares the great supper and invites us to come. We find this feast in the Word, in the Lord's house. Those who claim to be friends of the Lord—all Christians— have heard and recognized the invitation and are presumably willing to accept it, but when the actual time to partake comes—the time to study the Word, to go to church, to express our love for the Lord by doing His will—how often we begin to make excuses!

The Lord spoke this parable to the Pharisees. They had found fault with Him for not keeping all the regulations which they had added to the law of Moses. But He had pointed out that they themselves, while they kept the letter of all the laws, kept the substance of none of them. Because they saw the people flocking to hear Him, they maintained for a time a show of respect for Him, and He used all the opportunities they gave Him to try to teach them as He taught everyone. The Lord, as He said, came as a physician to heal the sick, and in His mind the Pharisees were suffering from a spiritual disease worse than those which afflicted the publicans and "sinners" whom they despised. So when He went into the house of one of the chief Pharisees "to eat bread on the sabbath day," He was carrying on His purpose. This time He attacked their desire for preeminence, first in plain teaching which might appeal to their worldly reason and then in the parable of the great supper, which might perhaps stay in their minds and have its effect later. We all need its lesson.

In their correspondence the three excuses in the parable picture three types of self-indulgence which we are likely to allow to come between us and participation in the spiritual feast to which the Lord invites us. The first man had bought a piece of ground and had to go see it. The ground pictures the mind. This is the man who is too interested in developing his own ideas to stop to receive instruction from the Lord. The second had bought five yoke of oxen and wanted to try them out. The oxen represent affection for useful labor. This is the man who has so much to do in his business and the woman who puts so much effort into her housework that they have no time to study the Bible or go to church. The third had married a wife and therefore could not come. This is the man who is really "wedded" to his own selfish ways and has closed his mind to anything which will interfere with his going his own way.

The invitation was accepted only by "the poor, and the maimed, and the halt, and the blind." These are the people who are humble-minded, who recognize their own sins and weaknesses and ignorance, and look eagerly to the Lord for guidance and strength. They are those mentioned in the blessings, the poor in spirit, the meek, they that mourn, they that hunger and thirst after righteousness.

The Lord's feast is perpetually spread for all of us. If we are rich in our own estimation, we shall make excuses; if we are poor in spirit, we shall accept and be fed. We should note the warning with which the parable closes: "For I say unto you, That none of those men which were bidden shall taste of my supper." Our opportunity is now—not in some vague tomorrow.

In the rest of this chapter a further lesson is drawn from the parable. The invited guests who acknowledged the invitation and then did not attend the supper are like the man who began to build a tower without first counting the cost, and like the king who started a war without estimating his forces, and like the salt which had lost its savor. In John 9:41 the Lord says to the Pharisees, "If ye were blind, ye should have no sin: but now ye say, We see: therefore your sin remaineth." To acknowledge truth and then recede from it constitutes sin. We all need the Lord's admonition: "If ye know these things, happy are ye if ye do them."

## Adult

The contrast between the Pharisees' attitude toward the Lord and His attitude toward them makes a good discussion topic, especially in view of the humanistic character of much so-called religion today. The ideas that man is inherently good and that human intelligence is the arbiter of truth are essentially Pharisaic. The three excuses also offer good discussion material.

Eating and drinking play a large part in our daily lives. Our bodies must be nourished regularly, and our food must be varied and wholesome. When we invite guests to a meal, we desire not only to do them good by feeding their bodies, but to enjoy the pleasure of association with them. Our associations with our friends are of the spirit, so that even with us, if we are in good states, eating together performs spiritual uses.

Many times in the Word the Lord spoke of eating and drinking, of feasts, suppers, wedding feasts. We can know that He was talking of spiritual uses. The food and drink which He offers us are His love and wisdom, good and truth to sustain and develop our souls, as natural food and drink nourish the body. But He offers us more than this. He promises to come in and sup with us, to be present with us, associating with us Himself. In the Word He spreads a perpetual feast for us, good and truth in every varied form which we may need and which will add to our happiness, and He is present there Himself ready to speak wise and loving words to us, to answer our questions, to help and encourage us in our problems and temptations, to delight us with new desires and thoughts.

But we are free to accept or to reject the Lord's invitation. In this world we choose the company with which we wish to associate. We can seek those who are wiser and better than we, and learn to become steadily wiser and better ourselves, or, if we like to show off our knowledge and virtues, we can seek those who, we think, know less than we, and so cut ourselves off from making progress and actually go backward. This is what the Lord teaches in our chapter in the parable of the wedding feast, which precedes the parable of the great supper. If we truly "hunger and thirst after righteousness," we will readily accept the Lord's invita-

tion, seek Him in His Word, accept the truth He offers, and
try to practice it and so receive its good, we will associate with
others who are learning of Him, and unite with them in work for
His kingdom. The Lord's Supper, of which we partake occasion-
ally, is the external symbol of our acceptance of His invitation to
sup with Him in His kingdom. It has reality and power for us in
proportion to our desire to receive the good and truth from the
Lord which the bread and wine symbolize, and in proportion to
our desire to associate with the Lord and with angels.

The Lord's invitation is given to all. It is repeated again and
again. Not only do we hear it in the letter of the Word in its general
form but in every truth which impresses itself upon us personally,
just as the servant was sent out to each guest. If we do not accept
the invitation, it is because we do not wish to. When we read the
parable, we wonder that any of the invited guests should have
refused so delightful an invitation; but we refuse it ourselves whenever we find other pursuits and other thoughts so absorbing that
we allow them to interfere with our associations with the Lord.

The three excuses symbolize all the types of preoccupations
which keep men from looking to the Lord for love and wisdom.
The first man had bought a piece of ground and must needs go to
see it. The ground, or more properly field, is the mind, intellectual
things, in this case leading away from the Lord. When we become
so interested in thinking our own thoughts and developing our
own theories that we have no time to learn of the Lord, to read
the Word, to go to church, we are making this excuse. The second
had bought five yoke of oxen and went to try them. The oxen
represent our affections for natural usefulness. When these are
turned to the Lord's service they are good, but when we are too
busy caring for our families and providing for their present and
future needs, or even too occupied with the external charities
which the world recognizes as good to look to the Lord and seek
to know Him better, we are making this second excuse. Both these
guests recognized that they ought to accept the invitation and
asked to be excused for this time. So we may feel that sometime,

when we have completed the study or the work which now absorbs our attention, we shall find time for the Lord and the church. But we cannot put off the building of spiritual character. Before long we shall be saying, as the third man did, "I have married a wife, and therefore I cannot come." We shall be so wedded to our own ideas and our own occupations that we shall reject the Lord's invitation outright.

The parable of our lesson was spoken to the Pharisees. The invited guests who made the excuses pictured the church, which had the Scriptures but had become wholly absorbed in worldly ideas and pursuits. The guests who were brought in to take the places of those first invited represented those who did not have the truth but desired it, first those in the streets and lanes of the city, those who had had some contact with the truths of the Word through living among the Jews, and then those in the highways and hedges, altogether outside of the city of doctrine, who must be "compelled," that is, drawn by the power of love rather than reached through the truth. " 'The poor, the maimed, the lame, and the blind,' do not mean such in a natural sense, but such in a spiritual sense, that is such as had not the Word, and were therefore in ignorance of truth and in lack of good, but still desired truths by means of which they might obtain good; such were the Gentiles with whom the church of the Lord was afterwards established." (AE 652[31]) See also AC 2336[4] and AE 223[22].

The last verse of the parable points to the serious nature of the choice offered us in the Lord's invitation: "For I say unto you, That none of those men which were bidden shall taste of my supper." Our reception of the Lord's love and truth depend upon our desire to obtain them. If we choose to go our own way, we close the door to the Lord and the time comes when even He cannot open it. Our life in this world is our opportunity to choose between self and the Lord, and the choice is made not in a moment but day by day, by putting away wrong thoughts and selfish desires and letting the Lord's truth and love take their places. Whenever we hold back from fully following the Lord, clinging to some idea or enjoyment which we love but know to be from self, we limit our ability to advance in the kingdom of heaven. If we really want the Lord to come in and sup with us, we must open the door to Him and keep it open, by ridding our minds and hearts of the self-esteem and self-love which shut Him out. This is the cost we must count, of which the Lord speaks in the parables which complete our chapter.

## From the Writings of Swedenborg

*Apocalypse Explained*, n. 252: "As suppers signify consociations by love and consequent communication of delights, therefore the Lord compared the church and heaven to a 'supper,' and also to a 'wedding'; to a 'supper' in Luke ... (14:16-24). (Nearly the same is meant by the wedding to which invitations were given in Matthew 22:1-15.) 'Supper' here means heaven and the church; 'those called who excused themselves' mean the Jews with whom the church then was; for the church specifically is where the Word is, and where the Lord is known through the Word. 'The poor, the maimed, the halt, and the blind,' mean those who are spiritually such, and who were then outside the church. Heaven and the church are here likened to 'a supper' and to 'a wedding,' because heaven is the conjunction of angels with the Lord by love, and their consociation among themselves by charity, and the consequent communication of all delights and felicities; the like is true of the church, since the church is the Lord's heaven on the earth."

## Suggested Questions on the Lesson

I. Why did the Lord put the story of Mary and Martha in the Word immediately after the parable of the Good Samaritan? *to help us learn how to love the neighbor*

J. Who were the Pharisees? *a strict religious sect*

J. In our lesson for today what fault did the Lord see in them? *they wanted the best for themselves*

P. What parable did He give them? *the great supper*

P. Whom did the man in the parable first invite to his supper? *friends*

J. What three excuses were given by his friends for not coming? *field, oxen, wife*

J. What fault in his friends did this show? *selfish thoughtlessness*

J. Whom did the man afterward find to enjoy his supper? *poor, maimed, halt, blind*

J. Whom does the man in this parable represent? *the Lord*

J. To what "feast" does the Lord invite people? *His Word, containing His love and truth*

P. Where is the Lord's house? *the church*

J. Who are the friends who make excuses? *all of us who call ourselves Christians*

J. Who are the poor people who accept His invitation? *the humble-minded*

I. What does eating at the Lord's table represent? *feeding our souls with the Lord's goodness and truth*

S. What do the three excuses picture?
   *(1) field: intellectual pride (mind)*
   *(2) oxen: wrong priorities in our affections (heart)*
   *(3) wife: "wedded" to selfish ways (act)*

# THE PRODIGAL SON
## Luke 15

This lesson follows easily upon the lesson of the great supper. Simply review the parable as a preparation for this lesson.

───────

## Doctrinal Points

*The Lord always is ready to forgive.*
*The truths of the Word are our spiritual riches.*
*As we lose truth, we lose our faith.*
*When we are unforgiving toward others, the Lord's forgiveness cannot reach us.*

───────

## Notes for Parents

The lesson in our chapter for today is a very beautiful one of the Lord's love and forgiveness. The scribes and Pharisees had found fault with Him because He received publicans and sinners. A publican was a Jew who collected taxes for the Roman conquerors; so the Pharisees despised him. In another place the Lord told the Pharisees: "They that be whole need not a physician, but they that are sick."

In our chapter the Lord answered His enemies with three parables. They all teach the same lesson, but each in a different way. Every one of us starts out in life with a "flock of sheep," that is, the innocent, trustful, loving states of a little child; but as we get a little older and our natural selfishness begins to assert itself, we are liable to let these heavenly feelings slip away from us one by one. Each one may become a "lost sheep." And when we are still children, each one of us acquires "ten pieces of silver," that is, truths which teach us what is right and wrong, especially the ten commandments. But again, when we find that one of the commandments forbids something we want very much to do, we hide the commandment away in the back of our mind. We let the dust of worldly reasoning cover it up. We have lost one of our bright "silver coins."

Finally, when we grow up, we want to take the talents and faculties which our heavenly Father has given us and use them to get as much pleasure as possible for ourselves. So we may leave our heavenly Father's home and go far away from Him where we may have our own way. We may even fall as low as the prodigal son did, and live for the satisfaction of our physical desires, which in symbol language are called "swine," and feed on "husks," the kind of thoughts which these lowest desires enjoy. But our heavenly Father has not really left us. Deep down inside somewhere we have a memory of Him and of the safe, happy home where we lived in our childhood. The Lord lives in that memory and is always trying to awaken it.

The chapter says of the prodigal son, "And when he came to himself . . ." To imagine that we can do without the Lord and win happiness by following our own selfish way is insanity. We "come to ourselves" when we realize this. But we have to do something about it. The prodigal son did not lie there among the swine and wish for his father to come and take care of him again. He arose and went back step by step over the long road home, wanting only to be a servant where he had once been served. We sometimes forget this part of the parable. The Lord is always ready to forgive, but we must go back to Him. We must change our bad habits, our bad thoughts, our selfish feelings, and get back into a state in which we behave like a child of God.

———————

## Primary

Emphasize our need of acknowledging our faults, being sorry, and trying to do better. Again the little ones can be introduced to some of the spiritual meaning. Stress the difference between the father and the elder son in the parable.

What fault in the Pharisees did the Lord rebuke in the parable of the great supper?

Whom did the man in that parable first invite to his table?
Why did they not come?
Whom did he invite then?
What does this parable teach us?

The Pharisees would not learn this lesson. They still thought they were better than anyone else. So when they were hunting for faults in the Lord, they said He received sinners and ate with them. And then the Lord tried to show them that the sinners who were sorry for their misdeeds and wanted to do better pleased Him more than all the people who thought they were so good that they did not need to learn anything from Him. He told them three parables.

In the third parable what did the younger son do?
What happened to him?
What did he decide to do?
How did his father receive him?
How did the elder son feel?

You see, the older brother in the parable was like the Pharisees. The younger son was like every one of us, because we all do wrong things. And the father in the parable was like the Lord, who is always ready to forgive us when we acknowledge our faults and try to do better.

---

## Junior

The Juniors can easily understand the general lesson of the three parables in this chapter. The teacher may suggest ways in which they in their school and play environment may be tempted to behave like the Pharisees, and also ways in which they themselves may be like the prodigal son. The emphasis should be on the necessity of recognizing our spiritual condition and retracing our steps before the Lord's forgiveness can come to us.

Who were the Pharisees?
What was their great fault?
How did they regard other people?
In our last lesson what parable did the Lord tell them?
Who were first invited to the supper?
Why did they not come?
Who did eat the supper?

There are three parables in our lesson for today.

What is similar about all three?
In the first parable what was lost?
What was lost in the second?
What was lost in the third?

The Lord spoke these three parables to the scribes and Pharisees. Read the first two verses of the chapter. The publicans were those who collected taxes from the Jews—their own people—for the Roman rulers; so they were despised by their fellow men. The apostle Matthew had been a publican (Matthew 9:9). The scribes, or the more learned ones who were called lawyers, were those who studied, copied, and taught the Old Testament Scriptures and all the additional regulations which their leaders had made up. They despised the Samaritans and all people of other nations. But the publicans and often the "sinners" were their own people. The scribes and Pharisees looked down upon them also, but only because they were not just like themselves. We know that today there are people of many different nations in our own country—people with different colors of skin, different religions, different customs—and that people are brought up with many different ideas of what is right and wrong, and that people also differ in the degree to which they live up to what they believe to be right. Because we are all naturally selfish, it is easy for us to take it for granted that we are right and that everyone who is different from us must have something wrong with him. It is hard for us to change this feeling even after we have learned better, but we must try hard to make this change, and even when thought and reason and experience have proved to us that in any particular matter we really are right and the other person wrong, we must not think of ourselves as better than he. We are like the scribes and Pharisees when we draw back from someone who has done wrong, and will not forgive him or help him to do better.

This is not the way in which the Lord treats us. The Lord sees to it that each of us has from babyhood an inheritance from Him which makes it possible for us, if we choose, to see and overcome little by little the selfish thoughts and feelings which are natural to us. If we lose one of these good feelings that He has given us to keep—as the one sheep wandered away from the flock—He tries to help us find it and bring it back. If we forget some truth we have been taught, He helps us to search our minds until it comes to light again; this is symbolized by the piece of silver that was lost. And we may even do worse than this. We may do so many wrong things that we get very far away from the good life we ought to live. Then we are like the prodigal son in the third parable.

*Prodigal* means "wasteful." The inheritance which the son wasted pictures all our talents and opportunities which our heavenly Father gives us freely. When we want to do as we please with our lives, we are like the prodigal son leaving his father and going to a far country and wasting his inheritance. We may even get to as low a state as he did. We know what we mean when we say certain people live like pigs. But if we recognize how wrong we have been, and turn back ready to serve the Lord, He will forgive us and restore us to our true place as His children.

What complaint did the elder brother make?
What did his father tell him?

The elder brother lived an outwardly good life, but he was hard and unforgiving like the scribes and Pharisees. Read what the Lord said about them in Matthew 23:23.

## Intermediate

The correspondences in the three parables will interest this class. In addition to those given in the pupils' notes, point out that it is the man—representing the intellect—which suffers the loss when the sheep is missing, and the woman—representing the affections—who has lost the coin. Tie this in with the third excuse in the last lesson and remind them of the meaning of the widow in the story of the widow of Nain. The teacher should have appropriate illustrations to give of all three kinds of loss.

The general lesson taught in all three of the parables in our lesson for today is that no matter how far one may wander from the

Lord, if he sincerely repents and turns to the Lord for help, the Lord will forgive, restore, and bless him. They also teach that, far from despising and turning from those who do wrong, we should seek them out with loving effort to restore and help them.

The three parables picture how we may go astray on one or another of the three planes of life: will, thought, and act. The lost sheep pictures one of our good affections, such as the innocent trust we had when we were little. Without it our whole flock of affections must wander in the wilderness without a leader. For this innocent trust is the very heart of all goodness. This is what the Lord means when He says: "Except ye be converted, and become as little children, ye shall not enter the kingdom of heaven."

The ten pieces of silver stand for the truths which the Lord has given us to guide our lives, especially the ten commandments. If we lose one, if we drift into neglect of any one of them, the loss is felt through every part of our life. The "house" we must "sweep" is our character, overlaid with the dust of worldly ideas and practices, and the "candle"—or more correctly the "lamp"—which gives us light for our search is the Word. "Thy word is a lamp unto my feet, and a light unto my path."

The prodigal or wasteful son is the person who does not want to be directed by the Lord in his actions. He takes his "inheritance"—all his talents and opportunities—and goes into a "far country"—a state of life far from the Lord—and wastes his substance in riotous living. Such a life leads directly to "feeding swine," that is, to indulgence in gross sensual evils, which is the same as living like an animal. It is really insanity, for the thing which distinguishes man from animals is his possession of a spiritual nature capable of knowing and loving the Lord. So the parable says, "And when he came to himself, he said . . . I will arise and go to my father." No matter how low we have fallen, when we "come to ourselves" and, lifting up our thoughts to the Lord, go back to Him with sincere and humble repentance, we shall find Him coming out to meet us more than halfway. Only the elder brother, who is a picture of the self-righteous Pharisees, fails to rejoice in the restoration of the repentant sinner.

Verse 10 troubles some people because they think it implies that it is better to sin and repent than not to sin at all, but this, of course, is not true. The Lord's attitude toward the people who do right is shown in the father's words to his elder son: "Son, thou art ever with me, and all that I have is thine." Only we must guard against self-righteousness and hardness of heart.

### Basic Correspondences

| | | |
|---:|:---:|:---|
| lost coin | = | a lost truth |
| our inheritance | = | all our abilities and opportunities |
| swine | = | affections for sensual things |
| lost sheep | = | a lost good affection |

### Senior

Stress the difference between evil and sin and the three planes in which spiritual loss may be suffered. Deal more fully with the third parable, pointing out that the cause of the prodigal son's disaster was his desire to go his own way. The teacher may know of particular books, movies or television shows which the young people have seen which may be pointed to as "husks," lacking in spiritual nourishment. Speak of the elder son and tie him in with the first two verses of the chapter.

The three parables in our lesson for today form a wonderful series. The scribes and Pharisees, in their pride and self-righteousness, had criticized the Lord for associating with publicans and sinners. The Lord answered them with these three parables, teaching them the same lesson which He spoke plainly in Matthew 9:12-13: "They that be whole need not a physician, but they that are sick. . . . I am not come to call the righteous, but sinners to repentance."

There are three ways in which we may commit sin: in heart, in mind, and in act. And sin is always the loss of something valuable which we have possessed. Swedenborg makes a distinction between evil and sin. [See AC 8925.] Evil is committing wrong unwittingly and unintentionally, as we all do again and again. Sin is doing what we know to be wrong or what we ought to know to be wrong, if we had thought about the truths which had been given us. So in these parables the lost sheep symbolizes some innocent affection we have possessed but have ceased to feel, the piece of silver stands for some truth we have known but have allowed to slip into the dusty recesses of our minds, and the prodigal or wasteful son is a picture of our efforts to do as we please in our outward life.

In this last parable the father represents the Lord, and the inheritance from Him is all our individual abilities and opportunities. The Lord does not withhold this inheritance from us when we choose to go our own way. He gives it to us to use freely as we like. He leaves us in full control of our abilities, our possessions, our strength, and our time, even when He sees that our free choice will be to go into a "far country"—far from our true spiritual home—and waste our substance. The Lord forces no one to remain in His house. This is because He wants us to be happy, and no one can be forced into happiness. We have to choose it freely. If we see early in life that there is no real happiness except in unselfish love and service—the qualities which are the Lord's—and choose the good life from the beginning, we can be spared much hard experience and suffering. But many prefer to try the other way, which looks so promising. Some even reach the state in which the prodigal son found himself before he learned his lesson.

Swine represent selfish, sensual affections or desires. The husks which feed them picture the superficial ideas which men accept instead of true spiritual nourishment when they think only of the worldly side of living. Many of the books and plays of today are such husks. They seem to give us something to think about and sometimes they look as if they might contain truth, but actually they are empty shells; there is no nourishing goodness in them.

A very little reason will show us that lasting happiness is not found in such things. To ignore the existence of God and of spiritual values is insanity. So the Lord says of the prodigal son, "And when he came to himself, he said . . ." That is, when he had suffered enough so that he could not help seeing that he had made the wrong choice, his mind was opened again toward the Lord,

and he said, "I will arise and go to my father." It is never easy for
us to admit that we have done wrong, and it is still harder to recognize that we must correct our ways before we can regain our position in our Father's house. Like the prodigal son, we have to rise
and retrace our steps with the intention of serving instead of being
served. One of the lessons of this parable is that the doctrine of
"faith alone"–which was one of the outgrowths of the Protestant
Reformation–is unsound. This doctrine teaches that the Lord by
His death on the cross paid all the penalty for the sins of mankind
and that if a person–no matter how evil his life has been–will
even at his last moment acknowledge that Christ died for him and
throw himself on the divine mercy, his sins will be washed away in
a moment. Fortunately all through the centuries many Protestants,
although they nominally accepted this doctrine, did not let it
actually affect their lives; that is, they lived as if they believed that
it was necessary to live good lives in order to be saved. But others
have used it as a loophole hoping to escape from the consequences
of their lifelong sins. We are told in the parable that the father saw
his son coming "while he was yet a long way off," and went out to
meet him. The Lord does give us every possible help and encour-
agement as soon as He sees that our intention to reform is sincere.

We easily see in the story of the elder son the lesson the Lord
was trying to teach the scribes and Pharisees. It is not enough to
keep the letter of the law. We must try to be like our heavenly
Father in our hearts and minds, knowing that we all do wrong and
constantly are in need of His forgiveness, and so ready to rejoice
with the angels in the return of any prodigal to our common spiritual home.

---

## Adult

Perhaps the best discussion topic for this class grows out of the quotation
from NJHD following their notes. The weak and selfish idea that the Lord is
so loving that He will forgive us whenever we ask Him, whatever our life has
been and without any real change on our part, has done much harm in our
modern world. The prodigal son had to take the long journey back before his

father could meet him, even though the father saw him coming "while he was yet a long way off."

Again we have the scribes and Pharisees contrasted with the publicans and sinners. The publicans and sinners "drew near unto him . . . for to hear him," and the Pharisees and scribes murmured. The intent of the three parables which follow is to show the nature of the Lord's love, in that it goes forth to all alike with desire to draw them to Him, examining each man to see wherein he has strayed, and seeking by all means to recall and restore what has been lost. In each parable it is made clear that if we will but recognize our departure from the Lord and try to reform, He can save us. The three parables picture this truth on the three planes of life.

In the first parable it is a sheep which is lost, representing loss of one of the innocent affections with which the Lord has endowed us. All our other affections suffer from the loss of the one—they are left in the wilderness, and the Lord Himself, the good shepherd, is pictured as following the lost sheep, finding it, laying it upon His shoulders, and bringing it back with rejoicing. Perhaps this "lost sheep" is the simple trust in the Lord which we had as little children but have lost in the course of acquiring worldly wisdom. The Lord leaves nothing undone to restore this trust. He shows us again and again in our lives that He is caring for us, by opening our way before us, smoothing out difficulties and dangers which we had feared, and delivering us from evils into which we might have fallen. And when the trust is restored, we are conscious of a sphere of relief and joy. The angels "perceive nothing more delightful and happy than to remove evils from a man, and lead him to heaven" (AC 5992). We are told that "to carry on the shoulder" denotes to preserve with all the power of the divine love, and that the " 'sheep that was lost and was found' denotes the good within the man who repents" (AC 9836[6]).

The parable of the lost piece of silver pictures the loss of some truth which we have known, its loss through failure to live according to it, and the need of searching for it with the light of truth from the Word and sweeping our mental house, that is, examining

ourselves thoroughly and rejecting the false ideas which have obscured the truth (AE 675[10]). Perhaps it is the truth that the real
life is the eternal life and that death is an orderly step which opens
the gate to that life. Little children accept this teaching readily
and have no fear of death, but as they grow older, they are likely
to slip into the prevalent attitude toward death, to shake their
heads when some friend dies and say, "It seems strange that this
should have come to him; it is hard to understand these things."
This is the accumulated dust of worldly ideas and points of view.
We need to sweep the house and find our piece of silver. Again
there is great rejoicing. The familiar saying, "We never miss the
water till the well runs dry" might well be interpreted according to
correspondence. It is true that we do not appreciate the goods and
truths which the Lord gives us until we have felt real need of them,
and sometimes it may be necessary for us to lose them altogether
in order to awaken in us this sense of need. Even in our everyday
life there is more rejoicing over the restoration of something we
have lost than over the possession of many treasures.

The third parable deals more directly with sins of external conduct. The father, of course, is the Lord. The inheritance which the
son wishes to have for himself is the goods and truths which come
to us from the Lord. When one becomes tired of looking to the
Lord for guidance and wishes to lead himself, he is like the prodigal son. Very soon he goes into a far country—far from the Lord—
and wastes his inheritance in riotous living. When our good affections and the knowledge we have of the truth are looked upon as
our own, the "substance" is gone out of them, for it is the Lord's
life in them which makes them good and true. "As the branch can
not bear fruit of itself, except it abide in the vine; no more can ye,
except ye abide in me." (John 15:4) When we look to ourselves
for light, we soon adopt worldly standards and come to live for
worldly pleasures and satisfactions, and may even descend to
"feeding swine"—gratifying the mere lusts of the body. Then
famine comes. For man is a spiritual being and can never be satisfied while his spiritual nature is starved. In the parable the prodigal

son is brought by this condition to realize his own fault and to determine to confess it and go back to right living under his father's command. So sometimes when we are willful, the Lord must permit us to suffer the penalties which belong to our evil ways, in order that we may see their true nature and be brought back to Him. When we come into a state of genuine repentance, the Lord's love comes out to meet us with forgiveness and rejoicing, restoring us to our place, clothing us again in the garments of true thoughts, and giving us a new love of doing good, represented by the fatted calf.

The elder son who remained at home represented the Pharisees, and pictures the Pharisee in us. When we live an outwardly correct life, doing the good works which community sentiment requires of us—as the elder son was "in the fields"—but are cold and critical toward those who have transgressed the external laws which we keep, and refuse to welcome them when they repent or even to believe in the possibility of their repentance or in the justice of forgiveness for them, then we are like the elder brother, for the Lord's love is not in our hearts and our good conduct is a mere hypocritical shell. See AC 9391[6] and AE 279[6].

The lesson in all three parables is that of the necessity of recognizing and repenting of our evils, and of the Lord's tender mercy and forgiveness which helps us all along the way and can make our sins as though they had never been. The elder brother of the parable, like the Pharisees, was not conscious of any fault in himself. As long as one is in that state, there is no possibility of his progressing into a spiritual state of life, no matter how carefully he may keep the letter of the law. The Lord's forgiving spirit is pressing upon us all the time, but it can gain no entrance until we see our need of being forgiven. And our confession must be more than a mere recognition that no man is perfect. We must see definite evils in ourselves and try to correct them. We must miss the particular "lost sheep" and the particular "silver coin," and we must, like the prodigal son, arise and go to our Father—lift our thoughts out of their worldly grooves and seek the Lord in His Word and ask to be helped to do right again. Each time we do this, we shall find the Lord's love waiting for us and experience the heavenly joy which is with the angels over one sinner that repenteth.

———

## From the Writings of Swedenborg

*Apocalypse Explained*, n. 279[6]: "By 'the prodigal son' those who are prodigal of spiritual riches, which are the knowledges of truth and good, are meant; 'his returning to his father, and his confession that he was not worthy to be called his son,' signifies penitence of heart and humiliation; 'the first robe with which he was clothed,' signifies general and primary truths; 'the ring on the hand' signifies the conjunction of truth and good in the internal or spiritual man; 'the shoes on the feet' signify the same in the external or natural man, and both signify regeneration; 'the fatted calf' signifies the good of love and charity; and 'to eat and be glad' signifies consociation and heavenly joy."

*The New Jerusalem and Its Heavenly Doctrine*, nn. 159-161: "He who would be saved must confess his sins, and do the work of repentance. *To confess sins*, is to know evils, to see them in one's self, to acknowledge them, to make himself guilty, and to condemn himself on account of them. When this is done before God, it is the confession of sins. *To do the work of repentance*, is to desist from sins after he has confessed them, and from a humble heart has made supplication for remission, and to live a new life according to the precepts of charity and faith."

———

## Suggested Questions on the Lesson

J. To whom was the parable of the great supper spoken?  *Pharisees*

P. Who were the Pharisees?  *strict religious sect*

J. Why did the Lord find fault with them?  *their pride*

P. In the parable what guests were first invited?  *friends*

P. What excuses did they give?  *field, oxen, wife*

J. What did these excuses show?  *selfish thoughtlessness*

P. Who were the guests who ate the supper?  *poor, maimed, halt, blind*

J. In our chapter today who came to hear the Lord?  *tax collectors, sinners*

J. What did the Pharisees and scribes say?  *murmured against Him*

P. How many parables did the Lord tell them?  *three*

P. What was similar about all these parables?  *something lost, then found*

P. In the first parable what was lost?  *sheep*

P. What was lost in the second?  *coin*

P. What was lost in the third?  *son*

J. What does *prodigal* mean?  *wasteful*

J. What did the younger son waste?  *money*

P. Where did he go?  *far country*

P. What happened to him?  *he became poor and hungry*

P. What did he decide to do?  *go home and serve his father*

J. How did his father receive him?  *joyfully*

J. How did his elder brother feel about this?  *he was jealous*

J. What did the father answer?  *all I have is yours*

I. What are pictured by the lost sheep and the lost coin?  *lost affection, lost thought*

S. What is the inheritance which the prodigal son wasted?  *all our abilities*

S. What is pictured by his arising and going back to his father?  *humbling self, correcting ways, trying again*

# THE UNJUST STEWARD
### Luke 16

Both parables in our chapter are important. We have centered the lesson on the first because its meaning is so often questioned. The lesson of both is the same: "No servant can serve two masters." It is a very important lesson and a hard one to learn, for children and adults alike.

---

## Doctrinal Points

*The Lord knows and makes allowance for our weakness.*
*The Word is eternally true. Its laws must be fulfilled.*
*Faithfulness to the Lord expresses itself in faithfulness to the neighbor.*
*Charity in the heart must be developed in this world.*

---

## Notes for Parents

There are two important parables in our chapter for today, both bringing out the lesson of verse 13: "Ye cannot serve God and mammon." We should know that *mammon* is from an Aramaic word meaning "riches." It is used in the Bible to mean all the things of the world—money, learning, social position, power—which men and women are likely to want for their own sake.

The Lord gives us all our gifts—our abilities, our material possessions, our place in the family, the community, and the world. All these things are entrusted to us to use for the benefit of everyone, for the advancement of the Lord's kingdom on earth. Every one of us is the Lord's steward, and our various possessions and abilities are the "servants" who owe the Lord their full measure of love and good deeds—the hundred measures of oil and wheat. If we are honest with ourselves, we know that we have not always been faithful stewards. We have often used our means and abilities to serve self instead of the Lord. We can never correct all our shortcomings of the past, never pay our full debt.

The steward in the parable, when he was found out, saw three possible courses: to dig, to beg, or to collect as much as was still possible from his lord's servants. To dig is a picture of trying to find some goodness deep within himself on which he could live—some people like to think they are just naturally good. To beg pictures asking the Lord to forgive us without making any real effort to change our lives. The steward chose the third course, and his master commended him and said he had acted wisely. On the face of it what he did looks dishonest, but it pictures making up as far as we can for the selfish and wrong things we have done and determining to try to hold our position as the Lord's stewards by being more faithful in the future. We make friends of the mammon of unrighteousness when we use all our worldly gifts unselfishly in the service of the Lord and the neighbor. The Lord gave this story of a steward in the world who made a wise choice as an example for the "children of light," who mean all who are really trying to live in the light of truth from the Lord.

And then the Lord gave the Pharisees another parable, because the Pharisees were not willing to admit that they had ever done anything wrong. They considered themselves wiser and better than others, whereas inwardly they were cold and uncharitable and domineering. You recall that the first of the blessings is: "Blessed are the poor in spirit: for theirs is the kingdom of heaven." In the Bible the rich are often condemned and the poor exalted, and we should see that by the rich are meant those who think themselves great, and by the poor are meant the humble-minded.

The parable of the rich man and the beggar Lazarus was given by the Lord to teach us that we must make our choice between God and mammon while we are in this world. This world is our "seed-time," when by our own free choice we give our souls the form according to which they will develop to eternity. We cannot change our ruling love after death. The great gulf between the rich man and Lazarus in the other world was not put there by the Lord but by the two men themselves. The Lord has given us in the Word all the truth we need in order to make our choice. People think sometimes that they would believe in God and heaven if they could see a miracle or a vision, but this is not true. If they did not want to believe, they would scoff at the miracle and the vision and explain them away. "If they hear not Moses and the prophets, neither will they be persuaded though one rose from the dead."

---

## Primary

The thought of our life as a kingdom which the Lord has given us to manage for Him is a good one to put in little children's minds, as well as the thought that we can never fully make up afterward for wrong things that we do.

What is a parable?

Can you tell why the Lord used so many parables?

Can you remember some of the parables we have had in the Gospel of Luke?

Today we have another parable which the Lord told His disciples about a man who had done wrong. The man was a steward. A steward was a trusted servant who managed his master's affairs for him.

In this parable what did the Lord learn about his steward?

How did he say he would punish him?

Why could not the steward afford to lose his position?

What did he decide to do?

What did he do for the first of his Lord's debtors?

What did he do for the second?

He knew that in this way at least part of his debt would be paid.

What did his Lord think of it?

We see clearly that the steward was not a faithful or an honest man.

Do you know that you are a steward too? The Lord has given each one of us a little kingdom to manage. This kingdom is our own heart and mind and life. The Lord wants us to manage our little kingdom in such a way that the world will be a better and happier place because we live in it. This is the service we owe to Him in return for all that we receive from Him.

The Lord gives us all our abilities and everything we have.

We are supposed to use them faithfully in His service.

Do we ever waste our Lord's goods?

Whenever we do what we know is wrong, we are like the unjust steward.

And the sad part is that we can never fully right the wrong.
But if we will do our best to make up for it, the Lord will forgive us.
This is what the parable teaches.

One of the sad things about doing wrong is indeed that we can never fully make up for it afterward. But our story teaches us that we should do the best we can to make up. If we do this, our parents will forgive us, and the Lord will forgive us, too. Only we must try to become more faithful stewards every day, because we cannot serve the Lord truly and be selfish at the same time.

Now read verse 13 of our chapter.
*Mammon* is from a Chaldee or Aramaic word for "riches."
It is used in the Bible to mean all the things we want selfishly.
So this verse teaches that we cannot serve the Lord and be selfish at the same time.
Let us read another parable which the Lord gave His hearers after this one.

———

## Junior

Take up both parables with this class, emphasizing the importance of choosing early in life to serve the Lord instead of self and of sticking to this choice from day to day.

Today we have two parables. The first is called the parable of the unjust steward. A steward is a man who takes care of another's property for him.

What did the master learn about his steward?
What did he threaten to do?
What did the steward say he could not do?
What was he ashamed to do?
What did he decide to do to save himself?
Would we consider this a good action?
What did his lord say of his action?

Notice that his lord did not say that he had been a good man, but only that he had acted wisely in collecting as much as he could of his master's debts. We must see that this is not a case of a man who has always done right, but of one who suddenly realizes that he has done wrong. We are all like this steward very often in our lives. We get into careless habits, and suddenly realize that we are in trouble. What is the best thing to do? We can never wholly undo the wrong we have done. Shall we merely say, "I know that I have done wrong and I am sorry, but there is nothing I can do about it"? Or shall we look around and see how much we can do to make up for our misdeeds?

Why do we not always do this? It is because we do not like to admit to others that we have been wrong. We care more about what other people think of us than we do about what the Lord thinks of us. This is what the Lord means when He says, "No servant can serve two masters . . . Ye cannot serve God and mammon." *Mammon* is from an Aramaic word meaning "riches," but it is used in the Bible to mean any of the things we want selfishly.

In the other parable "Abraham's bosom" means heaven, because the people venerated Abraham as the founder of their nation and looked forward to seeing him when they died. The rich man in the parable is sometimes referred to as *Dives*, which is from a Latin word meaning "rich." There is nothing in the first part of the story which tells us that Dives was a bad man and Lazarus a good one, but we know that the Lord does not mean that one went to hell because he was rich and the other to heaven because he was poor, although people have sometimes thought it meant that. By the poor the Lord always means the "poor in spirit," the humble; and by the rich He means those who are rich in their own self-esteem, as the Pharisees were. Our outward condition in this world does not determine our state in the other life. We are told that the Lord "looketh upon the heart." The rich man in the parable went to hell because he had cared only for his worldly possessions and had not learned to love heavenly things. Lazarus evidently had been a good man even though he had been a beggar. The great gulf that was fixed between them was fixed by the lives they had chosen in the world.

What did the rich man first ask of Abraham?
What did he ask next?
What did Abraham tell him?

The Lord tells us in the Word how we should live, and He wants us to read the Word and see its truth and choose freely to obey Him. This is the only way in which we can learn to love goodness, which is what everyone in heaven does. If a selfish person, who did not want to believe in the Lord and the future life, should see a vision, do you think he would believe it was true? No, he would explain it away as a dream or a hallucination.

Both the parables in our chapter teach us plainly that just as early in life as possible we must make the choice between selfishness and love to the Lord and the neighbor, because we cannot serve self and the Lord at the same time, and our eternal happiness depends upon our choosing to love the Lord and the neighbor.

### Intermediate

The general meaning of the two parables offers enough material for the teacher this time without too much attention to the particular correspondences, although some of these have been given.

The two parables of our lesson today both teach the truth of the Lord's words, "No man can serve two masters . . . Ye cannot serve God and mammon." *Mammon* means "riches" and is used to cover all the things we want selfishly.

The parable of the unjust steward has puzzled many people because in it the master commends the steward for doing what seems to us dishonest. But we see it in a different light when we realize that each one of us in the Lord's sight is an unjust steward who has wasted his Lord's goods, for everything we have comes from the Lord and is really His, given us to use in His service, and many times we have tried to serve self as well as the Lord, and we owe the Lord more than we can ever pay. What shall we do? We cannot live without what the Lord gives us, and we should be ashamed merely to beg the Lord to forgive us without trying to do anything ourselves about our debt. The Lord tells us in the parable that we act wisely if we do the best we can, once we recognize and acknowledge our shortcomings. The hundred measures of oil and of wheat mean all we owe the Lord of love and good deeds. The fifty and the fourscore (eighty) measures picture the fullest possible payment that we can actually make. The lesson is that when we have done wrong, we should admit it, undo as much of the wrong as possible, and go on from there, determined to do better in the future.

In the second parable the rich man—often referred to as *Dives*, from a Latin word meaning "rich"—represents those who have plenty of knowledge of goodness and truth but are satisfied with themselves and make no good use of their riches. The beggar Lazarus represents those who have little true knowledge and who may consequently live outwardly unlovely lives, but who are open-minded and eagerly receive even crumbs of truth from the Lord's table, making use of every bit they do receive. Dogs usually have a bad correspondence in the Word, because they represent our natural desires, which are usually selfish. Here, however, they are used in a good sense, and picture such natural tendencies to kindness and helpfulness as we may have, which can go some way toward making up for the evils we commit through ignorance.

In the other world, where we live inside out, the self-satisfaction and worldliness of the rich man led him to his place in the hells, where his selfishness appeared as a consuming fire—this is hell-fire. But the humility and desire for truth of the beggar led him to find his happiness in heaven. The great gulf is a very real one. It is fixed not by the Lord but by the great difference in the quality of the life each has learned to enjoy.

The essential qualities of a good life are humility and willingness to believe and obey the Lord. We cannot serve ourselves first and serve the Lord at the same time. If we want to think of ourselves first, no miracle or heavenly vision will cause us to change, because we will merely explain it away.

*Basic Correspondences*

wheat = goodness
one hundred = full measure

dogs = natural affections without
knowledge of self

hell-fire = love of self

---

### Senior

The idea of stewardship is important for young people of this age, as is the necessity of making the choice between serving God and serving self. Also discuss the reason why the selfish will not choose to go to heaven when they come into the other world.

On the face of it there seems little relation between the two parables of our chapter; yet the Lord expresses the principal lesson of both in verse 13: "Ye cannot serve God and mammon." *Mammon* is from an Aramaic word meaning riches, and it sums up all forms of self-aggrandizement.

All we have of goodness and truth, as well as all we have of natural ability and worldly opportunity comes from the Lord. We are His stewards. If we recognize this and use our talents in His service, we are good stewards. If we think of our talents as our own and use them primarily to advance ourselves in the world, we serve mammon. There is no middle course.

In the first parable the steward had used his master's goods for his own ends. But like the prodigal son he finally came to himself and realized the danger of his position. We are all, in one degree or another, guilty of this same sin. We often serve self rather than the Lord. When we realize it, what shall we do? We have nothing in ourselves which will enable us to pay our debt to the Lord—we cannot purchase salvation by our own merit. And we should be ashamed merely to throw ourselves on the Lord's mercy without making some effort of our own. The steward's solution was to call together his master's debtors—who represent our various faculties—and collect from each one as much as he could. We see in the debts of oil and wheat the full measure of love and obedience which we owe to the Lord, and in the fifty and fourscore (eighty) the measure of our limited ability to pay. We do wisely when we pay to the extent of our ability.

In the parable of the rich man and Lazarus, the rich man represents those who have the truth but use it to serve themselves. Lazarus represents those who are lacking in truth but who receive eagerly every crumb of it which comes their way. In other words the rich man served mammon and the beggar served God.

The vivid picture of the eternal results of these two opposite states is also presented. The fires of hell are the burning lusts of self-love, no longer checked by the considerations of outward expediency which were felt in the world. While we are in this world there is always the possibility that we may "come to ourselves." We may do right for the sake of appearance and so come to see that we are happier in doing right and learn to love it. But when the body is laid aside, the ultimates of action which influence our decisions here are gone. Our souls stand forth in the form we have chosen to give them. The great gulf between heaven and hell is fixed by our own life's choice.

The last few verses of the chapter are especially interesting. People who are unwilling to believe in anything but themselves and what they see around them in the world will sometimes say that they would believe if someone from the other world showed himself to them. But this is not so. Once the vision was over, their only thought would be to explain it away. We believe what we want to believe.

## Adult

The effort has been made in the Adult notes to give a constructive basis for the discussion of the first parable, which bothers many people. There are three current falsities which the chapter exposes clearly: (1) that man is inherently good and can shift the responsibility for his misdeeds to his environment and to other people; (2) that, since man can claim no merit for anything he does, all he can do is acknowledge the Lord as his savior, and therefore that he can throw himself on the divine mercy without living a good life; (3) that the Lord will somehow be able to save everyone eventually no matter how he has used his life in the world.

There are two well-known parables in our chapter for today.

The first is spoken to the disciples and the second to the Pharisees, but both teach the same lesson: "Ye cannot serve God and mammon." The emphasis in the two is different. In the first it is on what we may do while we are still in this world when we find that we have been serving mammon. In the other it is a stern warning that we must make our choice of master here, for the results are eternal. We might note that verse 13—as well as Matthew 6:24—should read "two lords" instead of "two masters." The Greek word is the same as that translated "lord" in John 13:13, where both *master* and *lord* are used, and Swedenborg tells us (AC 9167²) that *master* is predicated of truth and *lord* of good. So the verse really means *not* "Ye cannot serve truth and falsity" but "Ye cannot serve good and evil."

Good people have often been puzzled and troubled by the parable of the unjust steward. The master in the parable commends what seems to be rank dishonesty, and the Lord advises the "children of light" to take a lesson in this instance from the "children of this world," and to make themselves friends of the "mammon of unrighteousness." *Mammon* is from an Aramaic word meaning "riches." It is used in the Bible to cover all forms of possessions—money, learning, social position—which men may acquire and which so commonly lead them into self-satisfaction and contempt for others.

In giving this parable the Lord was speaking to all of us who claim to be His disciples. For every one of us is His steward. All our possessions, all our abilities, our knowledge, our responsibilities and opportunities are given us by the Lord to use in His service. And we know that every one of us is in some degree an unfaithful steward who has wasted his Lord's goods, using them selfishly instead of for the advancement of the Lord's kingdom on earth. From time to time, like the steward in the parable, we are brought up short and faced with our own unworthiness. The steward's words to himself in verse 3 are an interesting condemnation of the two "ways out"—both wrong—upon which Christian people have sometimes relied for salvation. "I cannot dig"—the idea that man is inherently good is false. "To beg I am ashamed"—it is unworthy of our human endowment to fall back on the Lord's mercy and think there is nothing we need do toward repaying our debt to Him. The steward's decision is—under the circumstances of the misuse we have already made of our Lord's goods—the only wise one. His lord's debtors, whom he called in, represent all our abilities which should serve the Lord. The hundred measures of oil and wheat which they owe represent the full amount of love and goodness which in the beginning might have been produced by their means. The fifty and fourscore (eighty) measures represent all that we now find ourselves able to procure with them. In other words, our duty is to recognize and acknowledge that we owe everything we have to the Lord. and to determine from this time forth to do all we can to correct our past shortcomings and serve the Lord wholly. We cannot go on trying to serve God and mammon.

This is not an easy decision to make, but the second parable teaches us that it is a decision which must not be put off. We have seen that there are various kinds of riches—worldly possessions, natural learning, knowledges of spiritual things. All these may be used in the Lord's service or in the service of self. The Pharisees and scribes had all three kinds and used them all for the service of self. They thought of themselves as rich and better than others because of their knowledge of the Scriptures as well as because of their worldly riches. It was of them and of all like them that the Lord said: "How hard it is for them that trust in riches to enter into the kingdom of God" (Mark 10:24). To these are opposed the "poor in spirit," those who recognize their own lack of knowledge and goodness and look to the Lord for help. In the second parable the rich man represents the Pharisees and all who, like them, feel that they do not need to be forgiven and taught by the Lord. The beggar Lazarus, whose name means "whom God helps," represents all those who feel themselves spiritually poor and weak and who "hunger and thirst after righteousness." The purple and fine linen in which the rich man was clothed picture the knowledges of good and truth which he possessed. The sores of Lazarus are the external evils into which we fall for lack of knowledge of what is right, the dogs which licked his sores the efforts of the merely natural good impulses to correct our outward conduct. There are many passages in the writings which explain these details. See AC 9231[3], 9467[5]; HH 365; TCR 215; SS 40.

The rich man did not go to hell because of his material riches, but because his whole enjoyment was in worldly and selfish satisfactions. Lazarus did not go to heaven because of his material poverty, but because he longed for even a little knowledge of how to be good—the crumbs which fell from the rich man's table. The great gulf that was fixed between the two in the other world was a spiritual gulf. In AC 10187 we are told that those in evils cannot stand the sphere of good. The Lord does not fix the great gulf. We fix it ourselves by the kind of life we have cultivated in this world. If we so live here that our whole delight comes to be in the satisfactions which we can get for ourselves, we shall find no more delight in heaven than we found in unselfish goodness here. If we have ever tried to speak of the Lord and the Word or even to give a little friendly advice to one bent upon having his own selfish way in some matter, we know how impossible it would have been for Lazarus to carry even a drop of pure water across the gulf to the rich man in hell. When we tell someone that in the other life people can go where they want to go, the immediate response is, "But then, of course, everyone will go to heaven." But the evil will not want to go to heaven any more there than they do here. They would not enjoy the company of angels any more than they enjoy the company of heavenly people in this world. The gulf is fixed in them. They have formed in themselves no capacity for enjoying the things of heaven. The only delights they enjoy are those they find in hell.

Many people think, as did the rich man in the parable, that we could be shown by miracles the realities of the other life, and that the Lord should so convince us. Swedenborg tells us very plainly in AC 7290, as well as in other places, both the reason why miracles were performed in the Lord's time and the reason why they are not orderly today. The Lord has given us the Word. Anyone who goes to it with the sincere desire to be instructed will learn from it the way to heaven. If we do not learn from the Word, it is because we do not choose to have our selfish desires crossed by the Lord's laws, because we want to go our own way. And if this selfish desire is in our hearts, we shall reject everything which opposes it.

## From the Writings of Swedenborg

*Divine Providence*, n. 250[5]: "In the spiritual sense 'the mammon of unrighteousness' means the knowledges of truth and good possessed by the evil, which they employ solely in acquiring for themselves dignities and wealth; out of these knowledges the good, or 'the sons of light,' must make to themselves friends; and these are what will receive them into the eternal tabernacles."

## Suggested Questions on the Lesson

J. To whom did the Lord speak the parable of the unjust steward? *His disciples*

P. What had the steward done? *wasted his master's goods*

J. With what was he threatened? *loss of his job*

P. What did he say he could not do? *dig*

P. What was he ashamed to do? *beg*

J. What did he decide to do? *take less than what debtors owed*

J. What did his lord think of the course he chose? *commended him*

I. What does this parable teach us? *recognize our shortcomings, do our best*

P. What does the Lord say about serving two masters? *cannot do it*

J. What is meant by *mammon*? *riches, things wanted selfishly*

J. What did the Pharisees think of this parable? *laughed at it*

J. What other parable did the Lord give them? *rich man and Lazarus*

P. Where did the beggar go when he died? *Abraham's bosom (heaven)*

P. Where did the rich man go? *hell*

J. What did the rich man first ask Abraham to do? *send Lazarus with water*

J. Why could not Abraham do it? *great gulf between*

J. What did the rich man then ask? *warn my brothers*

J. What did Abraham tell him? *they have Moses and the prophets*

J. What did the rich man think would convince his brothers? *if one went from the dead*

J. What did Abraham say to this? *this would not persuade them*

I. What does this parable teach us? *we decide here what we will be to eternity*

S. How can a course of action which in the letter seems dishonest be called "wise"? *wrong to feel oneself inherently good, unworthy to ask for "pure" mercy, thus the only course left is to serve the Lord as best we can*

S. In the second parable who are meant by (1) the rich man, and (2) the beggar?

*(1) those who think they are spiritually rich*

*(2) those who recognize their spiritual poverty and long for righteousness*

# PALM SUNDAY
## Luke 19

As the story of Zacchaeus is a very important and helpful one and is told only in Luke, part of the lesson time should be spent on it in all classes. It points up the preparation we should all make for receiving the Lord as our king, just as the cleansing of the temple shows what actually happens as soon as He has entered our hearts and minds to rule there.

## Doctrinal Points

*The Lord as king is the divine truth ruling in our lives. The Lord was the only one who ever fully mastered the natural reason.*
*Even the shortest stories in the Word have meanings which we can study forever.*
*If we really accept the Lord, we shall want to correct our misdeeds.*
*Humility is the ground of charity.*

## Notes for Parents

We know that the Sunday before Easter is called Palm Sunday because when the Lord rode into Jerusalem on the first day of the last week of His life on earth, the people cast palm branches before Him, hailing Him as king. He chose to ride that day on an ass's colt because it was customary for kings and judges to ride on asses.

We know also that it was only a few short days before the people crucified Him. What caused such a terrible change in their attitude toward Him?

The ancient Jews interpreted all the prophecies of the Old Testament literally. They believed that they were the Lord's chosen people and that sooner or later the Messiah or "anointed one" would come as a king who would overthrow all their enemies and establish them forever as rulers of the earth. In order to believe this it was necessary to ignore or to explain away many other things which are said in the Old Testament, but we know how prone we all are to believe what we want to believe, and also how firm a hold the beliefs in which one is brought up have on his mind in directing his reasoning. This belief accounts for much of their history.

It accounted for their treatment of Christ. The people who hailed Him as king when He rode into Jerusalem on Palm Sunday apparently expected Him to put Himself at the head of all the rebellious elements among them and immediately overthrow their Roman rulers. When He did not, they turned against Him, and the scribes and Pharisees, who had been hoping for just such a change in the strength of His support by the people, seized the opportunity to get rid of Him.

The Lord Himself knew just what was going to happen. He had told His apostles about it in advance, but they could not really believe it. His death on the cross was a part of His plan from the beginning, for He came into the world to show us how to live, and if He had not passed through death and appeared afterward unchanged, He could not have proved to us that we go on living forever, so that we would know that it is the things we do to our souls which are really important.

Our whole chapter for today teaches us the difference between humble acknowledgment of our sins and weaknesses like that of Zacchaeus and the stubborn determination to have our own way which was the ruin of the scribes and Pharisees. The Lord did not hate the scribes and Pharisees nor the people who put Him to death. Instead, He wept over Jerusalem because He knew that the people were really destroying themselves. He would have saved all of them if they had only been willing to listen to Him and choose the unselfish life, which is the only possible road to happiness.

This week, which is known by all Christians as "Holy Week," we should read with our children the story of the last week of the Lord's life in chapters 20 through 23 of Luke. We should think about this story very seriously as we read it and try to look into our own hearts and minds and find the feelings and thoughts there which are standing between us and the happiness which the Lord wants us to have. Let us, like Zacchaeus, receive the Lord joyfully and determine to correct our faults and to live as the Lord would have us live.

---

## Primary

The reading should be divided into two parts: first the story of Zacchaeus as an illustration of what the Lord's presence in our lives should mean—always being fair to others, trying to make amends when we have done wrong, and helping other people whenever we can. Then, after the teacher has talked about that with the children, the story of the actual entry into Jerusalem. Begin the lesson with the reason for calling the day Palm Sunday, as the palm branches are not mentioned in Luke.

Today, the Sunday before Easter, is called Palm Sunday because on this day long ago the Lord rode into Jerusalem as a king, and the people broke off palm branches from the trees beside the road and threw them in His path for Him to ride over. In those days in Palestine they did not have many of the ways of riding which we have today—trains, automobiles, airplanes. They did not even have many horses in the Holy Land itself. Most of the people walked wherever they had to go. But it was the custom for kings and judges to ride on asses. The colt the Lord rode on was an ass's colt. The Lord's followers and the people knew that this meant that He was coming as a king. They thought He was going to take command of their fighting men, overthrow the Roman governor, and make them a great nation again. But the Lord did not come to be that kind of king. His kingdom is in heaven, and in the heart and mind of everyone who loves Him and obeys His commandments.

What He really wants to do for us is shown in the story of Zacchaeus.

Where did Zacchaeus live?

What was his occupation?

What was a publican?

Why could not Zacchaeus at first see the Lord?

What did he do in order to see Him?

Why did the Lord tell him to come down?

What did Zacchaeus say which showed his character?

If we receive the Lord into our hearts and minds, we shall all be helped to be unselfish and to help other people.

─────────

## Junior

The Juniors can get some idea of the meaning of the Lord's entry into Jerusalem as its king, as well as of the story of Zacchaeus and the parable of the pounds. Be sure also that they know in brief what happened during Holy Week.

Next Sunday is Easter Sunday, which we observe every year in memory of the resurrection of the Lord after He had been put to death. As we read about the Lord's life on earth—the wonderful things He said and did, and His gentleness and kindness—it is hard for us to see how the religious leaders could have become so bitter against Him and how the people who had followed Him could have let them have their way. But that is what always happens when selfishness gets control of people. A selfish person hates anyone who interferes with his getting everything he wants, and often the people around him find it easier to let him have his way than to speak up and oppose him.

We remember from other lessons that the scribes and Pharisees had been trying all along to find faults in the Lord which they could point out to the people. Because He always proved them wrong instead, their hatred grew and grew. We all need to see clearly that crimes always begin in selfishness. This is as true in our own world today as it was in Palestine when the Lord was on earth.

On the first day of the last week of the Lord's earthly life He entered Jerusalem in the manner of a king and was received by the people as a king.

On what did he ride?
How did He get the colt?
Was the colt used to being ridden?
What did the disciples put on the colt for the Lord to sit on?
What did they cast in the road before Him?
What did the multitude cry?

This story is told in all four Gospels. Look up John 12:12-13.

Matthew and Mark both speak of their casting branches from the trees in the Lord's path, but only John says that they were palm branches; so it is from John's account that this Sunday before Easter gets its name of "Palm Sunday." We learn from the other Gospels that the colt on which the Lord rode was an ass's colt. Kings and judges rode on asses. The people thought that the Lord had come to overthrow their Roman rulers and set up their own kingdom again. That was the real reason why they welcomed Him. The Lord knew what they thought, but He had no such intention. It is in our hearts and minds that He wants to rule. His kingdom is the kingdom of heaven and He says it is within us. So His riding into Jerusalem as a king is really a picture of His coming into our hearts and minds to rule there.

It is to show us this that our chapter begins with the story of something that happened along the road before the Lord reached Jerusalem. It concerns a little man named Zacchaeus.

Where did Zacchaeus live?
What was his occupation?
What was a publican?
Why couldn't Zacchaeus see the Lord?
How did he manage to see Him?
What did the Lord say to him?
What did Zacchaeus say which showed his character?
What did the Lord tell him?

When the Lord entered Jerusalem on Palm Sunday, He knew that He would be put to death. He had told this to His disciples, but they did not believe Him. It was because He was about to leave them that He told them the parable of the pounds. The word translated *pound* was a sum called a *mina* amounting to about twenty dollars in our money today.

In the parable what did the nobleman give each of his servants?
What did the first make with his pound?
What did his master give him for a reward?
What did the second make?
What was his reward?
What did the third do with his pound?

What did his master call him?

This parable taught the disciples that, after the Lord left them, He would expect them to make good use of all the instruction and training He had given them. It teaches us that the Lord gives each one of us certain abilities and leaves us free to use them as we please, but that if we are wise, we shall make the best possible use of them in His service.

The Lord knew what the people were about to do to Him, but He did not hate them for it. He was sorry for them instead. He grieved because of the great disaster they were bringing upon themselves by their selfishness. Verses 45 and 46 show us that they had even come to use the temple itself as a means of making money. The Lord's prophecy about Jerusalem was fulfilled in A.D. 70 when the Romans completely destroyed the city.

---

## Intermediate

Bring out again the contrast between those whose minds are open to receive the Lord's teaching and those whose minds are closed by selfishness. The story of Zacchaeus is an important one for this age group, and they will be interested in its correspondence. In the Palm Sunday story proper, stress the Lord's attitude toward His enemies, as shown in His weeping over Jerusalem.

Today, as we know, is Palm Sunday, celebrated in memory of the Lord's entry into Jerusalem on the first day of the last week of His life on earth. The last few lessons we have had have been about things He did and said as He was coming down from Galilee for the last time and about the distinction which was becoming increasingly clear between His disciples and the scribes and Pharisees. Wherever He went, many "publicans and sinners" had joined the disciples who welcomed Him and listened to Him gladly, but this made the scribes and Pharisees hate Him all the more.

The Lord and His apostles were coming to Jerusalem to celebrate the Passover. He had told them that He was to be put to death and they had tried to persuade Him not to come, although they did not really believe what He said. But the Lord rebuked them. He came to His death willingly, as a part of the work He had come into the world to do. The Lord is pure, unselfish love.

We should note that the journey the Lord took in our chapter for today is the reverse of the journey taken by the man who fell among thieves in the parable of the Good Samaritan, where the man was going *down* from Jerusalem to Jericho. The Lord was going *up* from Jericho to Jerusalem, up from a period of outward ministration to the period of His deepest teaching and highest victory. The story of Zacchaeus with which the chapter opens may be linked with the parable of the Good Samaritan, for Zacchaeus was one who had spiritually "fallen among thieves." He pictures all of us little, erring people when we begin to feel our need to see the Lord. Zacchaeus climbed up into a sycomore tree. The Biblical sycomore tree was an inferior type of fig, and figs represent good works. The first thing for any of us to do, if we want to see the Lord, is to begin doing good as best we can. Then the Lord will come into our lives. "If a man love me, he will keep my words: and my Father will love him, and we will come unto him, and make our abode with him."

The parable of the pounds shows us that the important thing for us to do is to use what the Lord has given us as well as possible in His service, however much or little it may be. "He that is faithful in little, is faithful also in much."

We are all familiar with the Palm Sunday story. The Lord rode into Jerusalem on an ass, after the fashion of kings and judges. The ass is a picture of our "natural reason," our ability to think and judge wisely about worldly matters. The ass is a very sure-footed, but also very stubborn and unwilling to be directed by his master. Do you see how this is true of our natural reason? For instance, isn't it hard for us to believe that anything is really right and good which does not obviously "get us something"? The colt on which the Lord entered Jerusalem was one "whereon yet never man sat." That is, the Lord was the first ever to bring this power of the natural reason wholly under subjection to higher principles. The disciples and the multitude cast their garments in front of Him as He rode.

We may remember that garments represent the ideas with which we clothe our affections. The Lord's garments always picture truths of the letter of the Word, but our garments are not always truths, are they?

The people hailed the Lord as king, and the Pharisees objected. The Lord gave them to understand that the people were right, but He was grieved instead of angry with them, and wept over Jerusalem, prophesying its destruction. This prophecy was literally fulfilled some forty years later. But the Lord was really speaking of the ancient Jewish Church. It had the Word, with all the prophecies of Christ's coming, but it refused to recognize Him. So it could no longer be the church through which the Lord could be present in the world. The Christian Church was to take its place. The state of the church was summed up in the condition in the temple, where the very court was used for buying and selling.

In thinking of what Holy Week should mean to us, we should ask ourselves whether we are like those who rejected the Lord and tried to put Him out of their lives or whether we are His faithful disciples. We should welcome Him as our king, submitting all our thoughts and acts to His judgment, just as the disciples cast their garments before Him. We should recognize that to take up our cross and follow the Lord means to try to forget self in service to others. In fact, we should think of the cross as the symbol of victory over selfishness, a victory which each of us can win with the Lord's help.

### Basic Correspondences

$$\text{figs} = \text{external good works}$$
$$\text{the ass} = \text{the natural reason}$$

---

### Senior

With the Seniors this lesson offers a good opportunity to stress the importance of using certain periods in the church year, such as Holy Week, for special self-examination and renewal of their dedication to the Lord's service. The chapter contains many practical lessons for young people. Suggest to them that they read chapters 20 through 23 of Luke during the week.

We are all so familiar with the story of the Lord's entry into
Jerusalem at the beginning of the last week of His life on earth
that we need only review its meaning. Jerusalem represents the
place we have made for the Lord in our minds, and He reigns there
as king just so far as we actually accept the rule of divine truth. He
enters riding upon an ass when we submit our worldly reasonings
to the control of spiritual principles. We cast our garments before
Him when we are willing to give up our own ideas if we find that
they are contrary to His teaching. Then He can cleanse the inner
temple of our souls, driving out false thoughts and selfish desires.

The story of Zacchaeus, which is told only in the Gospel of Luke,
is a fitting introduction to the story of the entry into Jerusalem,
for the chief among the publicans—or tax-gatherers—represents our
affection for worldly success. Zacchaeus was "little of stature."
This affection is not an exalted affection. It is capable of leading
us into evil. But it is also capable of a good use. Zacchaeus desired
to see the Lord "who he was," and he "climbed up into a sycomore
tree to see him." Swedenborg says that the Biblical sycomore,
which was an inferior type of fig tree, represents "the truths of the
external church." Even such external truths, if we obey them, will
lift us high enough above the crowd so that we can see the Lord.
When the Lord saw Zacchaeus in the tree, He said, "Zacchaeus,
make haste, and come down; for today I must abide at thy house."
In other words, once our interest in worldly success has recognized
the Lord, it must immediately be put to use for Him on its own
plane. And the result with us, as with Zacchaeus, will be the recognition of our evils, the desire to correct them, and also joy and
salvation.

To those who murmured against the Lord for associating with
Zacchaeus He spoke the parable of the pounds, teaching that each
of us is responsible for the proper use of the place and abilities
given him by the Lord. Zacchaeus, when faithful and merciful in
his low office, was better than the scribes and Pharisees who failed
to use rightly the treasure of the Word.

The Lord's lament for Jerusalem and prophecy of its destruction referred literally to the earthly city and to the ancient Jewish Church, but spiritually the Lord longs to save all men. He spares no means of pointing out to us the sure ruin which will befall those who know the truth and are faithless to it. From the warning given in the Garden of Eden to the warnings in the messages to the seven churches in Asia Minor in Revelation the importance of our free choice of good or evil, life or death, is impressed upon us.

The week before Easter is called Holy Week. During this week we should make a special effort to think very seriously about what the Lord did for us in taking on our weak human nature in order that He might meet and overcome all the temptations which we feel, and in this way be forever present with us and help us from day to day. He "bowed the heavens and came down for our salvation." We should examine ourselves during this week to find our particular faults and weaknesses, and we should ask the Lord to keep us mindful of them and to give us strength to fight them.

---

### Adult

The story of the actual entry into Jerusalem, while it should not be slighted, is so familiar to all the Adults that it need take up little of the class time, while the story and parable with which it is introduced are given only in Luke and therefore should be developed. The teacher will find plenty of discussion material in them.

In our chapter for today the Lord, on His way to Jerusalem for the last time, came to Jericho, that city near the Jordan which Swedenborg tells us represents instruction in the knowledges of good and truth and consequently the good of life, because no one can be instructed in the truths of doctrine who is not in the good of life (AE 700[15]). We recall that in the parable of the Good Samaritan to go down from Jerusalem to Jericho meant to try to put spiritual knowledge into practice in outward conduct. The Lord had been teaching and healing in Galilee and in the cross-Jordan country—which represent the outer plane of life—and now He was ascending to Jerusalem for His deepest temptation and His greatest victory. At Jericho He found Zacchaeus the publican. Zacchaeus was rich in this world's goods, but he was "little of stature." Nevertheless, when He heard that the Lord was passing by, He "sought to see Jesus who he was." That is, he had a sincere desire to know the truth in regard to the Lord. The sycomore tree into which he climbed—an inferior type of fig—represents the external kind of truth and good of which the worldly man is capable (AE 403, 805$^{10}$). So we may think of Zacchaeus as a man lacking in spirituality who yet recognizes that external good works are "on the Lord's way," and determines to practice them, not from selfish motives, but to help him gain a better knowledge of the Lord. When he did see the Lord and heard that the Lord wished to enter his house, he received Him joyfully and immediately recognized and determined to correct his past evils. So the Lord could say to him, "This day is salvation come to this house."

The parable of the pounds is similar to the parable of the talents, but it is not identical. The emphasis here is on equality of opportunity. Each man was given a "pound" [actually a *mina*, worth about twenty dollars]. In AE 675$^{7-9}$ we have a simple statement of the correspondence of this parable: " 'The ten servants' whom the nobleman going into a far country called to him, mean all who are in the world, and in particular, all who are of the church . . . 'the ten pounds that he pays to the ten servants to trade with' signify all the knowledges of truth and good from the Word, with the ability to perceive them . . . and 'to trade' signifies by means of these to acquire intelligence and wisdom; those who acquire much are meant by the servant who from a pound gained ten pounds; and those who acquire some are meant by him who from a pound gained five pounds . . . the 'cities which are said to be given them' signifies intelligence and wisdom, and life and happiness therefrom . . . Those who do not acquire spiritual intelligence in the world through the knowledges of truth and good from the Word are evil." This parable is a picture of the way in which the Lord deals with each of us. In DP 210 the reason for this is given and strikingly illustrated: "Man would not be man except for the appearance to him that he lives from himself, and therefore thinks and wills and speaks and acts as if from himself. From this it follows that unless man, as if from his own prudence, directs all things belonging to his employment and life, he can not be led and directed by the Divine Providence; for he would be like one standing with relaxed hands, opened mouth, closed eyes, and breath indrawn, awaiting influx. Thus he would divest himself of humanity, which he has from the perception and sensation that he lives, thinks, wills, speaks, and acts as if from himself; he would also divest himself of his two faculties, liberty and rationality, by which he is distinguished from the beasts.''

The story of the last week of the Lord's life on earth is told in Luke in considerable detail, and we should all read and meditate upon it during this coming week, which the whole Christian world recognizes as Holy Week, and accepts as a period of special thoughtfulness and self-examination. The week begins today with Palm Sunday, the commemoration of the Lord's triumphal entry into Jerusalem.

The Lord's work on earth was almost finished. There remained the final temptation and then the full glorification or union with the Father. Many of the common people and a few of the leaders accepted Him as the Messiah. On Palm Sunday the Lord permitted His disciples to receive Him as their king, entering Jerusalem upon an ass—the beast of judges and kings—amid the worship of the people. He knew the dark days ahead of Him and that the shouting throng would desert Him, but His mission was to fulfill the Old Testament Scriptures, and the manner of His entry into Jerusalem had been foretold (Zechariah 9:9). And the letter of the Word was but the outer form of the truth which His life was revealing. Every act and word of His was to serve for the instruction of men for all time. He entered Jerusalem as a king as a symbol that divine truth must enter our hearts and minds as absolute ruler. The acknowledgment of the authority of the Lord's truth is essential to the Christian life.

Swedenborg tells us that the ass represents the affection for truth in the natural man and her colt rational truth which springs from this affection, or that the ass and her colt symbolize "the natural man as to good and truth" (AC 2781[7-9]). The Lord alone completely subjected the natural man; so the ass was one "whereon yet never man sat," and the Lord's riding into Jerusalem in this way pictures His subordination of all thoughts which came from the natural. The disciples placed their garments under Him and the throng that came out to meet Him cast their garments in His path. So our garments—the thoughts and ideas which are the expression of our individual personalities—should be submitted to the Lord and made to conform to His way. The palm branches which the multitude brought (John 12:13) were symbols of the recognition that divine truth was present in the Lord (AR 367). And the glorification "Blessed be the King that cometh in the name of the Lord: peace in heaven, and glory in the highest" represents the true disciple's acknowledgment that "in Jesus Christ dwelleth all the fullness of the Godhead bodily," and that by His life on earth He brought the heavens and hells into order, fulfilling the promise made by the angels at His birth. The Lord's entry into Jerusalem was significant in every detail.

"And when he was come near, he beheld the city, and wept over it." The Lord's deepest grief was because men refused to see the things which belonged to their peace. He came into the world not to condemn the world, but that the world through Him might be saved. On the cross He said, "Father, forgive them; for they know not what they do." The Lord had no desire to punish the people for their rejection of Him, but even to the last He longed to open their eyes that they might see the precipice on which they were standing. So, even in the last week of His life on earth the Lord cleansed the temple, driving out those who bought and sold, as a symbol of what His truth must do in the temple of our souls.

---

## From the Writings of Swedenborg

*Arcana Coelestia*, n. 5480: "That weeping is expressive of grief and love, is well known, and consequently it is expressive of mercy or pity, for mercy is love grieving. The Divine love is therefore called mercy, because the human race is of itself in hell; and when man perceives this in himself, he implores mercy. As weeping is also mercy in the internal sense, therefore in the Word 'weeping' is sometimes predicated of Jehovah or the Lord . . . Jerusalem, over which Jesus wept, or which He pitied and over which He grieved, was not only the city Jerusalem, but also the church, the last day of which, when there would no longer be any charity nor consequently any faith, is meant in the internal sense; and hence from pity and grief He wept."

## Suggested Questions on the Lesson

P. What is today called? Why?  *Palm Sunday; people spread palm branches (John 12:13)*

P. In our chapter, where was the Lord going?  *Jerusalem*

P. What place did He pass through as noted at the beginning of the chapter?  *Jericho*

J. What is the difference between this journey and that of the man in the parable of the Good Samaritan?  *going the other way*

J. Who was Zacchaeus?  *a tax collector (publican)*

P. Why couldn't Zacchaeus see the Lord?  *he was short*

P. What did he do in order to see Him?  *climbed a tree*

J. What did the Lord say to him?  *come down . . .*

J. What did Zacchaeus say which showed his character?  *"I give half to poor . . ."*

J. What did the Lord tell him?  *this day is salvation come to this house*

J. How did the Pharisees feel about it?  *murmured against Him*

J. What did the Lord tell them?  *parable*

J. What parable did He give them?  *pounds*

J. Can you tell this parable?  *ten servants, pound apiece . . .*

I. What does it teach us?  *use as well as we can what the Lord has given us*

P. When the Lord came near Jerusalem, what did He tell two of His disciples to do?  *go and untie colt*

P. What were they to say to the owner of the colt?  *the Lord needs him*

P. Was the colt used to being ridden?  *no*

P. How did the disciples prepare the colt to carry the Lord?  *put garments on it*

P. What did the multitude cast in the road before the Lord?  *branches*

J. What did they cry?  *blessed be the king*

J. What did the Lord tell the Pharisees when they objected?  *the stones would cry out*

I.  What did the Lord do and say as He looked at Jerusalem?  *wept, "if thou hadst dreamed . . ."*

J.  What did He prophesy?  *destruction of Jerusalem*

S.  What did He do when He entered the temple?  *cleansed*

S.  What did He say about the temple?  *house of prayer*

# EASTER
## *Luke 24:1-12*

This lesson is prepared with a view to covering the events of Holy Week rather than giving the meaning of the resurrection, which will be emphasized in the next lesson. In Sunday school, the story of Holy Week should be covered briefly, and the teacher should be prepared to do more with the resurrection itself.

---

### Doctrinal Points
*The Lord is life itself.*

*The "stone is rolled away" when we see that the letter of the Word was not man-made but was given by inspiration by the Lord for the sake of the inner meaning.*

*True faith is eager to understand.*

*Love in the heart is the first thing necessary if we are to see the glorified Christ.*

---

### Notes for Parents

We all know that on Easter Sunday we celebrate the resurrection of the Lord. The word *Easter* is not a Bible word.* It is taken from the name of the Teutonic goddess of spring. Easter always comes in the spring because the Lord was crucified on the day following the Passover feast, which is celebrated each year according to a certain phase of the moon near the vernal equinox, which marks the beginning of spring. This is also why Easter does not always fall on the same date in our calendar.

It is quite fitting, however, that the resurrection of the Lord should be associated in our minds with springtime, when nature is waking out of the sleep of winter, new shoots are pushing up out

---

*This is quite correct, despite the KJV passage in Acts 12:4, where it should read "after Passover" as in later versions. —*Ed.*

of the ground, and returning birds are beginning to wake us in the morning. For the Lord's resurrection brought new life and hope to the world.

When the Lord was crucified, the apostles were completely discouraged. They forgot that He had told them that He would be put to death and would rise on the third day. It is hard for us to understand how they could have forgotten until we think of our own experience with trouble. All of us have had troubles and we have always come through them and we also know the Lord's promises, and yet when a new trouble strikes us, we find it very hard to think of anything hopeful, to "look on the bright side." The apostles either went back to their old work or sat together lamenting and wondering what to do.

But the women who had loved the Lord, while they had no more hope than the men, found something they could still do for Him. They prepared the spices which were used to anoint the bodies of the dead for burial, and early Sunday morning they brought them to the sepulcher. So it was the women and not the apostles who found the stone rolled away, and they were the first to be told that the Lord had risen. There is a simple lesson in this for all of us. When trouble and death enter our homes, we should not give way to our grief and spend our time mourning and questioning the ways of divine providence. We should look for active, useful things to do, and so find new life and hope opening to us.

When the apostles themselves saw the Lord after His resurrection, they lost all fear and doubt and went out and preached the Gospel—the good news—throughout the world, and so founded the Christian Church. We need never doubt that the resurrection was a fact. We see the proof of it in the history of the world as well as in the lives of all those individuals who really accept it as a fact.

The resurrection teaches us two wonderful things. The first is that we need have no fear of death. It is a normal step in life, the closing of one chapter and the opening of another. When we die, we merely go to sleep in this world and wake up in a brighter and more beautiful one, in which we really are now, although our consciousness of it is prevented by our physical bodies.

The other thing we learn is that the Lord is not someone far away. He said to His apostles, "Lo, I am with you always," and He says the same to us, He sees our hearts and our thoughts and hears us when we pray. As we learn of Him and try to live as He would have us live, He draws us ever closer to Him, guiding and supporting us and in every experience that comes to us preparing us for eternal life and happiness.

## Primary

Make the connection with the Palm Sunday lesson and then try to show the children why the people turned against the Lord and put Him to death, and why the Lord let Himself be put to death. Speak of death and resurrection as part of the normal life of everyone.

You know that today is called Easter Sunday. Last Sunday was also a special Sunday. Do you remember what it was called? And in December we had another special Sunday. You all remember that one. Whose birthday do we celebrate at Christmas?

You know that the Lord came into the world long ago to show us the right way to live. He let Himself be born as a little baby, just as we are, and He grew up in a home, just as we do. And finally, when He was fully prepared, He began to teach and preach and heal. He was so wonderful that great crowds came to hear Him; but they did not all like what He told them, just as we sometimes do not like to be told the truth because we don't want to stop doing wrong.

The people who had received the Lord as king on Palm Sunday were disappointed and angry when they found that He was not going to be the kind of king they wanted.

Then the scribes and Pharisees saw their chance to get rid of the Lord. How did they do this?

His body was laid in a tomb and a great stone was rolled in front of the door.

The Lord had told His disciples just what would happen to Him and also that He would rise from death on the third day.

But you know that when we are in trouble, we often forget what we have been told.

The disciples lost all courage and hope.
Who went to the tomb on Sunday morning?
What did they bring?
The spices were to anoint the Lord's body.
What did the women find?
What did they *not* find?
Who appeared to them?
What did these angels tell them?
Of what did they remind them?
When the women told the apostles, what did they think?
What did Peter do?

You see, the Lord let His enemies put Him to death to show us that what we call death is nothing we need to be afraid of. It is just the beginning of a new and happier life.

## Junior

A considerable amount should be done in this class with the story of the last week of the Lord's life on earth, including the Passover feast, the betrayal, trial and crucifixion, and ending with the Lord's purpose in permitting His enemies their brief apparent triumph, and finally the meaning of the resurrection.

What was last Sunday called?
What did the Lord do on that day?
What kind of animal did He ride?
How did the people receive Him?
What did thy think He was going to do for them?
Where did He say His kingdom is?
Who were the Lord's enemies?
Why did they hate Him?
Who were His friends?
Who was Zacchaeus?
What did the Lord do for him?
When the Lord entered Jerusalem, what did He do in the temple?

We know that this was to be the last week of the Lord's life on earth. He and His disciples had come to Jerusalem to celebrate the feast of the Passover.

When was the first Passover celebrated?
Why was it called the Passover?

The Lord spent the first two days of the week teaching in the temple. At night He went out to the village of Bethany and lodged at the home of Mary and Martha and their brother Lazarus. (When we study the Gospel of John, we shall have the story of how the Lord had raised Lazarus from death.) By Tuesday night the people had begun to realize that the Lord had not come to drive out the Romans, and they were beginning to believe the Pharisees and priests, who said He was an impostor and should be put to death. So after that the Lord stayed in Bethany until Thursday night, when He came into the city again and ate the Passover feast with the twelve apostles.

It was at this last Passover that the Lord instituted the Holy Supper, which all Christians have celebrated ever since instead of the Passover. The Lord called the bread and wine of the Holy Supper His body and blood. Bread is the symbol of goodness because it nourishes the body just as goodness nourishes the soul. The Lord was perfect goodness, and it is His goodness on which our souls live. The wine and also the Lord's blood picture the truth about Himself, about the soul, and about heaven. This was why the Lord spoke of the bread and wine as His body and blood. It was also at the Passover feast that the Lord told His disciples that one of them would betray Him to His enemies.
Which one was it?

After the feast the Lord went out to the Mount of Olives, near Jerusalem, to pray. There Judas and the multitude found Him. Judas had told the soldiers that the one he would kiss was the one they wanted to arrest. So it is said that Judas betrayed the Lord with a kiss, and this is often said when someone does an injury to another while posing as his friend. The Lord was tried first before the high priest, who condemned Him and sent Him to Pilate, the Roman governor, for sentence because the Jews were not allowed by the Romans to pronounce the death sentence on anyone. Pilate tried to avoid pronouncing sentence by sending the Lord to Herod— this is the Herod who beheaded John the Baptist, not the one who tried to destroy the Lord when He was a baby. This Herod mocked the Lord but was afraid to be responsible for His death; so he sent Him back to Pilate. Pilate did not want to condemn the Lord, but the priests and the people insisted.

When the Lord was crucified—which happened on Friday—the disciples all ran away. They thought He had failed and that they had been mistaken in believing Him to be the Messiah. They forgot all He had told them. But the crucifixion was a victory, not a failure. The Lord could have saved Himself, but He had to show men that death is only a step in life, and He could not show this without passing through death. He let men do their very worst to Him to show that they had no real power over Him. The cross was not the end of the story.

After the crucifixion the soldiers divided the Lord's garments among themselves and cast lots for the inner garment, which was woven without seam. The Lord's body was laid in a new tomb, which a man named Joseph of Arimathea offered for the purpose, and a great stone was placed at the opening of the tomb and sealed there, and soldiers were set to guard it so that His body could not be taken away. During Saturday, the Hebrew sabbath, the body lay in the tomb.

It was early on Sunday morning that the women who had loved the Lord came to the tomb bringing spices which they had prepared to anoint His body, as the custom was. Read Mark 16:3.

What did they find? (Read Matthew 28:2.)
Who appeared to them?
What did the angels tell them?
What saying of Jesus did they remind the women of?
What did the apostles think when the women told them?
What did Peter do?

We shall have the rest of this chapter of Luke in another lesson. On Easter Day we should rejoice in the Lord's resurrection, for it changed the whole history of the world. The Lord permitted His enemies to do their worst and to put Him to death so that we might all know that there is nothing about death of which we need to be afraid. It is just a normal part of our life. We begin our lives in this world of nature and make them what we choose to have them, and then, when the Lord sees best, we go to sleep in this world and wake up in the spiritual world where our real homes are. And our homes there will be just what we have chosen by our life here.

―――――――

## Intermediate

The principal lesson for this class is in the meaning of the sealing of the tomb, which comes naturally from an account of the events of Holy Week, and then the correspondence of the Easter story, stressing the fact that it is only as we really love goodness that we can be enlightened by the Lord.

When the Lord and His apostles were coming to Jerusalem for the last time, He told them that He was to be put to death. Although they did not fully believe Him, they tried to persuade Him not to go, but He rebuked them. He came to His death willingly as part of the work He had come into the world to do.

On the first day of the week He rode into Jerusalem as a king. He wept over Jerusalem, seeing it as a symbol of the church which was being brought to ruin. He cleansed the temple of the money-changers and vendors of doves, who were doing business in its very court. During the first two days of the week He taught in the temple, but at night He went out to the little village of Bethany on the Mount of Olives and rested at the home of His friends Mary, Martha, and Lazarus. On Thursday evening He celebrated the Passover feast with the apostles in an upper chamber in Jerusalem, and instituted the Holy Supper. Afterward He went out to the Garden of Gethsemane on the Mount of Olives to pray, and there Judas betrayed Him. He was brought back the same night and tried by the high priest, by Herod, and by Pilate. On Friday He was crucified and His body was placed in a new tomb belonging to Joseph of Arimathea. The tomb was closed with a great stone and sealed, and a guard of soldiers was set. During the Hebrew sabbath His body lay in the tomb.

We can understand the crucifixion of the Lord better if we remember one of the things He said about Himself: "I am the way,

the truth, and the life." The scribes and Pharisees and priests put
Him to death because they did not want to follow the divine way,
to know the divine truth, or to live the divine life. They wanted
only their own way, their own ideas, and the life of the world.
People today may do the same thing. The Lord always does everything He can to show us the way to happiness, but we may choose
to close our minds against Him and to believe in our own selfish
ideas instead.

You remember that the scribes and Pharisees had so covered up
the Scriptures with their own interpretations and regulations that
the people did not know what the Word really taught. This false
interpretation of the Scriptures is pictured by the great stone
which was rolled in front of the entrance to the sepulcher.

You may remember too from an earlier lesson that morning
always pictures the beginning of a new state. Women picture affections. The women who loved the Lord came to the tomb to do
what they could for Him even though they could not understand
what had happened. The spices they brought to anoint His body
represent an inner understanding about Him prompted by their
love. Because they were trying to serve the Lord even when He
seemed to have left them, they were the first to learn of His resurrection. The apostles had given up hope when they saw Him die
and saw nothing more they could do. They did not even believe
the women's story of what they had found.

This shows us the difference between a belief based on the love
of goodness and a belief based on merely seeing with the mind.
For after the short rest of the sabbath the tomb was burst open
and a new era in the lives of men began. Even the Lord's closest
disciples thought everything was finished when He was crucified.
But His death, like the death of every one of us, was merely the
close of one chapter and the beginning of another. The Lord's
death on the cross marked the end of one church era and the beginning of the Christian Church era. The Christian Church began first
with the apostles whom the resurrection transformed from broken
and disheartened men into strong, invincible messengers of the

Gospel, able to go out and evangelize the world. The resurrection put the seal of truth upon every word the Lord had spoken and every miracle He had performed. Without the resurrection there would have been no Christian Church.

The Lord passed through death to prove to His disciples and to us that He is really the "resurrection and the life," that the death of the physical body is nothing but an upward step in our lives and does not change us in any way. If someone says to you, "I can't believe in a future life; no one has ever come back to tell us about it," your immediate answer should be, "The Lord Jesus Christ came back to tell us just that." Anyone who calls himself a Christian should accept this answer. The Lord's life as recorded in the Gospels is the only foundation which the Christian Church has. Fairy tales do not change history.

### Basic Correspondences

| | | |
|---:|:---:|:---|
| the stone which closed the tomb | = | a false interpretation of the Scriptures |
| morning | = | the beginning of a new state |
| women | = | affections |
| spices | = | interior truth from good |

### Senior

The Seniors need the application to their own lives of the closing of the tomb and its opening. Some of them will be going to college soon, where they are likely to meet teaching based on a fundamental misconception of the nature of the Bible, and they should be prepared to think independently while submitting to such instruction.

The thought that Christ is not God closes the door of the mind against light from heaven as it comes to us through the Word. Because Peter, James, and John believed Jesus to be the Messiah, their spiritual eyes could be opened to see Him transfigured. So our eyes can be opened to see Him in the inner meaning of the Word. Swedenborg also tells us that our ability to see the Lord in the other world is measured by the understanding of Him which we have gained in this world. If we have not thought of Him as a person, we shall never see Him "face to face," but shall be conscious of Him only as a diffused light, even though we accept the fact that Jesus is God from our angel instructors, as everyone must who enters the heavens.

To understand the Easter lesson we need to review the last week of the Lord's life on earth. The triumphal entry into Jerusalem on Palm Sunday was, as the Lord knew, really the beginning of the end. The temporary support of the multitude, however, gave the Lord an opportunity to denounce the scribes and Pharisees openly and to cleanse the temple. In very much the same way, there are moments in our lives when our sense of the Lord's kingship there is so strong that we can see our own sins and hypocrisies in clear light and condemn them. We may soon lose this fervor amid the temptations of our daily environment, but its effect will persist and strengthen in us the small beginnings of regenerate life.

There is, of course, a deep spiritual reason why the Lord was crucified during the celebration of the Passover. He is called the paschal lamb. The crucifixion was the culmination of the long succession of struggles and victories by means of which He overcame the hells, the powers of evil which had grown so strong in the world that no man could resist them from his own power. As the Passover commemorated the deliverance of the Jews from bondage to Egypt, so the Holy Supper, instituted by the Lord to take its place, commemorates our deliverance from hell by means of His earthly life and death.

The Lord could have saved Himself from the cross (see Matthew 26:53). But if He had stopped short of physical death, He would not have shown us the way through it. He could have saved Himself by so mighty a miracle that all His enemies would have been forced to acknowledge Him as God. But their hearts would not have been changed. They might have obeyed Him through fear, but they would have been no happier. They would have become slaves to Him instead of to the devil. The Lord does not want slaves. Swedenborg tells us that the Lord's final and supreme temptation was this very temptation to save men against their wills.

We sometimes wonder how the apostles, who had had so many evidences of the Lord's power, and who had even been told what was to happen, could have given up hope and forsaken Him when He was crucified. But we have only to remember how hard it is for us, when we are in the midst of a severe trial, to remember all that the Lord has done for us and all that we know of His promises, and to be steadfast and trusting.

It was the women who were first told of the Lord's resurrection. The women represent our affections. These women did not understand—any more than the apostles did—why the crucifixion had been permitted, but their thought still clung to the Lord and they occupied themselves with doing something for Him. They prepared spices to anoint His body. Spices represent interior truth in the natural from good there. Swedenborg often speaks of the "simple good." These are the people who, without any faculty of deep understanding of the truth, simply want to be good and so are open to heavenly influences and can be given to recognize the truth in the letter of the Word as they read it. So it was the women who found the stone rolled away from the sepulcher. The stone was a symbol of the false interpretation with which the church had closed the Word, and so rejected the divine truth in the person of the Messiah.

The Lord had told His disciples that His kingdom was "not of this world." But even the apostles persisted in thinking of His mission in terms of worldly success. This should not surprise us. We too know—better than the apostles did—that our thoughts and affections are more important than our bodies, and yet we shun physical pain and discomfort and give up spiritual things again and again for the sake of physical ease and pleasure. We may despise Peter for denying the Lord, but then turn around and deny Him in our own daily lives. We wonder how the disciples could have failed to understand and remember the things He had told them about His death and resurrection, but how well do we understand and remember His teachings?

The Lord must rise for us as really as for the disciples. Do we believe the report, or are we like the apostles when the women returned from the sepulcher with the wonderful news: "And their words seemed to them as idle tales, and they believed them not"?

---

### Adult

The effort has been made in the Adult notes to cover the major questions which people ask concerning the Lord's crucifixion and resurrection. It is suggested that the teacher ask the class for questions to begin with and take up whatever phase of the story the questions suggest. The teacher should of course be prepared, if there are no immediate questions, to outline briefly the events of Holy Week and then discuss the meaning of the resurrection for the world and for the individual.

We should not pass from the Palm Sunday to the Easter lesson without having clearly in mind the events of the last week of the Lord's earthly life and their general significance. The week began and ended in triumph, but in between—in the space of a few short days—came the culmination of the evil states of the church and the Lord's last and deepest temptation, which was the longing to save men even against their wills.

The first two days of that week the Lord spent teaching in the temple, unhesitatingly exposing the worldliness and hypocrisy of the scribes, Pharisees, and priests. At night He went out to Bethany and lodged with Mary and Martha and their brother Lazarus. On Thursday evening He came into the city again and ate the Passover feast with His twelve apostles. At that feast He laid the ritual basis for the transfer of His presence to the Christian Church by instituting the Holy Supper to take the place of all the sacrifices and feasts, telling His apostles plainly that it was a symbol of His own sacrifice, and that they were to observe it in recognition of the fact that He gave His life for them: "This do in remembrance of me." He also told them that the bread represented His body and the wine His blood. We recall that the paschal lamb represented innocence, which is the good of love to the Lord, and that its blood sprinkled upon the doorposts represented divine truth applied to life. The Lord is love and wisdom, His body representing His love and His blood His wisdom or truth. The bread and wine of the Holy Supper have the same representation. So when we partake of the Holy Supper we are testifying to the fact that we recognize that all good and truth are the Lord's, and expressing our wish to receive them from Him.

We are told that throughout the period of the ancient Jewish Church the Lord was present in the world through the correspondence of their worship, because the interior life of men was so perverted that He could no longer be conjoined to them in any interior way. But by His life on earth He put in order the spiritual forces which had been perverting man's internal life and so opened the way to genuine conjunction. From that time on, it was no longer necessary for men to observe the detailed rituals of that church, since they could live out the Lord's love and truth in their daily lives in affection, thought, and conduct. But still some formal, periodic recognition and worship are necessary to keep ever in our minds our dependence upon the Lord, to keep us from setting ourselves up as good and wise. So we have our church services, and particularly we have the sacraments of Baptism and the Holy Supper, which the Lord Himself ordained. If we observe these with an understanding of their meaning and a sincere desire to learn about the Lord and to do His will, they become effective means of conjoining us to the Lord. They are necessary to the Lord's closest presence with us. If we sincerely wish to follow the Lord, we shall always look forward to fulfilling this outward symbol of His presence with us. It is a spiritual feast to which the Lord invites us, and He promises to be present with us when we partake of it: "That ye may eat and drink at my table in my kingdom" (TCR 702-710; AE 329).

Swedenborg links together the temptation at Gethsemane and the temptation on the cross as constituting the last great temptation of the Lord. The Lord assumed a human in order to meet temptations and overcome them, for the hells could have no possible access to the Divine in itself. Also, the Lord as to His assumed human had to be in freedom just as we are in freedom, if He was to meet and overcome the forces of the hells. So—at times called states of "exinanition"—He was conscious only on the plane of the assumed human, and at such times He prayed to the Father and struggled as a man against the attacks made by the hells upon that human. Such was the final struggle. In the Garden of Gethsemane He prayed that the "cup"—the temptation of the cross—might be removed from Him if it were the Father's will, just as we pray daily, "Lead us not into temptation." He felt, as we feel it, the weakness of the human nature and the strength of evil. But He also prayed, "nevertheless not my will, but thine, be done." "And there appeared an angel unto him from heaven strengthening him." Swedenborg says that the angel was the divine of the Lord, of which He always became conscious again when He was victorious in temptation, every state of exinanition being followed by a state of "glorification." The temptation of the cross and that of Gethsemane were not a shrinking from physical suffering or even from the sorrow of desertion by His followers and misrepresentation before the people, but the temptation to show forth His power and compel the world to see and be saved (AC 2821, 10528).

To have yielded to this temptation and avoided the cross would have been to defeat the whole purpose of His incarnation. Elsewhere we read, "Now is my soul troubled; and what shall I say? Father, save me from this hour: but for this cause came I unto this hour." (John 12:27) The Lord did not come into the world to compel men to believe in Him but by passing through all men's possible states and overcoming all their temptations to enable them to overcome in His strength. He passed through death to show its powerlessness to destroy the real man. He permitted His enemies to do their worst to show how ineffectual that worst was.

The Lord was tried before three tribunals: the Sanhedrin, Herod, and Pilate. The council, composed of the chief priests and elders, actually condemned Him; the others merely consented to His crucifixion. Priests always represent the will side, and the priests in the time of the perverted church picture evil in the will. This is what really condemns the Lord and rejects Him. The Lord told the priests explicitly that He was the Christ, and they took that very claim as their excuse for condemning Him. The evil will recognizes the claim of the Lord to divine authority and for that very reason rejects Him. Herod, the Jewish ruler, represents the false principle which governs the selfish life. He was anxious to see Jesus, hoping for a miracle, and asked Him many questions, but the Lord gave him no answer. So the rational of an evil man may examine the testimony concerning the Lord out of curiosity, but cannot possibly receive any enlightenment. Pilate, the Roman governor, symbol of worldliness ruling in the outward life, also recognized the Lord's claim to be divine and actually found no fault in Him, but was willing for his own interests to concur in the judgment of the evil will, washing his hands of the whole question.

The passion of the cross was the final temptation necessary to the complete overcoming of the power of evil which attacked the Lord through the assumed human. By it He put off finally all of the finite humanity and united His own Human to the Divine, completing the process of glorification which had been going on throughout His life, as He met and overcame temptations. The earthquake (Matthew 28:2) pictured a complete change in the state of the church which took place at that time (AE 400). The darkness at the time of the Lord's death represented the falsities of the last time of that church era. The parting of the Lord's garments among the soldiers represented the picking to pieces of the letter of the Word by those who profess to accept it, and the casting of lots for the inner vesture, woven without seam, represents the fact that the internal sense could not be injured. The two thieves on the Lord's right hand and on His left are like the sheep and the goats, those who are saved by genuine acknowledgment of Him and those who are lost because they reject Him. The rending of the veil of the temple represents "that the Lord entered into the Divine Itself by dispersing all appearances; and that He at the same time opened the way to His Divine Itself through His Human made Divine." (AC 2576[5]) Before the crucifixion, the Lord could reach men only through the mediation of the heavens, always appearing to them in the form of an angel, but after the crucifixion the Lord could come in direct contact with men in His divine human. It is in this sense that Jesus Christ is the mediator. If the Lord had not passed through the states experienced in the death on the cross, there would still have been temptations possible to men through which He had not showed the way, states which He could not reach directly. Now we have direct access to divine power in our every possible need, and in Jesus Christ glorified we can see our heavenly Father face to face.

We know that without the resurrection the founding of the Christian Church would not have taken place. The Gospels show clearly that in spite of the plain statements of the Lord as to His death and resurrection, the crucifixion left the disciples in a state of doubt and discouragement. So doubtful were the apostles that they would not believe the statements of those who first learned that the Lord was risen. They had to be convinced by the evidence of their own eyes. The testimony of the Gospels is quite contrary to the claim of materialistic critics that the apostles made up the story of the resurrection. After the resurrection they were ready to live and die for their faith in the Lord and His teachings. The fact that a small group of men, simple for the most part and not at all remarkable intellectually, could go out into a world of strangers and, in spite of persecution and even the death of some of them convince so many of the truth of their message that the Christian Church was permanently established is a sufficient testimony to their own conviction as well as to the power of the message.

What did the resurrection mean to the disciples? It meant that the Lord was really the Messiah, as they had believed, that all His promises and words were true, that He was master over the grave, that He was unchanged, still the loving friend and tender Father of His "little children," that He was present with them even when they could not see Him, that death was the gateway to a more glorious life, and that nothing which men could do to them could affect their eternal happiness if they remained true to Him. In the strength of this assurance they went forth. In the strength of this assurance the Christian Church was established and grew. Take away belief in the resurrection with all that it implies, and Christianity becomes a mere man-made philosophy, powerless to transcend the level of civil and moral life, with no strength for the present or power for the future.

Let us examine a little more fully the meaning of this event which we celebrate on Easter Sunday. The Lord had told His disciples that He would pass through death and rise again on the third day. He had said, "Therefore doth my Father love me, because I lay down my life, that I might take it again. No man taketh it from me, but I lay it down of myself. I have power to lay it down, and I have power to take it again. This commandment have I received of my Father." (John 10:17-18) He had several times shown His power to raise men from the dead, but to lay down His own life and take it again was another thing. The mockers at the cross recognized this when they said, "He saved others; himself he can not save." The disciples recognized it by giving up hope after the crucifixion. When the Lord rose without the help of any outside agency, He proved that He had life in Himself as no finite human being has. Swedenborg in many numbers notes the difference between the Lord's resurrection and the resurrection of men (DL 35, AC 25, 108, 1729, 2083, 5078, and others). Only God has life in Himself (DLW 4-6), and the Lord's resurrection therefore showed Him to be God. So Thomas, when finally convinced of the reality of the risen Lord, said "My Lord and my God" (John 20:38).

The certainty that the Lord Jesus Christ is God immediately gives all His words and promises final divine authority. If Jesus had been a mere man, no matter how great and good, He might have been mistaken. But the Lord makes no mistakes. We can be perfectly sure, as the apostles were, that if we follow the Lord and trust in Him, all will be well with us, and that, whatever may happen to us in this world, our efforts to do right will bear fruit and will be crowned with eternal life. Some men claim that belief in another life is an "escape mechanism," a fiction invented by men to help them endure the hardship and injustice of life. Rather, it is a reasonable assumption from the general order of the universe, in which struggle is essential to growth and development, and men voluntarily sacrifice lesser things in the present for greater things in the future. The Lord's resurrection makes this belief a certainty instead of an assumption. "Because I live, ye shall live also."

If we genuinely believe in the Lord's resurrection, we shall not only not fear death, but we shall look forward to it as the crown of life. But the resurrection gives us more help than this. It proves to us that the Lord not only came to earth many centuries ago and lived for a few years in a human form similar to ours, but that He still lives among us in His divine humanity, the same wise, strong person whom the apostles knew and followed. They did not see Him again after the ascension, but they knew He was with them. We do not need to think of God as some far-off being or as some impersonal force. We can think of Him as a man, in whose image we are made, a loving Father, always watching over us and standing near ready to help, if we turn to Him. "For where two or three are gathered together in my name, there am I in the midst of them." (Matthew 18:20) "Lo, I am with you always, even unto the end of the world." (Matthew 28:20)

## From the Writings of Swedenborg

*Apocalypse Explained*, n. 400[14]: "It is recorded also in the Word that there was an earthquake when the Lord suffered upon the cross, and also when the angel descended and rolled away the stone from the mouth of the sepulchre (Matthew 27:51, 28:1-2). These earthquakes occurred to indicate that the state of the church was then changed; for the Lord by His last temptation, which He endured in Gethsemane and upon the cross, conquered the hells, and put in order all things there and in the heavens, and also glorified His Human, that is, made it Divine; for this reason 'there was an earthquake, and the rocks were rent.' 'The veil of the temple was rent in twain from the top to the bottom' signified that His Human was made Divine; for within the veil was the ark in which was the Testimony, and 'the Testimony' signified the Lord in respect to His Divine Human . . . 'The veil' signified the external of the church which was with the Jews and Israelites, and that covered their eyes that they might not see the Lord and Divine truth, or the Word in its own light."

*Arcana Coelestia*, n. 4748[2]: "The reason why frankincense and incenses were used in sacred rites among the ancients, is that odor corresponds to perception, and a fragrant odor, such as that of spices of various kinds, to a grateful and pleasing perception, such as is that of truth from good, or of faith from charity. Indeed the correspondence is such that in the other life, whenever it is the good pleasure of the Lord, perceptions themselves are changed into odors . . . In general they [spices of various kinds] signify interior truths in the natural, but such as are from good therein; for truths by themselves do not make the natural, but good by truths. Hence its varieties are according to the quality of the truth conjoined with good; for good has its quality from truths."

## Suggested Questions on the Lesson

P. Whom did the Lord meet at Jericho on His way up to Jerusalem? *Zacchaeus*

J. Can you tell the story of Zacchaeus? *(see Luke 19)*

J. Why did the Pharisees object to the Lord's going to the house of Zacchaeus? *he was a hated tax collector*

J. What parable did the Lord tell them? *pounds*

I. What does this parable teach? *do our best with what abilities we have*

P. How did the Lord enter Jerusalem on Palm Sunday? *riding an ass*

J. Why did He ride on an ass? *kings and judges rode them*

J. How did the people receive Him? *as a king*

P. Where does Palm Sunday get its name? *branches spread on road*

J. What did the Lord do in the temple after He entered the city? *cleansed it*

J. Where did He lodge during the week? *Bethany*

J. What did He do on Thursday evening? *ate Passover*

J. What new feast did He institute? *Holy Supper*

J. Who betrayed the Lord? *Judas Iscariot*

J. How was the Lord put to death? *crucified*

P. On what day did the crucifixion take place? *Friday*

P. What was done with the Lord's body? *put in new stone tomb*

P. Who came to the tomb on Sunday morning? *women*

P. What did they bring? *spices*

P. What did they find? *stone rolled away*

P. What did the angels tell them? *He is risen*

J. What saying of Jesus did they remind them of?  *that he would rise the third day*

J. How did the apostles receive the news?  *did not believe*

J. What did Peter do?  *ran and looked*

S. What does the resurrection teach us?  *the Lord has power over death*

# THE WALK TO EMMAUS
## Luke 24:13-53

The teacher will simply need to review briefly the story of the last week of the Lord's life and the Easter story, as an introduction to this lesson.

———

## Doctrinal Points

*The heavenly doctrines of the New Jerusalem open the Scriptures for all mankind.*

*If our hearts are fixed on worldly things, we will be unable to see the truth.*

*We must study and believe the Scriptures as preparation for receiving and understanding the heavenly doctrines.*

———

## Notes for Parents

The Gospel of Luke does not tell us that the women who went to the sepulcher on the first Easter morning saw the risen Lord, but we learn from the other Gospels that Mary Magdalene was actually the first to see Him. The men who had followed Him—because they were preoccupied with their own blighted hopes—could not immediately see Him. The story of how He gradually made His presence known to them is told in our lesson for today.

We are all very much like the two disciples on the way to Emmaus. We have the Scriptures. We ought to know what was prophesied about the Lord, and we ought to believe His promises. But we are likely to be so absorbed in what is happening to us right now that we do not look either back or forward. The Lord said to the two: "O fools, and slow of heart to believe all that the prophets have spoken." Are we not all too often "slow of heart to believe"? Our hearts are fixed on the things of this world.

The Lord did a wonderful thing for the two disciples and later for all the apostles. He "opened unto them the Scriptures." We all

350

know how many different ideas people have of the Bible and that quite opposite teachings are drawn from it by various groups. This is because people do not pay attention to this teaching of the Lord that the Word needs to be "opened" if we are to understand it, and that in reality it teaches throughout of Him—not of the history of the Jews and other external happenings. If we insist on thinking that the literal sense of the Bible is all there is to it, we shall never know what it really means, for the letter of the Bible is full of apparent contradictions. Some sects, for example, just take certain statements which they want to believe and ignore the statements which contradict their chosen beliefs. Paul recognized this when he wrote, "The letter killeth, but the spirit giveth life." (II Corinthians 3:6)

We all know what parables are—we have studied some of them. We can see that there is a deeper meaning within a parable. In our lesson for today the Lord teaches us plainly that the Old Testament as a whole—Moses and the Prophets and the Psalms—is a parable, with a deeper meaning which is about Himself.

The post-resurrection appearances of the Lord, and His ascension, which took place at Bethany forty days after the resurrection, taught the apostles two things: that He was always near them, whether they could see Him or not, and that He was God Himself. In that belief they went forth and founded the Christian Church.

---

### Primary

Begin with the Easter story very briefly, then read the lesson from the Word, and then tell briefly the events of the rest of the chapter so that the children will know of the Ascension. Stress the Lord's presence with us even though we do not see Him. Point out the opening of the Word and make the connection with the Second Coming.

What did we celebrate on Easter Sunday?
Who were the first to learn that the Lord had risen?
What did the apostles think of the women's story?
When did the events of our lesson for today take place?
Where were the two disciples going?

Emmaus was a little over six miles from Jerusalem.
What were the two disciples talking about?
Who came and walked with them?
Why did they not recognize Him?
When they told Him why they were sad, what did He say?
How did He explain these things to them?
What were they doing when they finally recognized Him?

When the Lord vanished from their sight, the two disciples went right back to Jerusalem and told the apostles about the wonderful thing that had happened to them, and while they were talking about it, suddenly there was the Lord again standing in the midst of them, and this time they all saw Him and talked with Him.

They were afraid because they thought He was a ghost.
But He proved to them that it was He Himself.

He showed them, as He had showed the two disciples on the way to Emmaus, the inner meaning of the Scriptures, and how the books of Moses and the Prophets and the Psalms taught about Him.

The Lord was seen from time to time by different people during the following month. Finally one day, when the Lord had gone out with the disciples to Bethany, the little village where Mary and Martha and Lazarus lived, they saw Him ascend into heaven. So then they were sure of two things, one that the Lord really was, as He had told them, God Himself come into the world, and the other that, even when they could not see Him, they could know that He was always close to them. The Gospel of Matthew tells us that one of the last things He said to them was, "Lo, I am with you always." We can know both of these things, too, and we should think of them often. Hundreds of years later the Lord opened the understanding of Emanuel Swedenborg to see these same things in the Word and had him write them down, so that now we may all know them if we want to.

―――――――

## Junior

With this class much should be done with the importance of this chapter to the New Church. Show the children what a privilege we have in being able to

learn the very things the Lord told the disciples about the real meaning of the
Word and even much more than He could tell them.

What event did we celebrate on Easter Sunday?
Who were the first to learn of the Lord's resurrection?
Why had the women come to the sepulcher?
What did they find?
Who told them the Lord had risen?
What did the apostles think of the women's story?

The two disciples of our story for today were not apostles, but
they had evidently been devoted followers of the Lord. They were
talking of all that had happened and they were sad, even though
they had heard about the women's report. They could not really
believe what they had been told. That was why, when the Lord
came and walked beside them, "their eyes were holden that they
should not know him." Before they could believe, He had to remind them of all that the prophets had said would happen to Him
and show them that His resurrection was just what they should
have expected, and He also had to show them some of the deeper
meaning of the Scriptures.

By the time they reached Emmaus, which was over six miles
from Jerusalem (a furlong is a little over six hundred feet), they
were ready to believe, and so the Lord could open their eyes to
recognize Him as they were eating together. This story means a
great deal to New Church people, because in it the Lord Himself
tells us that there is a deeper meaning behind the literal story of
the Old Testament, a meaning which tells about Him. He opened
the understanding of the two disciples and later of all the apostles
to see this meaning. The disciples were simple men. Their hearts
burned within them while He opened the Scriptures to them, but
afterward they did not remember or write down what He told
them. People of that time were not ready for this deeper knowledge.

But hundreds of years later, after men's minds had outgrown
the simple ideas of those early times, the Lord again opened the
understanding of a man to see the deeper meaning of the Scriptures, and this time He commanded the man to write down what

he had learned so that all who wished could study the Word in its inner meaning. This man was Emanuel Swedenborg. The opening of the Word in this way for all mankind was the promised Second Coming of the Lord.

What did the two disciples do as soon as the Lord left them?
When did the Lord first appear to the eleven apostles?
What did they think at first?
How did He reassure them?
What final event took place at Bethany?

We learn in Acts 1:3 that the ascension did not take place until forty days after the resurrection, and the other Gospels tell us of some of the Lord's other appearances.

———————

### Intermediate

From this lesson the Intermediates should get at least the thought that the Lord is always present with us and that it is very important for us to study the Word and believe it—to want to know what the Lord is saying to us. The Scriptural proof of the existence of the internal sense of the Word should be stressed.

When the women reported to the apostles that they had been told that the Lord had risen, the apostles did not believe them. And even after Peter himself had been to the tomb and found that the body of the Lord was really gone, the disciples were still only puzzled. They still thought of death as the end of everything.

So in our lesson we find the two disciples on the way to Emmaus talking over the events of the day but still sad—without any real belief. This was why, when the Lord came and walked beside them, "their eyes were holden that they should not know him." And when they told Him why they were sad, He said: "O fools, and *slow of heart to believe* all that the prophets have spoken." He was pointing out that if they had chosen to believe the prophets instead of just what their own eyes had seen, they would not have been discouraged by the crucifixion.

Then the Lord began to remind them of what the Scriptures prophesied concerning the Messiah and also to explain to them some of the things which the Scriptures taught of Him. That it was the inner meaning which He gave them we know, because they said, "he opened to us the scriptures." And later in our chapter we read that He did the same for the apostles when He appeared to them all. From our lessons on the book of Psalms you will remember that one of the important things we learn from this chapter in Luke is that the Psalms are a part of the fully inspired Word, although the ancient Jewish canon did not recognize them as such.

From this chapter in Luke as well as from the traditions they received from the apostles the people of the early Christian Church knew that the Law and the Prophets and the Psalms had an inner meaning, and during the first few centuries of the church many efforts were made to discover or to work out such a meaning. But the Lord knew that man was not ready to use the knowledge of the inner meaning properly and so He had not given the apostles any specific principles by which it could be obtained. The attempts of the early Christian "fathers" resulted in some fantastic explanations which turned many people against what they called "allegorizing." In John 16:12 we read that one of the things the Lord said in His long talk with the apostles at the last supper was, "I have yet many things to say unto you, but ye cannot bear them now." It was to be many hundreds of years before the world reached the point in its development when the Lord could open the inner meaning of the Word in such a way that everyone who wished might have access to it. We know now that this opening of the Word was what was meant by His promised Second Coming, and that it was accomplished in the middle of the eighteenth century, when Emanuel Swedenborg was chosen and prepared by the Lord to receive and write down for us the basic principles by which the Word may be understood.

The four Gospels give us four different accounts of the appearances of the Lord after His resurrection. The account in John is the fullest. From our chapter for today we might think that the ascension took place almost immediately after the resurrection, but we must remember that in all the accounts of the Lord's life lapses of time between one event and another are often unnoted. From the book of Acts (1:3) we learn that the Lord was seen on earth for forty days after the resurrection. In that book also (1:1-14) Luke gives us a fuller account of the ascension than he was inspired to give in his Gospel. But it is in the Gospel that we learn that the ascension took place at Bethany, which you remember was the home of Mary, Martha, and Lazarus.

We should note something else which we learn from our chapter. The Lord satisfied His apostles that He was not merely a ghost by showing them His hands and His feet, telling them to "handle" Him, and eating food in their presence, and He said, "A spirit hath not flesh and bones as ye see me have." When we die, we leave behind us with our physical bodies our ability to see and hear the things which go on in this outer world. The bodies we have in the other world are made of spiritual substance. But the Lord, we are told by Swedenborg, made even the "ultimates" which He took on by birth in this world divine, so that He continues always to be in direct touch with this world. And yet we must not think that the Lord appeared after the resurrection in the finite physical body which He received through Mary, for that was a human, not a divine body. If He had risen in that body, the two disciples on the way to Emmaus would have known Him immediately, and also He could not have appeared and disappeared at will as He did. The best way for us to think of the Lord when we pray to Him and when we are trying to understand His teaching is as He appeared to John in Revelation 1:12-16. This gives us the thought of Him as a person and yet as one very different from any mere finite human being.

We have not tried to take up the correspondences in this chapter because the general lessons give us so much to think about. But we might notice that the Lord made Himself known to the two disciples in the breaking of bread, which is a picture of conjunction by means of good, and that the food which the apostles gave Him was broiled fish and honeycomb, the broiled fish representing their natural knowledges made serviceable through love and the honey-

comb natural delights. Swedenborg tells us that here the broiled
fish and honeycomb mean the letter of the Word and its pleasantness. This was what the Lord was able to share with His apostles.

*Basic Correspondences*

|  |  |  |
|---|---|---|
| breaking bread | = | conjunction by means of good |
| broiled fish | = | natural knowledges made useful by love |
| honeycomb | = | natural delights |
| the broiled fish and honeycomb together | = | the letter of the Word and its pleasantness |

## Senior

The lesson should center in the nature and purpose of the Lord's post-resurrection appearances and the importance of this chapter for the New Church.
Finish with emphasis on the need of constant study of the Word and of the
writings.

The Gospels give us four different accounts of the post-resurrection appearances of the Lord. It is interesting to sit down and read
them one after another—in the last chapter of each Gospel—and
even to list the facts mentioned. We notice that the Lord appeared
and disappeared. Sometimes, as in our chapter in Luke, He was
not at first recognized. Yet He was able to show Thomas the prints
of the nails in His hands and the wound in His side, and at least
twice He appeared to eat food with His disciples. And the physical
body which had been placed in the tomb disappeared, although
the linen cloths in which it had been wrapped were left. All this
adds up to what the Lord says in our chapter: "A spirit hath not
flesh and bones as ye see me have." He rose differently from the
way in which we rise after death. When we leave our physical
bodies behind us, we leave with them all conscious contact with
the outer life of the natural world. But the Lord, as Swedenborg
tells us, had in the gradual process of glorification made even the
"ultimates" divine, and so lives with us always, even in our outward lives in the world.

In the two appearances which are described in our chapter His purpose was to impress upon the apostles—and upon us—the importance of studying and believing the Scriptures, and also to give the assurance that within the letter of Scripture is divine truth. He "opened their understanding that they might understand the scriptures." There is no record of what He told them at that time, but the glimpse they had added depth to their later preaching. We have infinitely more than they had, for in these latter days the Lord has come again and not only opened the Word to the understanding of Swedenborg but caused, through him, the publication of the basic principles of its interpretation together with sufficient examples so that all who wish to make the effort may study it with assurance. We should all ask ourselves how far we are taking advantage of this wonderful thing which the Lord has done for mankind. Do our hearts "burn within us" as we read the Word in the light of the Second Coming?

The Lord said through Isaiah, "What could have been done more to my vineyard, that I have not done in it?" The Lord speaks to us today through His Word and opens our understanding by means of the writings of Swedenborg. If we really love Him and want to be taught by Him, we can see Him rise from the sepulcher and walk with us by the way. When we doubt and fear, He says to us, as He said to the disciples: "O fools, and slow of heart to believe all that the prophets have spoken," and "Why are ye troubled?"

The Lord, forty days after the resurrection (Acts 1:3), ascended to heaven in the sight of His disciples. He ascends for us when we see that He is our Father in heaven as well as our savior, the only God of heaven and earth, from whom alone truth and goodness flow.

And He says to us, as He said to the apostles, "Ye are witnesses of these things," and promises to be with us always if we will tarry in Jerusalem until we have been endued with power from on high. To tarry in Jerusalem is to study faithfully the Word and the doctrines until we are so sure they come from God that we can give them to others without letting ourselves get into the picture.

In preparing for our occupations in the world, we know that we need to learn all we can in order to be effective. We should realize that this is equally true of our occupation as "witnesses" for the Lord. It is not our ideas but the Lord's truth in which is the power to enlighten and to save men.

## Adult

Possible discussion topics are the nature of the Lord's post-resurrection body, the opening of the Scriptures, and the charge to "tarry in Jerusalem." This charge and the promise of the Holy Spirit were literally fulfilled for the apostles. They should be spiritually fulfilled for us.

Our lesson today is a portion of the Gospel of Luke which we all need to study and make part of our equipment as New Churchmen, as well as to ponder for its personal meaning for us. There have been differences of opinion in the church as to the nature of the Lord's post-resurrection body, and our chapter puts this problem squarely before us. The body was gone from the tomb, but the linen cloths in which it had been wrapped were left. The two disciples on the way to Emmaus walked and talked with the Lord for some time without recognizing Him. As soon as they did recognize Him in the breaking of bread, He vanished from their sight. He appeared suddenly standing in the midst of the apostles. The body in which the Lord appeared after the resurrection was obviously not the finite physical body which He had worn before the crucifixion. Yet it was more than the spiritual body in which each of us lives after death. He told the apostles to handle Him, and said, "A spirit hath not flesh and bones, as ye see me have." And He also ate in their presence. Swedenborg tells us that the Lord, by the process of glorification, made the very "ultimates" divine and so rose with the whole body. But the divine body is necessarily infinite, and matter is finite. There we have our problem—a challenging one—about which we may and do come to different conclusions in this world. But without solving it we may be sure that the facts by which it is presented are all true, and these facts give us the assurance that the Lord is present in the world actually, as He says in Matthew: "Lo, I am with you always." By His life in the world He not only overcame the hells, but He established a direct, permanent, personal contact with men on earth which He had not had before.

The two on the way to Emmaus did not at first recognize the Lord, but as He explained the Scriptures to them, their hearts burned within them, and later they knew Him in breaking of bread. The fact that they urged Him to abide with them pictures their desire to preserve the truth which they were receiving, and their sitting and eating with Him their desire to apply it to life, and thus they received good from Him and so recognized Him. Swedenborg tells us that to break bread and give it to the disciples signifies "to instruct in the good and truth of faith, by which the Lord appears" (AC 9412).

The New Church accepts this story and the incidents which follow as the Lord's own testimony to the fact that the Word has an internal meaning, and that the whole of the Word of the Old Testament treats inmostly of Him. He said that He came to fulfill the Law and the Prophets, and now we are told that, "Beginning at Moses and all the prophets, he expounded unto them in all the scriptures the things concerning himself," and later: "These are the words which I spake unto you, while I was yet with you, that all things must be fulfilled, which were written in the law of Moses, and in the prophets, and in the psalms, concerning me. Then opened he their understanding, that they might understand the scriptures." We think what a wonderful privilege it must have been to hear the Lord Himself expound the Scriptures; but today we have that same privilege, if we will make the preparation necessary to enjoy it, for the Lord in His Second Coming has opened the Scriptures so that all who will may understand them.

In Acts 1:3 we are told that forty days elapsed between the resurrection and the ascension. The Gospel of John records several appearances of the Lord not mentioned in the other Gospels. The instruction given the disciples during these days was of a more

interior character than before and was designed to strengthen them
for their mission. Then the Lord led them out as far as Bethany,
and was parted from them and carried up to heaven. The faith of
His disciples had now reached a point where His visible presence
was no longer necessary to them. Indeed, He did not want them to
depend upon His visible presence. He tells Thomas, "Blessed are
they that have not seen, and yet have believed." And John adds,
"And many other signs truly did Jesus in the presence of His disciples, which are not written in this book: but these are written,
that ye might believe that Jesus is the Christ, the Son of God; and
that believing ye might have life through his name." (John 20:29-
31) The Lord must ascend in our minds. We must not cling to the
thought of His earthly life as something that happened long ago,
to the thought of His infancy, childhood, miracles, and suffering
on the cross as the reason for our loyalty to Him. These all have
their place in preparing us for His service, and in the internal sense
they describe the stages through which our concept of the Lord
must pass if we make orderly progress in the Christian life. But our
thought of the Lord should rise above the merely natural phenom-
ena of His life and center in His glorified human, of which we have
a correspondential picture in the first chapter of Revelation. The
Lord is not only our personal friend and savior; He is our heavenly
king. As Isaiah tells us (Isaiah 9:6): "His name shall be called Wonderful, Counsellor, The mighty God, The everlasting Father, The
Prince of Peace." The Bible story does not leave the Lord hanging
on the cross. It goes on through the resurrection to the ascension.
The Christian thought and the Christian appeal should never leave
the Lord on the cross. We should not give the Lord pity; we should
give Him worship.

The last promise of the Lord to His apostles was the promise of
the gift of the Holy Spirit. They were told to tarry in Jerusalem
until they should be endued with power from on high. Jerusalem
represents doctrine. We must all tarry in the study and practice of
doctrine until the Lord's power can come to us through it. Divine
love works always in accordance with divine wisdom. We can do

no more good than we know how to do. If we go forth with our own ideas, merely using such passages from the Word and from the writings as we think support what we have decided to believe, we may do more harm than good. The truth is not always what we wish to believe, and we do not arrive at the truth by our own observation and reasoning. We too may go forth "in the power of the Spirit," but the spirit comes to us only through the Word, and in this new age through the Word as opened for us with the help of the writings. Some scholars today try to change the Word or discount certain passages in it so that it will mean what they think it ought to mean. And the same destructive method may be used with regard to the writings of Swedenborg. But we should see clearly that these attempts spring from the pride of self-intelligence and are falsifications of the truth.

We may read in Acts 2 of the literal fulfillment of the promise to the apostles made in our chapter. The crown of Christian discipleship is the ability to bring the Lord's truth to others, to bring others to the recognition of the Lord and to acquaintance with the means of learning of Him. To have this power we must put self aside. Our hearts and minds must be "continually in the temple, praising and blessing God."

―――――――

### From the Writings of Swedenborg

*Arcana Coelestia*, n. 5620[14]: "The 'honeycomb and broiled fish' that the Lord ate with the disciples after His resurrection, also signified the external sense of the Word (the 'fish' as to its truth and the 'honeycomb' as to its pleasantness) . . . It appears as if such things were not signified, because their having a piece of broiled fish and a honeycomb seems as if fortuitous; nevertheless it was of providence, and not only this, but also all other, even the least, of the things that occur in the Word. As such things were signified, therefore the Lord said of the Word that in it were written the things concerning Himself. Yet the things written of the Lord in the literal sense of the Old Testament are few; but those in its internal sense are all so written, for from this is the holiness of the Word. This is what is meant by His saying that 'all things must be fulfilled which are written in the law of Moses, and in the Prophets, and in the Psalms, concerning Him.'"

## Suggested Questions on the Lesson

P. What happened on the first Easter Sunday? *Jesus rose from death*

P. Who first learned of the Lord's resurrection? *the women*

J. What did the apostles think of the women's story? *idle tales*

P. What were the two disciples talking about later the same day on the way to Emmaus? *all that had happened*

P. Who came and walked with them? *Jesus*

J. Why did they not recognize Him? *their eyes were "held"*

J. What did He say when they told Him why they were sad? *"ought not Christ . . . ?"*

J. What did He teach them? *about Himself in the Scriptures*

P. What happened as they were eating together? *they recognized Him; He vanished*

P. How did they say they felt when the Lord was talking to them? *heart burned within*

P. What happened later as they told their story to the apostles? *Jesus appeared*

J. What did the apostles think? *He was a ghost*

J. How did the Lord reassure them? *let them touch Him; ate some food*

J. What did He eat? *fish, honey*

J. What did He then teach them? *inner meaning of Scriptures*

J. What did He tell them to do? *wait in Jerusalem for power*

J. What promise did He make to them? *I am with you always*

P. How was the Lord finally separated from them? *ascended into heaven*

P. Where did the ascension take place? *Bethany*

I. What does "breaking bread" represent? *sharing in love*

S. How can we now know many of the things in the Word which the Lord revealed to the disciples? *the heavenly doctrines*

S. How did the Lord's post-resurrection body differ from the one He took on from Mary? *glorified, divine substantial*